~~Jack Hamilton~~

THE GOOD BALKANS

To Tony,

with best wishes

John

17 iii 2009

London, 2009

Published in 2007 by Wild Man Books
1/12 Pembridge Crescent
London
W11 3DY

First published in Bulgarian translation by MaK Izdatelska Kushta, Sofia, in December 2006 under the title Чашата на Гадателката (Chashata na Gadatelkata)
by John Hamilton

The following texts are reproduced courtesy of Michigan Slavic Publications from Monumenta Bulgarica, ed. Thomas Butler (1966)

Excerpt from Slavo-Bulgarian History, Paisij Hilendarski
Excerpt from a *Letter to Mr Nikolaj Canovic Cuski*, Neofit Hilendarksi Bozveli
An incantation against a devil
A Bride, a Golden Apple

ISBN   978-0-9557969-0-6

A full CIP record for this book is available from the British Library

For my parents
In memory of my father

Acknowledgements

It has taken me a long time to research and write this book. The list of people who helped me understand Bulgaria over the past decade would be as long as the book itself, so I must thank many people without mentioning their names. There are however those to whom I owe special thanks for their love and care, for being great hosts and travelling companions, for opening doors, for giving great advice and telling great stories, for helping me to learn Bulgarian and to learn about Bulgaria. They are Robin Brookes, Matthew Brunwasser, Niki Chavdarov, Itso Dechev, Maya and Neven Dilkovi, Mitko Dimitrov, Elga Kirakova, Aglaya Kotseva, Ken and Galia Lefkowitz, Kalin Manolov, Dimi Panitsa, Johnny and Tanya Pojarlievi, Carolina Ramos and Hristo Stoyanov. Thanks also to Piers Russell-Cobb for his great encouragement and to Justine Ettler for her editorial advice.

CONTENTS

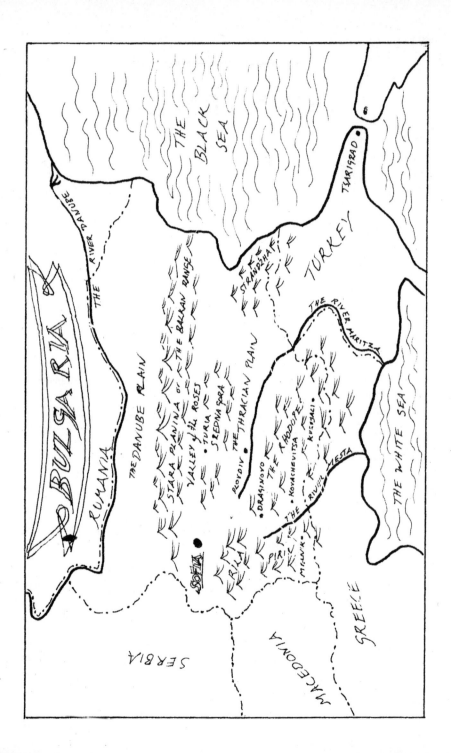

Across the Frontier

Of the whole Slavic race the most glorified were the Bulgarians: they were the first to appoint tsars, the first to have patriarchs, the first to be Christianized, and they conquered the most land. So that of all the Slavic race they were the most powerful and most honoured, and the first Slavic saints issued from the Bulgarian nation and tribe.

Slavo-Bulgarian History, Paisij Hilendarski (1762)
Translated by Thomas Butler

A Blank Spot on the Map

"IF YOU can work out what is going on in Bulgaria, you can work out what is going on anywhere. Everything happens under the surface there."

As soon as the East European editor said these words, I knew it was the idea I had been searching for. What better reason could there be for going to a place? What better challenge could there be for someone starting out in journalism in their mid-20s?

I wanted an adventure and that meant going to a place outside my imagination. When I tried to think of what contemporary Bulgaria might be like, I could bring no images to mind. It was 2000 miles from London, yet it might have been on the other side of the world or on another planet.

I gazed at the large European wall map on his office wall and the possibilities of the little rectangular country on the western edge of the Black Sea seemed to jump out at me. It was small, formerly communist, part of Europe, part of the Balkans but also in the east and Slavic too. I gazed at the space it occupied on the map. It was just north of Greece. Less than the length of my thumb separated the capital Sofia from the approximate location of the village in the Pindus Range from where my Vlach Great-Grandmother Anastasia had come from (I had always been drawn to that quirk in my family history).

Another short stretch of the thumb and forefinger reached to Istanbul to the east. The Danube ran along its northern border. The fractured states which were once Yugoslavia lay to its west, and through its centre ran the spine of the Balkan Range, so the Balkans were in Bulgaria as well as the other way round. The national airline was called "Balkan". It was probably the only place in the world where that troubled word was used to connote something positive. The good Balkans.

As the editor and I gazed at the map, he told me about the country and its place in the region. It had been a democracy since 1990. But its transition from communism had been different from the other countries of the communist hinterland. Mostly they had thrown off their oppressive regimes with passion and fury: Poland with determination, Czechoslovakia with flair, Romania with vengeance. Or else, like Croatia and Bosnia and Serbia they had gone to war. Bulgaria had done neither. It had slipped into the democratic era with a shrug and a quick glance over its shoulder. What had happened since? I decided that instant that I would go to Bulgaria to find out.

• • •

That was eleven years ago. Since then I have made friends, fallen in love and for a while I thought I would never leave. I was transfixed by Bulgaria's fantastic unpredictability, its false starts and its bizarre political experiments, such as making the former monarch the democratic prime minister. Sometimes I felt that during five minutes of Bulgarian politics, the whole political history of Europe, from monarchy and fascism through socialist dictatorship to contemporary advertising-driven democracy, was flashing before my eyes. Only this history didn't follow an orderly line. It hit me in a confused lump.

There was a reason for this. I had stumbled into the country during the best chance it had ever had to make good. One could almost feel the weight of history shifting off the backs of the people.

And what a weight! Since it became part of the Ottoman empire in medieval times, Bulgaria had been on the wrong side of every major geopolitical conflict. It missed out on the renaissance, joined the losing side in both world wars and spent the Cold War in the Soviet freezer.

In 1989, Bulgaria was the most loyal satellite of the Soviet Union. The dictator, Todor Zhivkov, once suggested to Brezhnev that it become the U.S.S.R.'s 16th republic. But fast forward to the present day and Bulgaria, unready, poor, corrupt and disorganised as it is, has slipped into the European Union – the last country likely to do so for a long while. For the average Bulgarian even this lightning change hasn't come fast enough.

This change made Bulgaria feel like the most exciting place in the world, even when no one outside the borders gave a damn about what was happening there. The country may have been cruddy and falling down in places. The politicians may have been vain, corrupt and greedy. It may have been frustratingly hard to get by. But the Bulgarian people were grasping at their destiny. And I was with them.

Tomorrow begins today

Promise me nothing for tomorrow
I'm counting every minute today.
So what if there will be flowers,
In my home, my hall, in my block?
Yes Iwant a flower, but I want it now,
Because tomorrow begins today.

Anti-Communist Pop Song, 1997

Balkan Winter

I ARRIVED in the middle of January. The Balkan winter, so vicious that it prevented even the bloody-minded Yugoslavs from fighting one another, had the city in its grip. It was so cold and clammy that I had to push the bed up against the hot water pipes which ran through a corner of my damp budget hotel room. At night I huddled rather than slept. Sofia was enveloped in a dank freezing fog and a sense of helpless confusion. In these first weeks I must have considered abandoning this crazy adventure and going back to England to resume my three-month old career writing up the end-of-year results for the least important publicly quoted companies on a freelance basis at the *Financial Times* nearly every day.

This was how I began my career as a freelance foreign correspondent. I didn't have much to work with, a handful of contacts scribbled in my notebook and the vague promises of the *FT's* East European editor. That was it.

The situation in the country was chaotic. Banks had been collapsing all the previous year, each one taking nother chunk of the nation's saving with it. A former prime minister had been assassinated on his doorstep. The government was on the skids. New Year had come in with food shortages and triple digit inflation. Bread and oil had were running out. Factories had stopped production. They couldn't pay their workers or buy raw materials.

Map in hand, I traversed the grey city on foot, soaking up every detail of the confused and traumatised country that I saw around me. One by one I ticked off my contacts. Most of them inhabited offices lodged in the back of dowdy blocks or in grand and forbidding ministry buildings.

Sofia was not a beautiful or dramatic city, like Prague or Budapest. On a good day, when the freezing fog was not smothering the streets, it was a fine place. If you raised your head you could see the white peak and crisp snowy slopes of Vitosha Mountain from almost everywhere in the centre. This view alone transformed the city into something out of the ordinary. Suddenly the streets were no longer mundane. It was all right so long as you kept on looking up.

The old women were the ones who most depressed me. There was one who begged in the dark concrete underpass leading to the garden on the other side of the boulevard next to the Soviet Army monument. (This vast grey quadrangular pillar, surmounted by a stout headscarved woman and chubby Russian soldier waving a machine gun commemorated the Soviet "liberation" of 1944.)

As I walked up the cracked concrete steps, she tugged my sleeve.

"*Dai edna baba stotinki za hlap.*" Even without my studies into the Bulgarian language, the desperate whine in her voice needed no translation.

"Give a granny some small coins for bread."

I could hardly bear to look at her pinched face, the misery and fear in her eyes, the supplication in her trembling outstretched hand. I felt a wave of disgust and fumbled for my wallet.

"My lad, my lad," she cried. I thrusted some notes at her, the equivalent of 20 or 50 pence, a loaf of bread or two, and strode away as fast as I could with her blessings following me like a curse.

A poky dark stairwell of an old and vandalised block led me to the office of a well-known political scientist. It was like stepping through a portal into another world. One side of the threshold was dark, antiquated and smelly. The interior was light, bustling and modern. I don't know what I expected. What I found was a bearded pony-tailed rebel, who wore his hirsuteness as a proud badge of dissidence from a decade before. He greeted me absently as he strode around his office like a general in his war room. Paper was strewn everywhere. Excited young protesters rushed in and out with papers and news delivered in excited, breathless bursts. It was impossible to have a continuous conversation. The rebel talked to me over his shoulder between flurries of instructions and telephone calls as his minions scurried around him.

"We must be prepared," he muttered darkly. "If the government declares martial law there will be a civil war."

"Is that likely?" I wondered. It seemed incredible.

"We will be ready, in any case. There is no way that these criminals can continue to hold power." There was anger and excitement in his voice.

This bearded politico-warrior was agitating in the cause of the anti-communist president, who had been elected two months before, and was shortly to be inaugurated. By voting for him, the Bulgarian people had asked for change. But Bulgarian presidents fulfil little more than a symbolic role. Power still lay in the hands of a deeply hated and compromised government led by the Bulgarian Socialist Party, formly the Bulgarian Communist Party.

This government had been elected two years previously in fair and legitimate elections. Bulgaria was no dictatorship. But since gaining power the government had done nothing but rob the country blind. So it wasn't much of a democracy either. The same people from the old communist elite, who had ruled the country as a one party state for 45 years, were now profiting hugely from the demise of the old regime. This was not what democracy was supposed to be about.

I was amazed to hear these things. Could it be true that a battle was still raging here against a regime that I thought had been swept out from this part of Europe when I was still a schoolboy?

The rebel had no doubt. Far from being dismayed by the riot that I had heard reported on the radio in London, he was enthused by it.

Protestors had rampaged through the parliament building, smashing furniture and computers. Then a crowd nearly 50,000 strong had barricaded more than 100 deputies inside for a whole night. They refused to let them out until the government agreed to hold fresh elections. The government had refused. Squads of baton wielding policemen had broken up the siege and released the deputies.

The tension created by that outburst of violence had grown and grown. The unions had called a national general strike. Factories had closed everywhere. The oil refinery had stopped working. Sofia airport was open for just an hour or so each day. Roadblocks had closed city streets, roads and rail links throughout the country. Protestors in the second largest city of Plovdiv had blocked the highway and railway lines, cutting off the main route to the Black Sea ports in the east. Other demonstrators south of Sofia had blocked the way to Greece.

This was revolution, he told me excitedly. The forces of communism were finally being shaken out of the crannies where they had lodged for too long.

"Come to the demonstration this afternoon," he implored. "Things are going to change."

I left the political scientist to his ringing telephones and war planning. Back in the street there was no energy at all. Everything was dirty and the colour of oxidised lead. Even the air. The pavements were blocked with crappy old cars with dusty windscreens and flat tyres. There were not many people about. Sacks of garbage mouldered in corners where packs of stray dogs rummaged and bickered. Was this what incipient civil war looked like? I wondered if I could believe what I had just been told.

My next meeting was with an economist. Another block. Another dirty set of stairs. The heavy metal security door clanged behind me. This place was a haven of calm. The economist - a cheerful middle-aged man, twirled on an expensive office chair. He waved a receipt at me as if it were the joke out of a cracker.

"I have just filled my car with petrol. See how much it cost me." I looked at the paper he held out to me.

"See the price per litre," he pointed. "12 US cents a litre! That is less than what they pay in Saudi Arabia!" The government had forgotten to permit — or had not let — the refinery adjust its prices in relation to the hyper-inflation. "And still no one can afford to drive!"

On a rough sheet of paper he sketched out what had bankrupted half the banks in the country in the past months. Almost anyone with the right contacts could set up a bank, he explained. The managers of state-owned banks had lent millions of dollars to their friends without security. Some of these loans had been used as capital to set up new private banks. These banks had then made more unsecured loans in their turn. And so on. None of the loans had been paid back or could be. The chain of unpayable debts ultimately led back to the national bank, the lender of last resort. It was as if the national bank had opened its vaults and allowed people to walk in and simply take the money away.

"If we get a new government it must be honest," he told me. "They can't be corrupt. This is the country's last chance. So much has been stolen, so many chances have been missed. The public won't stand for anything else."

After leaving the economist I noticed how the eyes of every pas-ser-by on the pavement slid sideways when passing the boards pro-.claiming the latest exchange rate in the bureaux de change which had cropped up in every other window, next to deserted boutiques sell-ing German kitchenware and Italian suits. The rate changed every half an hour. One had to change money several times a day. I could almost feel the crummy Bulgarian Levs, with their many zeros, dis-solving in my pockets.

The streets were clogged with parked cars but none were on the road. I crossed Boulevard Maria Louisa, one of the city's main arter-ies without looking. There were no cars. In the big market on the way to the railway station crowds of panicked old men and women mobbed a row of tin kiosks piled with bags of rice, flour, sugar and dried milk. Successful shoppers staggered away with big bags of food. They were obeying newspaper advice on how to live in a time of hy-per-inflation, buying storable goods as soon as they got any money. Mass hoarding was creating shortages and prices had soared. In the provinces bread, the chief staple, had already run out. News of this was creating more panic.

Again, it was the old women who were more noticeable. Perhaps because they were more pitiful. Many wore fur coats, relics from a more prosperous time. But the orange, and purply aubergine tints with which they had dyed their hair (the Balkan equivalent of a blue rinse) were growing out, revealing lengths of snowy root. Was it pos-sible to calculate the depth of the economic crisis by the length of time that pensioners had not been able to afford hair colouring?

Answering these questions was no longer just a question of find-ing work and making a successful career. I was seized by a stubborn determination to find out. What I had not understood back then, and did not understand until it was all over was that I had stumbled into the country at a historical moment of crisis. This was Bulgaria's turning point, it was the moment when it definitively chose the path to Europe, and to the west. A little section of the world was being defined.

It may take another generation or more for the country to over-come its spiritual thraldom to the communist past, to become "west-ern" in spirit as well as intention. But by good fortune I was in the country when its people took a massive step along that long path.

The Bulgarian National Anthem 1886–1944

Maritsa rushing,
Blood-stained, gushing
A widow is wailing
Wounded to the quick.

Chorus:
March, march,
Our general with us!
Into battle leap
The enemy to beat.

Youth of Bulgaria
The whole world is watching
Onwards to victory,
Gloriously let's advance.

Chorus

The lion of the Balkans
Flies into battle
In a giant fight
Against enemy hordes

Chorus
We are the nation:
For glory and freedom,
For our sweet land
We know how to die.

Chorus

Nikola Zhivkov (ed. Ivan Vazov)

Europe's First Post-communist Revolution

BULGARIA'S revolution didn't have a name. Now they would probably call it the blue revolution, but at the time everything just seemed grey to me. But then it seems that revolutions never happen in the green of summer. All of the post-communist revolutions that have taken place since Bulgaria's have happened in the depth of winter, the time when life is hardest. Ukraine's Orange Revolution happened in December 2004, Georgia's Rose Revolution in December 2003. Bulgaria's revolution took place in January and February 1997.

The streets filled with protest marches every afternoon. Every day, I marched with the vast crowds that blocked the the main streets of central Sofia. Every day the crowd was bigger. Tension mounted.

One afternoon in early February, I craned my neck to look over the heads of the people who pressed around me, and I could see that I was in the middle of the biggest march yet. In spite of the bitter clammy cold, tens of thousands of people had turned out. Here at last was the feeling of crisis and danger that had been perplexingly absent in the streets after I had visited the civil war-preaching rebel on my first day in the city. The slogans were strident and angry. Some protestors waved placards painted like "No Left Turn" road signs, a witty way of showing that they did not want to be led back into communism. Everyone I spoke to was sure something would happen today.

The crowd advanced along the main east-west boulevard towards the gold-domed Saint Alexander Nevsky Memorial Church in the very centre of the labyrinthine capital. We were marching along a boulevard that cut through a cross-hatching of straight narrow streets. The city seemed to have been built on a series of skewhiff grids that didn't quite fit each other. This main avenue then sliced through the grid. The church was built to the left of it on a slight hill. It was the chief landmark.

It was a much more fitting monument to Russian soldiery than anything the Soviet's ever produced. It was dedicated to the great holy prince of Russia and commemorated the soldiers who died to make Bulgaria free in the Russo-Turkish war of 1877. Dome was heaped on dome in a great triangle leading up to the central gilded cupola. Verdigris from the lower domes had leached down the white marble walls streaking them like peppermint creams. It looked pre-posterously like a vast Edwardian jelly mould, but was built with such symmetry and daring that it effortlessly vaulted over the ridiculous to the sublime.

It was here, during an environmental rally in 1989, that ordinary people had shocked themselves by voicing forbidden dreams. In the middle of this officially sanctioned protest the first cries of "Dem-O-krats-Si-Ya!" had rung out – for a few seconds only, followed by a stunned silence. It was, though they didn't know it then, the death knell of one party rule. Just weeks later the East Germans were tearing down the Berlin Wall and huge numbers of people had gathered again on the broad cobbled square in front of the cathedral. But after all that, the ghost of communism had continued to haunt Bulgaria. Eight years on and the country was still divided between communists and anti-communists.

It was a middle-class protest, fuelled not by working class anger nor by intellectual radicalism but by the bourgeois disappoint-ment. The people close to me in the crowd wore smart clothing. There were women in fur coats and men in suits. My two guides at the march were Johnny and Tanya Pojarlievi, whose flat I had started lodging in. They were typical of the people I saw around me. Tanya, a cheerful, neat woman in her mid-50s looked meek and respectable in a tartan skirt, thick sheepskin jacket and woollen hat. I thought she appeared slightly surprised to be on a march, but determined too. Later I learned she had honourable experience of the first protests which had brought down the regime in 1989. She had recently re-tired from her job in a chemistry lab was an avid reader of *Demokrat-*

sia, the anti-communists' official publication. She was a passionate supporter of the "blues" – the coalition of anti-communist political parties. She spent all day listening to the radio and discussing politics with her friends, all of whom were as politically committed to the anti-communist cause as she was.

Johnny, her husband, looked rumpled and slightly distracted in a brown trilby and blue anorak. He was a professor of organic chemistry at the Bulgarian Academy of Sciences. A natural sceptic, he had refused to join in with his wife's enthusiasm at the recent political changes, but was still protesting along side her.

As we marched he told me about hee wary of grand political movements. "What you must know is that there was no proper dissident movement here. We didn't try to oppose communism until late in 1989 when it was nearly over anyway. From the beginning we never resisted. When I was nine I watched the Soviet troops come into our country. We cheered them as they came through the streets. They called it liberation."

"Johnny is a proletarian," ragged Tanya. "Proletarian!"

He spoke English with an insistent mixture of strong southern European consonants and flat Yorkshire vowels, inherited together with a love of PG Tips tea from his mother, who was born in a village near York. The friends whom they had joined on the march were fellow academics, lawyers, housewives, civil servants. All of them had come out onto the streets hoping to overthrow their freely elected government.

It all seemed very foreign to me. I looked carefully at their faces to see if they appeared very different. They were perhaps slightly darker, with a different shape to the cheek-bones, Bulgarians are Slavs after all. But they seemed much like anyone whom I could see in the street at home. It was just that here they had been forced onto the streets by the total collapse of the Bulgarian economy. Democracy had brought them nothing but falling living standards. After all the hope and trust they put in the new era, this is had been the bitterest insult imaginable. The country was bust. They had lost their savings in bank crashes. Hyper-inflation had reduced the value of the average pension to two US dollars a month. On every side angry people shouted slogans and wave banners.

"Communists Out! Elections Now! New Future for Bulgaria Now!" A line of sombre politicians marched in front. A row of

black robed priests in pill box hats followed them. Enthusiastic
youths and defiant looking men brandished a thicket of multi-
coloured banners and flags. The blue anti-communist banner was
most in evidence, but there were also purple trade union flags, orange agrarians, and the sinister black and red of the Bulgaro-Mac-
edonian nationalists.

On the edge of the cobbled square a wild and unshaven man
perched unsteadily on a step-ladder. He was draped in white bandages, a pot of red paint precariously slung on one arm. He had tied
up all the lower branches of the young lindens around the square as if
they were broken limbs and then daubed them in red paint. Half the
trees already look like wounded soldiers. I asked him why.

"The bleeding trees are a symbol of what is happening to his
country," Johnny translated for me.

A mob of energetic students charged by us wearing pyjamas and
bedclothes. They waved alarm clocks and yelled:

"Wake up! Time for elections!"

They had taken their inspiration from the students of Belgrade
who were pulling similar stunts in the mass protests coincidentally
also blocking the streets there. (President Slobodan Milosevic had
refused to comply with local election results.)

Tanya was full of admiration.

"Yesterday they dressed in shrouds and carried mocked-up cof-
fins. They were burying communism. Every day they think of a new
stunt for the TV cameras."

She spoke good English with exaggeratedly rounded vowels that
betrayed the careful language coaching of Bulgarian schools.

"This time we must succeed," she added.

"Eight years ago, the regime changed on the surface but underneath the same people continued to wield power. Now they have
brought Bulgaria to the brink for a second time. We won't give them
a third chance."

I wasn't sure. The trade unions, waving their blue and purple
flags in the front row seemed faint shadows of Poland's Solidarity,
or indeed, the miners of Romania. The shop-worn "new" democrats
who gathered to rally the crowds from the cathedral steps did not
inspire me with confidence. They were grey, tired and definitely not
in command. How would this uninspiring, loosely united group de-
liver the new elections that the demonstrators were demanding? As

their speeches crackled over the tannoy system, Johnny gave me a dry commentary of what was going on.

"It is impossible for such a demonstration to go ahead in Bulgaria without the *chengeta* taking an interest in who attends. Impossible!" he stressed. He was talking about the secret police. In 1989, the DS had openly scrutinised the crowds and wrote down the names of anyone they could recognise.

"Uurrgh! Horrible men in black leather jackets! They were quite obvious!" chirruped Tanya with a shiver.

I looked around, suddenly spotting a potential spy behind every leather jacket or unfriendly face.

"How can you spot them?"

"They are here for sure," said Tanya.   As if on cue a rhythmic chant began to echo round the square. It was the cue for everyone around me to start jumping on the spot. The whole crowd undulated like someone shaking waves through a blanket.

"Come on! Jump, Jump!" they urged me.

"What is everyone shouting?"

"It's an old favourite. Whoever isn't jumping is a red!"

Tanya was hopping vigourously on her toes. Johnny bounced more sedately, slightly unsure of his dignity.

"We used to do this in 1989. We could tell who the *chengeta* were because they wouldn't join in. For them it's too ridiculous."

As I jumped up and down on the spot I looked around again. I had no idea if I should be concerned or not. I wanted to dismiss the idea of a secret police conspiracy. Surely this sort of thing was part of history now? But then how could so many people be wrong?

To my right, on the edge of the square, beyond the waves of jumping people I could just see the white square face of the *Narodno Subranie* building. It was surrounded by riot barriers and showed signs of the violence that marked the beginning of this protest three weeks before. Its doors and windows were covered with wooden boards.

Would this crowd erupt into violence again? Perhaps the army would be brought in? But would they obey orders?

"Bloodshed is quite possible, even civil war," Johnny told me in his quiet professorial way.

"I'm frightened, of course I am," added Tanya. But fear had not stopped her protesting.

Up until that day the crowds had dispersed in the evening after meeting in front of the cathedral. But that night no one wanted to go home. The new anti-communist president had been inaugurated. The protests had become a conflict between the State and the people, but now the president was on their side.

After the rally in the cathedral square, the crowd surged back along the streets towards a large unevenly shaped plaza lined on three sides by the grandiose Stalinist façades of government offices. This entire complex was imposed on the centre of the city in the 1950s as a kind of textbook compendium of Stalinist superiority.

The grey portico of the Presidency looked across diagonally to the granite temple-like front of the Party House, formerly the headquarters of the Bulgarian Communist Party. The angry crowd milled outside, shouting its slogans louder and more shrilly.

"Murderers! Red Mafiya! *Cherveni boklutsi!*"

"That means 'Red rubbish!'" Johnny told me. "But I don't suppose they are listening," he added glumly.

As night fell it became bitterly cold, but still no one went home.

"If we are here in the morning they will send in the army," he predicted. No one contradicted him.

"How do you know?" I asked. He shrugged.

The first sign that something might have happened was a commotion around the heavy wooden double door leading into the presidency building. The doors opened and a mob of photographers and TV camera men burst out.

A cry went up. "Victory, Victory!"

Then another group of men pushed out into the crowd. In their centre was a youngish man with dark, neatly parted hair and square glasses resting on a beaky nose. He had the air of a modern, western-style politician and the clothes too, a neat black overcoat and a silk tie. Some men hoisted him onto their shoulders. The president of Bulgaria floated above the crowd like a football star. The halogen light of the TV cameras exaggerated every detail of this former divorce lawyer: the full expressive mouth with thick lips, the red and white megaphone that he held in one hand. He didn't look real. It was as if he was on a movie set. But he had the look of victory on his face.

The crowd yelled in enthusiasm. The journalists shouted questions but nothing could be heard. In the dim background, flags waved and placards bobbed. One read: "Inadequate Mutants! The time is already ours!"

"The government has given up its mandate. There will be early elections," he shouted. More yells of "Victory!" shook the square.

"I am with you. I do not promise that you will be richer or live better. But under the next government I will be honest and you will be masters of your lives. We will not build a factory of dreams," he continued.

It was a sober warning of difficulties to come. But that evening no one paid any attention.

Along the curved granite steps of the St. Kliment Ohridski University, the jublilant faces of shouting and laughing students were illuminated in the orange of a great bonfire. What had been a road-block on the main road into the city had been turned into a blazing pyre of tyres and wood. The students cavorted around it, waving bottles and protest flags. Little mobs of demonstrators roamed the streets, unwilling to go to bed on their success. Cars flying opposition flags raced through the streets, honking horns as if the national football team had won the World Cup. It had been a bloodless coup, a velvet revolution of sorts. It was Europe's first post-communist revolution.

To the English

You tricked us and we tricked ourselves,
We followed and we trusted you,
Now it's shown up and revealed,
What is in your unclean stew.

Sensitive people, and enlightened,
So-called noble, decent race!
In the guise of brother Christians
You first before us took your place.

"England pities, will protect you"
Isn't that just what you said?
"Her thoughts are with you, watches o'er you,"
But what happened here instead?

Can you deny that your object,
The outcome that you wanted most
Was Turks to hold dominion over us
And our total wretchedness.

And for them aren't you ready
Against the will of Christendom
To keep us bound in manacles
In slavery and shame.

You didn't act, did not forestall
The slaughter of our women, children
Does that not make you one and all
A race with hearts of stone?

Petko Slaveikov, 1877

Ex-patriates

WHAT happens after a revolution? Most editors lose interest in the country again. But the problems don't stop. In fact they multiply.

I had become hooked. It was not just a stubborn determination not to return to London with my tail between my legs which drove me onwards. I was fascinated. The country was changing before my eyes from a place where change seemed impossible, to one where everything changed, almost on a daily basis: sometimes for good, sometimes for bad, but always unpredictably.

I was lodging with Johnny and Tanya in their flat in the very centre of the city. The whole building was solid 1930s construction, strong and attractive, particularly compared to the shoddy 50s and 60s era panel blocks where most people had to live in the suburbs. It had been built by Tanya's grandfather and arranged on slightly Chekovian lines. Three female cousins had inherited it, one to each floor.

It was, in every respect, a bourgeois throw-back to the pre-communist era. Everything about it was too good. It had wooden parquet flooring that Tanya kept at high polish. The reception hall, neatly ready for visitors at all times, was arranged with dark art nouveau arm chairs and elegant occasional tables covered in fine laces.

My own bedroom was huge, with a large bay window and a bookcase crammed with English books. The older editions, probably school books, showed a strong bias towards the approved socialist end of the literary canon: Jack London, John Steinbeck, C P Snow, and also, wonderfully, Evelyn Waugh's *Decline and Fall*. I wondered if communist schools had taught this as a set text on the evils of the British class system.

I had set up my laptop on an old wooden table covered in chipped light blue formica in the back pantry. This was where the telephone socket was. The pantry had a faded black and white tiled floor and a vast porcelain sink in the corner. In the late-30s, when it was built, it must have been as chic as you could get in this part of the world. Now it was worn and comforting, from a time when things were made to last.

Here I spent my mornings with telephone, computer and newspapers. But life of another sort was all around me. The old-fashioned wooden cupboards were crammed with glass jars of pickled fruit and vegetables: jars of bright crimson peppers and deep red tomato paste, pallid squirls of cabbage and the baroque mixture of cauliflower and dissected bell-peppers, bottles of home-made tomato juice, golden apricot jam, purple-brown plum jam and dark puce fruit compotes. These jars were part of the Bulgarian way of life, even in the city, Tanya explained to me. They were what everyone lived on through the winter.

"In every house you can be sure there is one of these jars full of dollars too," she said.

This was my introduction to the "jar bank". Instead of converting their savings into gold, Bulgarians bought foreign currency: then US dollars or Deutschmarks, rolled them tight and stuffed them in a jar, hidden under the floorboards, or in the cupboard alongside the pickled fruit.

"Here try some of this from last year." Tanya took down a small pot from the cupboard and opened it for me.

"You can smell the mountains in it," she told me, wafting the jar under my nose. It was wild strawberry jam, crammed with whole fruit. I spread some on a slice of bread. It tasted like nothing I had ever experienced before.

"It is from a village where we have a cottage. You see now why we Bulgarians like things in jars."

The blue formica table was where I wrote my stories about Bulgaria's vast economic problems for *The Sofia Independent*, which had its newsroom in the front room of a grubby ground floor flat just round the corner. If instead of walking round by the street, I nipped round the back of my block, jumped over the wall, using an upturned bathtub half-covered in weeds for a leg up, I could get into the building without having to go on the road.

On Thursday nights I helped the editors to meet the deadline. The scene was always the same. In the foyer, Roland, the Norwegian translator, scribbled frantically, surrounded by sheets of paper, while at the end of the table the TV mimed silently to the porn channel that no one had bothered to switch over. On the wall there was a crusading mission statement:

"We will report the truth as we find it, without fear or favouritism."

The *Independent* was one of the two English language newspapers in the city. Neither made any money. It proprietor liked to think he was bringing civilization to the Bulgarians as well as news in English every week. He was an American property developer with a William Randolph Hearst-type flair for self-promotion, if not for making money out of newspapers. In spite of eight years in Bulgaria he still had that hearty American openness, which non-Americans found so difficult to understand. This was perhaps the origin of the rumour that appeared in the newspapers from time to time that he was the local CIA resident. He did little to discourage it.

"You wouldn't believe how useful it is when dealing with *mutri*," he brayed. "If they threaten me, I record their conversations and I threaten them back. No one wants to get on the wrong side of the USA."

But while most of Sofia seemed to think the proprietor was a spy, he was convinced that everybody else was. He was obsessed with *groupirovki*, the sinister and powerful business groups that had taken control of the economy and the country since the end of communism. He was sure they had their origins in the fearsome and pervasive communist era secret police.

"Everybody knows that communism didn't go away in Bulgaria. That's why this country is so screwed up. The people who were abusing the country before are still doing so now," he used to tell me. It was his favourite rant.

My closest friend in the newsroom, the man who had pretty well dragged me from the street to give me a job at the paper, was Matei Brunwasser, the assistant editor. He had arrived in Sofia a year early, more or less by chance. Travelling on the night train from Istanbul to Buchurest he got off at the first stop.

"I liked it so I stayed," was his explanation.

I hardly ever saw him without a Victory cigarette dangling from his lip. (A completely unintentional piece of post-communist irony, only ever remarked on by visitors from England, was that Bulgaria's leading brand of cigarettes shared its name with the brand smoked by Winston Smith in Orwell's 1984.).

His clothes typified his approach to life. He was unshaven with short black curly hair and a few grey hairs at the temples. He was always resolutely un-smart, often wearing the same t-shirt, combat trousers and old anorak for days. He didn't try to impress anyone because the mainstream wasn't very interesting to him. When he looked at any major event he always tried and find some way to make it unusual or rather to show what was unusual about it.

"I get the feeling here that I am on the frontier. I never get bored here. It's the most completely unpredictable country I have ever lived in. You can never say what's going to happen next," he told me.

This, for him, justified the edgy informal existence that those on the margins of the expatriate world are forced to live in Sofia. His long stay in the country had been semi-legal at best. He had to renew his visa every month by crossing the border. It was a ridiculous ruse. No one was quite sure why it worked so well.

The idea had been pioneered by Norwegian Roland who had been a tourist in Bulgaria for five years already, thanks to the endless renewal of his 30-day tourist visa.

Roland came in on press nights to transform dodgy Bulgarian articles into reasonable journalistic English. He was emblematic of a particular type of ex-patriate jetsam that seemed to wash up in Bulgaria. He had been raised by his father in Norway but abandoned it, driven by some never fully expressed discontent.

Thanks to his mother he had an American passport. But he refused to go there. Many of our mutual Bulgarian friends could not understand this. They dreamt of being able to go to the USA, and discussed jealously the Green Card lottery and the possibilities of getting sponsorship to study in American colleges. Yet here was someone who could go to the US and even work there legally any time he liked. Yet Bulgaria had become his refuge.

To begin with he had come to Sofia because of a woman. The same thing that had attracted many foreigners to Bulgaria. The reason why many stayed was that it was a very cheap place to live. This was important to Roland expecially as he had to adjust his standard of living to what he could earn teaching English, sub-editing on the newspaper and translating. It seemed this was an even worse living than could be made writing journalism.

He was a big man, not only tall but broad. But not powerful. He had the clumsiness of a child about him. And he had a huge head with a great lantern jaw. I often wondered what he would look like if provoked into a rage. What would it take to galvanise him into violent action? I never found out. He did everything slowly, walking talking, eating and drinking. This could have looked like deliberation, but it came across as aimlessness.

Several years later, after the newspaper had closed and we had all gone our separate ways, I would occasionally see him in one of the bars that we used to frequent. He always looked exactly the same. It seemed his life hadn't changed in any detail. He was still living (illegally) in his girlfriend's bedsit in a tower block in the Student Town on the edge of the city and drinking cheap beers in the "non-stop" all-night cafes with their plastic chairs and tables and the smell of stale cigarette ash. Even then, much later on, he was still an eternal tourist, still only officially passing through.

"I get stamped out of Bulgaria. Then I walk around the corner and get myself stamped in again. They don't seem to mind," he told me in slow precise Scandinavian English. Strangely, the authorities seemed relaxed about it. Even when he had forgotten to go for a month or two, they still let him pass. Perhaps the officials thought that anyone who has to resort to such a feeble enterprise to stay in a country whose inhabitants all seemed desperate to leave, could hardly be worth touching for a bribe.

Back then no one knew how long it could go on for. There were rumours that the visa regime would change now that the government was aiming to take the country into the European Union. So one day, Matei and Roland might cross the border and not be allowed back in again.

Falling in Love

Bandit Song

My day I day in hidden places,
My night I night in unknown by-ways
I have no father,
And no mother.
Father, for me to groan,
Mother, for me to moan.
Woe is me, white peaks of Pirin
Alas, alas strong brandy of Odrin

My foe I foe, measure for measure,
My friend I befriend, together forever.
I have no brother,
And no sister.
Brother, me to hail,
Sister, me to wail
Woe is me, death dealing carbine,
Alas, alas dark Tsarigrad wine.

God he is God. Let him be so,
The Tsar is Tsar, but forever, or no?
I have no love,
No true first love.
In me to believe,
And then to grieve.
Woe is me, sharp, bloody blade,
Alas, alas slim Salonica maid.

Peyo Yavorov

Disappearing Treasures

THE first thing I noticed about the girl waiting for the press conference in the foyer of the grandiose presidency building was her straight, natural honey-brown hair which fell half way down her back in thick strands. The next thing I noticed were her eyes, which were large and light brown and almost unnervingly steady, like the eyes of an owl. She had an oval face, high cheekbones and pointed chin. She gazed around the heavy marble hall, where the journalists were gossiping and smoking and waiting for something to happen, with a detached look containing an indefinable challenge that might or might not be contempt.

"I'm not a journalist," she told me in soft simple Bulgarian, realising that I was foreign.

"I'm an artist. My name is Yana."

"So what are you doing here?"

I had been learning Bulgarian as fast as I could and could just about keep up with her.

"Waiting for a friend."

"Here?" It seemed improbable.

"How did you get in?"

I was thinking of the formalities I had to go through: showing passport and press card to the security thugs on the door.

"If you know the right thing to ask, the right way to ask it and the right person to ask it to, you can do anything, go anywhere and get what you like in this country."

She said this with a mixture of pride and cynicism. Could the rules coulbend like plasticine for everybody?

I was waiting for an American economist to give his press conference. He had been telling the President how the country could fix its economic problems. Soon he would come down the red-carpeted staircase and announce his panacea to the country.

"Bouhhh! Those guys! What do they know about Bulgaria? One economist says one thing. Another says different. Whatever we do, nothing changes for us ordinary people. Don't bother with him. Come and drink coffee."

We slipped out through the heavy double doors as the economist and the President sauntered down towards the microphones. Outside we were just in time to catch the changing of the presidential guard. They goose-stepped raggedly past us in white braided tunics, high shiny boots, eagle feathers in their woollen caps. But they had nowhere to march to. 20 yards down the street they rounded the corner and without waiting for an order, immediately broke ranks and started hunting through their pockets for cigarettes and lighters, which they shared with the girls who waited at the small doorway in the side of the building.

In a little café near the archeological museum Yana told me about her life.

"My father doesn't want me to be an artist. I disappointed him by not becoming an economist like him. An economist! Can you imagine? He is unemployed now, so what good has it done him? At least I have a job."

She had trained as a restorer of antique icons, mosaics and frescos, but worked as a graphic designer. Even then the money was not good.

"I came to Sofia to study at the Arts High School. I lived with my aunt, but she was a bitch. She said I looked like a gypsy. I had to say who I was going out with, when I would be back home. So I left. The next year I lodged with a woman and her daughter. I think they were prostitutes. Not on the streets, but you know, men would come in from time to time. They had no other way of getting money, apart from my rent. I fell in love with a cocaine addict. It was a bad time."

My understanding of Bulgarian was being tested to the limit. Yana knew no English. *In extremis* we resorted to French. She was fluent but I had a dimly remembered 'O' level. I carried a dictionary in my pocket and brought it out frequently, but she pushed it back and explained her words using other, more simple Bulgarian words that I knew.

"Don't always look at your book. To understand you must talk. You must learn to listen!"

She told me about the last days of communism. It sounded like a great adventure.

"It was so exciting! Even before the changes it was exciting. You could feel that things were changing. More things were allowed. They stopped criticising us so severely for listening to western music. We started to take risks. After the changes we thought for a while that everything would be so different. But now..."

She stopped and gestured.

"You see what we have now."

• • •

For Orthodox Easter we borrowed a car and headed to a little village where Yana's cousin had a house. We travelled eastwards across the wide expanse of the Upper Thracian plain. The broad prairies stretched out on either side towards the mountains. They were still bare after the winter, although in some fields great flocks of black rooks swooped and swirled like funereal confetti, feasting on newly sown crops.

To the north were the low rolling slopes of the *Sredna Gora*, the central highlands. The purple-grey rounded forested peaks of the Rhodopes, spread along the distant southern horizon. From there they stretched for a hundred miles almost to the shores of the Aegean.

Throughout the plain, conical mounds jutted incongruously from the field, many of them shaggy with grass and small trees and pock-marked with holes dug by hundreds of generations of looters. These Thracian burial tumuli had been pillaged for centuries, up to the present day. But it drove Yana wild with anger.

"Bulgaria is full of treasure. But every year the thieves and bandits with their metal detectors dig it up and sell it. *Prostatsi!* Simpletons! Our country is being stripped to the bone!"

Close to the road the prairies were divided into small rectangular parcels where groups of people planted something, or hoed or weeded: bending and straightening their backs to cultivate fields which under communism must surely have been ploughed and sown and sprayed by tractor. We passed herds of sheep watched over by solitary men who leant on their long sticks, or sat on the verge and gazed at nothing

Plovdiv appeared on the far horizon like a cluster of vast tumuli. It is a city, like Rome, on seven hills. It straddles the River Maritza, known as the River Hebrus in classical times. It is the river down which the still singing head of Orpheus floated, after he had been torn to pieces by a horde of women in a Bacchanalian frenzy. Generations of Bulgarian nationalists, up to and including the communists were very enthusiastic about Orpheus. They liked to think that his musical genius had been transmitted to the modern world in the complex and haunting folk music of the Rhodopes, which is certainly unlike any other music you will ever hear.

The Rhodope mountains are not high. They have no jagged peaks. It's as if they have been smoothed down by time. They spread in an irregular oblong over the south western corner of the country, straddling the border with Greece. We arrived in a village where a score of houses clung to the side of a steep valley that fell sharply away below to a stream, just visible through the still bare branches of the beech trees. There was a permanent roar of water cascading over stones, and the wind in the branches. The stone and mud houses scrabbled across the slope, bunched like a herd of sheep. They were connected by rocky little footpaths where grannies shooed chickens and dogs loitered. Half the houses were deserted. A few, like the one we are staying in, had become family holiday homes.

That evening, Easter eve, we went to the church of the neighbouring monastery. Batchkovo is one of the country's greatest monasteries. Its high stone walls make it appear more like a fortress than a church on the side of a dark and narrow valley.

We arrived a little before midnight. Crowds of people thronged up the steep roughly cobbled road to the main gate. The entrance was a heavy round arch. The old metal studded wooden doors (the similarity to a fortress even more striking here) were wide open. To the left of the gate, water gushed from a line of metal spouts into a stone trough.

Inside the whole aspect of the building changed. The dark shadow of a classic orthodox church in the Byzantine style, occupied the centre of a crowded courtyard. I could just make out the shape of its dome against the inky sky, with no trace of ambient light. The high walls, which looked so forbidding from without, were ringed with tiers of wooden balconies, like a great Shakespearean theatre. The whitewashed walls were lined with doors, each one a monk's cell. The balconies were the corridors and were linked by a network of staircases. People crowded everywhere. Yana and I pushed into the church, squeezing past a long line of worshippers waiting to buy candles. Inside it was unusually bright. Orthodox churches derive their mystery from the darkness. They are low buildings, often half-submerged, with only a couple of tiny windows. The wall paintings in the farthest corners should be almost invisible. But this evening every lamp and candle in the massive brass candle holders blazed with light and hundreds of lemon curd-yellow votive candles dropped hissing beeswax onto the floor. It was hot and the honey smell of the beeswax mingled with the spice of burnt incense. Several hundred people had squeezed in to light ever more candles and kiss icons. They waited expectantly, grasping unlit candles in their hands, waiting for the coming of Easter day.

A few minutes before midnight the priests hidden behind the iconostasis began a fresh chant. The twin doors in the centre of the wooden screen opened and the Easter procession emerged. The first monk carried an icon of Christ. A bishop in a glittering bulbous mitre followed. He carried two bunches of crossed candles. A third priest rushed across from the side, to hand him his crook, just in time, before a crush of worshippers closed round him, trying to light their candles from his blessed flame. This seemed like old religion, mixed with superstition, far away from what I was used to. Another priest emerged carrying the Gospels.

"*Hristos Voskrese!*" bellowed the first priest.

"*Voistina Voskrese!*" came the reply from the whole church, intoned in unison. The procession slowly forced its way out of the church into the courtyard where the cry was repeated for the hundreds of worshippers gathered outside.

"Christ Has Risen!"

"Indeed He Has Risen!"

The reply rippled through the crowd. There was a crackle of breaking eggshells. Yana called to me. "Come on!. Where's your egg?"

Everyone had brought hard-boiled eggs with coloured shells.

"Fat end first," she indicated and cracked hers on mine, which broke. We turned them over and I cracked the pointed end down on her egg. Mine broke again.

"I win, I win!" She cried.

It was a game of conkers. A stranger cracked her egg and turned victorious to challenge someone else. We peeled our defeated contenders and ate them straight away.

"Oh, I was hungry!" gasped Yana between eager mouthfuls.

I was not surprised. She had fasted all day, taking neither food nor water. Very few people still fast this way at the end of Lent, and most who do, tend to be women. The priest's candle flame had multiplied many hundred-fold. All around us the firefly glimmer of the slim yellow candles illuminated faces with an orange glow. The carriers of the flames guarded them skilfully against the wind in their cupped hands. Yana lit her candle from the man who broke her egg.

"We must take it home with us without it blowing out. Then we can bless the house."

• • •

During the next months, Yana took me to monasteries and nunneries that she had helped to restore. There were many in the mountains around Sofia. The Balkan Range just north of the city is known as the Sofiiska Holy Mountain. It used to be a kind of mini-Athos. Now there are so few monks and nuns that many of the monasteries are deserted, or have just a single inhabitant.

One of them overlooked the huge steel plant that squatted east of the city like a rusty stain on the edge of the plain. It was where Yana's mother had brought her to be christened as a young teenager. Her eyes are alive with the recollection.

"Oh, you cannot hope to understand the importance of that moment! Everything had to be done in secrecy because, you know, the thing the communists hated most was for children to be taught religion. They would allow American films to be shown every year on Easter and Christmas Eve – anything to persuade us not to go to church. They let our parents worship if they chose. But it was bad for them if they did. They were spied on and could hope for no career or promotion. But for us, we were not allowed. At school we had to be very careful to say nothing about it."

As we walked up the path through the trees, the little monastery looked like a little farm. Chickens scurried in the yard out front and there was a small vegetable patch. It was only when we were up close that I noticed the white piece of paper stuck to the gate-post. Yana stopped dead, hand over mouth. Then gripped my arm and dragged me forward.

"Oh look! She is dead."

The paper was a "necrolog". It was a death notice, a printed sheet surmounted with a large back cross that announced a death with the name of the deceased. The Abbess had died just the day before. Beside the church a pair of scruffy old men were already digging a grave. One was inside it, one on the edge. They leant on their spades and watched us as we walked by.

Yana had worked on the restoration of the church where the Abbess was now lying in her coffin. We went in. A single nun was praying by the coffin. She pulled back the black covering. The Abbess looked like she was made from yellow wax, more of a thing than a person. Her face was framed by a crisp black nun's veil. She had an unfriendly tight-lipped expression – not at all how she was in life Yana told me later.

I stifled a panicked desire to laugh, looking around while I pulled myself together. The church had a new plain roof because it had been shaken down in an earthquake. The walls were covered with extraordinarily vivid late 15th century frescoes – Archangel Michael was a stern Roman soldier with great gold wings spread behind his crimson cloak. St John the Baptist, bowed with care, with straggly hair and beard, stared piercingly through the centuries; his face and expression were surprisingly vivid and naturalistic. The paintings were riven with great cracks. Yana had filled the great cracks with white plaster and cleaned away the centuries of tallow grease so the surviving pictures could shine again. The church was now being left to a single old nun. She had the chickens and the vegetable patch. I wondered if she would stay and what will happen to the place.

Yovano, yovanke

Yovano, Yovanke,
By the Vardar ever sitting,
In the stream your linen cleaning
Ever upwards gazing, darling
O my heart, my Yovanke

Yovano, Yovanke,
Ever for you am I waiting,
Waiting for you, for your coming
But you never come, my darling
O my heart, my Yovanke.

Yovano, Yovanke,
Your mother, O, your mother, alas
Will not let you, does not allow you
To come near, to be near me, darling
O my heart, my Yovanke.

Traditional Macedonian love song

Crossed Lines

"**D**ID you know your telephone is bugged?"

I was working at my formica table top, with the throbbing of the old fridge and the humming of my old laptop in the background. I had to listen hard to tell what the tinny distant voice was talking about.

This voice belonged to the East European Editor of the *Financial Times*, who once upon a time had been expelled from Moscow in one of the "tit-for-tat" spy rows, and therefore might have known what he was talking about.

"It's not surprising," he added. "Old habits die hard."

As he said this, the line clicked and whirred ominously. Things hadn't worked out with the *FT* like I had hoped. Their local stringer, who claimed to have been getting death threats, and was all set to move to England, had decided not to quit after all. Instead he was complaining about me. At least the newspaper had given me a letter of accreditation. But now that was causing problems, which is why I was having this conversation about phone-taps with the editor.

"You are making life very awkward for our man there," he told me on the crackling line. "People keep on asking him who the other correspondent is. Haven't you picked up any other strings yet?"

"I'm working on it," I told him. "But please believe me, I'm not the one who's making these claims. It's the Foreign Ministry. I'm down on their list as the *FT* correspondent because of the letter you wrote."

"Well, don't do any interviews calling yourself our correspondent," he warned. "But I hope things are OK for you out there otherwise. Get some other strings as quick as you can. Try some radio. And careful what you say on the telephone."

As if on cue the line clicked and buzzed some more.

I had put all those background noises and the regular soft ticks down to the immense decrepitude of the telephone system.   But maybe I was being listened to. If so, I pitied the poor spy who had to do the job. Sometimes I hardly knew myself who I was talking to.

Often stray voices would cut across my conversations. There were several murmuring grumbling men and an old woman who always seemed to be complaining. But the most frequent background chatter came from a pair of incorrigible gossips. Most often their voices were faint, like a radio turned down too low or neighbours overheard through a party wall. But sometimes they drowned out the voice of the person I was trying to reach.

Occasionally I didn't even have to dial, I could just pick up the telephone and hear their cackles and exclamations and I would strain to decipher what scandals and secrets they were relaying to each other. They must have spent half their day gossiping. Perhaps they had started gossiping about me.

I was talking to Yana one afternoon when we suffered a particularly bad interruption. The gossips were laughing and cawing at each other so loudly that it was impossible for us to speak over them.

"This is a bit annoying," I yelled. "We can hardly hear one another. Perhaps we should speak later."

Yana had a different plan. Instead of replying to me, she shouted at the women something I couldn't understand, possibly quite rude. Whatever it was, it shocked them. For a blissful moment, they were silent. Then just when I thought the problem had been solved a rapid and furious three-way dispute broke out. I couldn't follow it at all. In any case I had been forgotten.

Finally there was a pause.

"What's going on?" I asked.

"I told them to stop their conversation. But they won't unless we do too. We must all hang up and try again."

Once we had established this rule, things became easier. I even got to meet one of the women. Svetla was a plump, vacant shop assistant wearing too much make up. We met up for coffee and she pestered me with personal questions about my relationship with Yana.

"It is better to be alone. Bulgarian girls are no good. If you have a Bulgarian girlfriend and do not buy her clothes, and CDs and take her out and give her gold, she will leave you," she told me.

I wondered what the spies thought of it all, if they existed at all. Although everyone believed in them, I had my doubts.

"Don't worry about them," Yana shrugged. "If they want to listen, let them. Why should we still be frightened?"

It was a good question. But the sad truth was that even in the mid-90s many Bulgarians were still very scared of the regime that they had so recently left behind.

Yana lived alone in a small dark apartment in a block just outside the centre. I spent as much time there as I could. It had bars on the windows. Although it was supposed to be a smart area of the city, at night it still echoed to the sound of gunshots. Private security vehicles and stray dogs prowled the streets after dark. During the day, the dusty-grey strays sprawled on the steps outside the flat with lolling pink tongues.

Yana's neighbour fed them scraps and put collars on them so the city council didn't take them away and destroy them.

In the evenings, Yana curled in a plastic chair in her little kitchen drinking intense herbal teas sweeted with honey and brandy and smoking cigarette after cigarette. She patiently told me everything about her past in a soft deep voice with both laughter and sadness in it. Even when I was so tired that the words no longer made sense, I loved to listen to the music and rhythm of her language. As she talked she brushed her long hair. It was one of the things I liked best about her. She didn't dye it, like most other Bulgarian girls.

Learning Bulgarian was like learning a new way of thinking. I even learnt a new body language. Yana shook her head for yes and nodded for no. In fact the yes was more of a head wobble, quite a cheerful little movement, but lackadaisical and conditional. Her nod for no, however, was curt, dismissive and infuriatingly laconic. Sometimes she accompanied it with a short sucking clack of her tongue against the upper palate or a swift wag of her index finger. What pleasure she got from it, and from my confusion. Never had saying no seemed so bloody-minded, been so much fun.

I sometimes wonder if the historically terrible relations between Greece and Bulgaria would have been any better if nodding and saying "Ne!" didn't mean no north of the border and yes south of it. How can near neighbours be so mutually incomprehensible?

According to legend, the Bulgarians got their opposite body language thanks to Turkish attempts to convert Christian peasants to Islam. The Janissaries would hold a knife under the throats of the poor Christians and ask them if they accepted Islam. A shake of the head was taken to mean yes. Or perhaps nodding the head would have brought the point of the knife into soft underside of the victim's jaw. Either way, no was taken to mean yes or vice versa.

I don't know if I believe that tale. Perhaps it is rrather that Bulgarians have got used to neither giving or receiving a straight answer. This is certainly true where politics is concerned. No one ever believes the first thing they are told or accepts any event or development at face value. As my friend Tanya once told me "We think one thing, say a second and finally do a third thing." But Tanya also told me that this was nothing to do with age old legends of the Ottomans. This was just how everyone got by living under communism.

• • •

Every so often Yana got death threats. The first time it happened the telephone woke me in the middle of the night.

"*Mutri,*" she told me padding back into the bedroom.

"Shouldn't we be doing something?" I was panicking. Mutri were gangsters, ex-wrestlers, burly shaven-headed graduates from the elite communist sports academies who wore sinister dark suits and drove their shiny black limousines with darkened windows too agressively through the Sofia streets. The word derived from the Bulgarian for a dog's snout. It meant "mug", "ugly face" or perhaps "plug-ugly".

If they were calling in the middle of the night it was time to be worried. Yana seemed more angry than concerned.

"Bastards!" she said, curling up in the bed. "They're just trying to scare me. What would they gain from killing me? Don't worry. Go back to sleep!"

These mutri threats came and went at unpredictable intervals. Weeks or months could go by without any disturbance. Then one afternoon as she sat on the plastic chair in her kitchen with her feet on my lap and long hair bundled up with a clip, Yana told me she had had a visit on the day before. It was clear what she meant.

"How many?"

"Just two. They had guns. I didn't know what to do. I told them I had nothing of value and that I didn't know anything. They had a look around and left."

Part of me wished that I had been there. Another part was thankful that I was not. What would I have done? The thugs were looking for money – payoffs still owing from when Yana's sister Maria was running a cigarette scam from this flat. The scam had folded a couple of years previously when Maria had packed up and left for Greece. She had been friends with many of the city's most well known criminals, gangsters and racketeers.

"Why don't you move?" I asked.

"And you think they wouldn't find me if they wanted to? If they were going to do something to me they would have done it by now. They know what the situation is. They know I have nothing."

She didn't sound like she had convinced herself but shrugged wearily, a gesture that had already become familiar to me in conversations about Bulgarian life.

• • •

Sometimes I felt like a monkey in the zoo when I sat on Yana's balcony. It was encased with thick bars for security. But it caught the sun nicely. I was reading there one afternoon when I saw Maria's convertible VW Golf pull up in the car park below. The top was down and back seat was ostentatiously piled with presents.

Maria liked to come back to visit from Greece without warning. She looked like what all Bulgarian women want to be: a woman of the world, with plenty of money. She was in her late thirties, polished, confident, but somewhat overdone: beige business suit and high heels, shiny Gucci handbag, heavy gold earrings, wrists clanking with thick braclets, a pair of sunglasses with an obvious Gucci label pushed up into her short dyed blond hair.

"I'll make some calls," she promised, when Yana told her about the threats. "They won't touch you."

For her this seemed to be just another problem as tiresome and every day as a blocked drain or a burst pipe.

I pulled some glasses and a bottle of rakia from the cupboard. Yana sliced some white cheese and tomatoes, sprinkling them with salt, sunflower oil and vinegar. This was lunch.

"I knew all the biggest scams in Bulgaria," confessed Maria with enthusiasm, even with pride. She reeled off the names of people about whom I had heard only bad things, for instance the boss of a racketeering group who had just been arrested for firing his gun in a crowded nightclub. Several others were now dead: murdered.

"Yes, they were crooks, and some of them killers, but they were still good friends. Anyway, most of them are much better behaved now," she said. "Particularly the dead ones."

She saw those rapacious years of the early nineties as a game, in which she had been a player for a while. It had been entertaining to fill her villa on the slopes of Mount Vitosha with notorious, dangerous men. She had possessed both glamour and money.

Maria's particular scam was cigarettes. She had been the local representative for a major international tobacco company. Her job was to market its cigarettes throughout the country.

"It was impossible. There was no way I could sell enough cigarettes to pay for this office and the staff, let alone the villa and the parties. The simple answer was to re-export the cigarettes as duty-free. All I had to do was to bribe some customs officials. I gave them money and presents and opened a free club for them in my villa. They came every night to drink my whisky. I must have avoided $1 million in taxes."

The cigarette company had not been pleased to find itself being undercut by its own produce on the black markets in Greece and Italy and other European countries, which was where the lorry loads of tax-free cigarettes had ended up. The trail seemed to lead back to Bulgaria but they couldn't prove anything.

"They got suspicious. They sent an inspector to see what was going on. I had to persuade him that I was selling the cigarettes here. At that time I was selling an amazing quantity of cigarettes abroad. I had smuggled everything I had out of the country except for a few cartons. So we organised ourselves in two cars. In one car we had the cigarettes, the promotional materials, umbrellas and posters. I was in the other with the man from the company. He bought a packet of cigarettes from every kiosk we visited. I drove him round in circles, while everything was packed up and rushed by a different route to the next bar or kiosk and set up again."

"So what happened? Why did you leave if it was going so well?"

"We were forced out."

"Forced out?"

"Oh, yes. Some much bigger thugs than us came into the market so we had to go. Why do you think Yana is still getting these threats? People get killed in this business."

Maria went back to Greece. I never worked out what she did or said to stop the mutri from bothering Yana any more. Yana knew but refused to tell me.

"You don't want to know," she said.

But I did want to know. I wanted very much to know everything about the mutri that I could possibly discover.

They gave the gypsy a kingdom and he asked:
What about bread?

Popular Bulgarian saying

Adventures with the Underclass

A LL I had to do was to stick with Yana and eventually I would learn. A few months later, Maria returned to Yana's flat, flashy as ever in designer jeans and a new peroxide hairdo. She poured a cascade of little gold trinkets onto the plastic table on the balcony.

"What do you think of this? Pretty, huh? Nice presents? I got them in Istanbul." She held up a handful of little gold hearts, which dripped through her fingers on slender chains. They looked like very nice presents.

"Who are you giving them to?"

Maria didn't answer. She and Yana went out together and didn't come back until the evening. They had been touring the main western European consulates, Yana told me, giving little presents to special friends at each stop. It made life a lot easier when the time came for applying for visas, she said.

The visa application business was a sideline that Maria had operated alongside her cigarette business. Unlike her cigarette smuggling scam, it was still just about going. Demand had shrunk dramatically since the introduction of the European Union's Schengen system. It would vanish altogether once the EU finally agreed on visa free travel for Bulgarians.

But until then Bulgaria still seemed like a prison. Getting visas was a much-admired skill in the atmosphere of semi-acceptable criminality that had its roots in disappointed hopes. Yana boasted with justifiable artistic pride that she had obtained fraudulent visas from almost every consulate in Sofia.

Spas "The Greek" was one of the last remaining customers. He had travelled all over Europe thanks to the sisters' combined arts.

Maria's gift-giving tour of the consulates had greased the wheels for his future travels.

"Spas is fun. He's a *pich*, a wild guy!" Yana told me one afternoon as we waited in her flat for him to visit.

"But watch out for him. He's cunning as a fox. No, as a wolf. He may seem foolish when he speaks. He makes laughable mistakes in Bulgarian that only foreigner or child could make. But in his world we appear very foolish too. So don't be tricked."

Spas made his entrance like a showman. He paused briefly on the threshold, glowered at me for a second and then came in beaming broadly arms outstretched to embrace Yana. He was wearing a soft very long greeny blue overcoat, reminiscent of comic book Chicago gangsters from the prohibition period. Its soft opulence suggested a garment not really designed for wind and rain. It flapped open to reveal a bright blue Bugs Bunny tie and an exaggerated, almost zooty, double breasted suit, the green of a troubled sea. Heavy gold flashed from his person as he strode into the room. Fingers winked with thick rings, a deliberate shake of the wrist rolled a chunky bracelet from under his cuff. Expensive fillings glittered amongst the decay of his smile.

He greeted Yana warmly and then turned to me. We shook hands warily. My eyes watered from the aftershave which enveloped him in a bitter cloud. He had a full, mobile mouth and sharp eyes. His dark colouring and thick-set features immediately distinguished him as a Roma gypsy.

"Let's go out," he suggested.

At the Happy Kebab bar and restaurant, Spas insisted on ordering everything himself. The waitress brought big plates of food and large glasses of beer.

"Eat! Eat my friends!" the gypsy urged us.

Yana nibbled, cool, relaxed, and watchful.

Later she told me that he always bought the drinks because he wanted to create an obligation. He wanted us to feel we owed him because sooner or later he was going to ask for something.

Yana had been working on the opposite tack to make him feel an obligation in return. She presented him with a batch of business cards that she had designed and had printed specially for him. They proclaimed his name in large, bold italic: **Spas Gruka..**

"Spas the Greek".

"Why are you Spas the Greek? Why not Spas the Rom?"

He grinned broadly and winked: "Well, you know what the Greeks are like? A Rom can cheat a Bulgarian but only a Greek can cheat a Rom! No one is better than they are."

As he said this he twirled his fingers in the deft twisted grasping motion that throughout the Balkans is the classic symbol for light fingeredness. It seemed like an advertisement: "I am going to con you."

Pleasantries over, he and Yana got down to business. Spas wanted to visit America. Yana shook her head. This was a more complex proposition than the usual business of getting a European visa. The US consulate was much stricter than the others. There was no one there who would take a gold bauble and wink as the application went through. It would have to look completely official and above board. That would be difficult and expensive.

"I have to get this visa," Spas said. "Whatever it takes."

Yana decided that he must travel as a representative from the travel company, which her sister kept going for just this reason. She could prepare all the necessary employment documents on elegant company letter headings – in full colour. Spas would have to produce bank statements and property deeds. What couldn't be obtained legitimately would be carefully forged. It would be expensive – 1000 German marks.

Spas winced. He pushed his chair back and stood up abruptly. "Too much."

He paced to the door and back biting his thumb in worry and disappointment.

"You are taking advantage of me," he protested.

Yana sat unmoved.

"Its not an easy job. If you know someone who will do it for less money, why are you bothering me?"

It had been a bad year he complained glumly.

"One of my enemies has put a curse on me."

"A curse?"

"Yes. He must have gone to a witch and asked her to jinx me. In Sliven, where I am from, they will do that. It must have been a strong curse because it has been difficult for my own witch to remove it."

He sighed again, grumbled, cursed, paced back and forth, sighed and pleaded some more.

My resolve would have wilted a dozen times at the pathos of this preposterous tale. But Yana was firm. Spas extracted from her a single important concession. He would pay the price but only on receipt of the visa. As Yana agreed, the cloud of the curse seemed miraculously to evaporate. They shook hands, great satisfaction evident on both sides.

"Why exactly do you have to go the US?" I asked.

"I have business."

He refused to say exactly what, grew edgy under my questioning. "Just business, you know."

"How will you get by? How much English do you know?"

He trotted out a few words: "Hello, thank you, good bye…" and grinned proudly.

"That's it?"

"I have friends. I get by."

"Don't ask me how, but he does," added Yana. "Show him your passport."

Spas took the document from the inside pocket of his lurid suit and passed it to me. It was stuffed with stamps.

"Look! Nederlands, Osteriech, Fransia, Germania, Englerland."

"Maria and I got them all for him," said Yana proudly.

Spas had loved visiting Europe. He had picked up a smattering of almost every European language, just enough to satisfy his needs, which like his impressions, were basic. Amsterdam had pleased him most.

"I had two, two at once!" He crowed lasciviously. It wasn't necessary to ask two what?

"One blonde and one brunette!"

Yana left the table and he nudged me again.

"Tell me. Yana? What's she like?" He wagged his finger obscenely. "Come on. Tell Spas."

We left him chortling and drinking. Back at her flat, Yana took out her electric typewriter and a sheaf of company letterheadings.

"First we give him all the official company documents. Spas is an employee of our travel agency. We are sending him abroad to set up some tours for us. The next most important thing is money. Fortunately Spas has access to funds. We must make sure there is a large amount in his account and then get a balance statement for that day. Finally, we must show that he owns property in Sliven and has his family there. The good thing about Spas is that he always comes back. He never makes a mistake, it's too important to him."

"What is?"

"His business, whatever it is."

She and her sister had often asked him about this and never got a reply either.

"It must be something criminal. Perhaps he is a pick-pocket."

"More likely a drug smuggler."

Yana snorted with derision. "He's not part of any gang."

"Doesn't it bother you what he might be getting up to?"

"It's just business. I'm not responsible."

• • •

A week later, Spas went for his interview at the US consulate. I waited with Yana at a café five minutes walk away. He arrived, resplendent as ever in his inky green suit and bugs bunny tie. But he had added a pair of spivvy very dark glasses to his accessories. They failed to disguise a large black eye.

"I got into a fight at a disco," he confessed sheepishly lifting up his shades to reveal the full extent of the damage.

Yana was furious.

"How could you? I thought this was important to you. Well, it'll be your fault if you are refused. You should pay me anyway."

Accepting payment on delivery was always going to be risky for her. This had made it more so. It was risky for Spas too. If the consular officials spotted any subterfuge he would be refused entry to the US for ever.

While he queued we waited in the café. Yana fidgeted over her coffee. She needed this money desperately. Her job was not going well. The graphic design project she was working on had been rejected and her boss was threatening to reclaim some of the advances he had paid out on her wages. To make matters worse a restaurant where half of her paintings were on display had gone bust. The creditors had taken her pictures away along with the kitchen equipment and the tables.

"Can't you get them back? Why don't you just go and talk to the administrator or the court?"

"What administrator? The creditors have just taken everything. These are not the sort of people you can just ask for things from."

A poor old man was stopping at each table in the café fiddling with an old book bound in orange plastic. He opened it to reveal four leafed clovers pressed between its yellowed pages.

"For luck... for health...?" he croaked.

Yana refused with a nod and a tongue click. It left no room for appeal. Sometimes she was capable of great compassion, but she had a hard streak too.

I gave the man some *stotinki*. He left one of the clovers on our table and shuffled away. I could hardly bear to see the many pathetic ways that old pensioners tried to earn money. Babas would sit on street corners behind a set of bathroom scales: 50 stotinki to weigh yourself. I had never seen anyone take up the offer. But selling clovers was not much better.

"That man must have a whole bush of four-leafed clovers at home," I suggested not really believing it. The more likely alternative was that he spent days searching for them in the fields and then sold them for a pittance.

"Tch....tch..." nodded Yana again in the emphatic negative. "They belonged to his wife, who collected them when she was young. She's now dead and so he's selling them off."

She stared at me defiantly, waiting for a comment on her cynicism.

"Does it still make you feel lucky?" she asked. "You have to make your own luck here you know."

"I brought mine with me. Your bloody country! At least I can leave when I want to."

"Whenever you want!" spat Yana in fury. "I hate it when you are foreign and I hate your pity. Don't condescend to me. I'm proud to be Bulgarian. Whatever happens to me or to this country, I will always be proud to call myself a Bulgarian!"

The argument had swung out of nowhere and left us both surprised and speechless. We sat in furious silence until Spas returned, swaggering cockily, sniffing at the remains of the hard words between us like a dog on a scent.

"Anything wrong? Something I should know about?"

Yana shook off the enquiry. "What happened to you?"

Somehow Spas had passed the interview and got his visa. Now it was time for payment. He counted ten 100 German Mark bills from a thick wad onto the flimsy table. Yana picked them up and put them into her bag.

"You didn't count them!" protested the gypsy.

"I counted them as you were putting them down. Anyway you wouldn't cheat me, Spas. You need me too much."

"Count them. Please!" he begged. He was grinning a big joke smile.

"OK. As you wish." She took the little wad and put each note down on to the table just as he had done.

"One, two, three... seven, eight...nine."

Spas's grin grew wider. Yana counted again to check. The same result.

"Seven... eight... nine."

"You see. You are way too trusting."

He picked up the notes, pulled another blue 100 mark bill from his notecase, and counted them back out to ten again on the table with exaggerated flips of his thumb. Yana put the money away again with a laugh.

"No! no! no!" yelled the gypsy. Sighing, Yana counted the wad for a third time, pedantically thumping each note on the table.

"Five...six...seven." 300 marks short.

Spas watched smugly then roared with laughter.

"How did you do that? Where did they go?"

As if out of thin air three more notes appeared in Spas's fingers. He handed them over with a flourish.

"Is this how you make your living? Is this what you are going to be doing to those poor Americans?"

He wouldn't tell us.

"Where shall we go to celebrate?" he asked.

• • •

The issue of crime and the Roma minority in Bulgaria reveals human nature at its worst. Most of the country's gypsies live in squalor in ghettos on the edge of major towns or villages. The streets are rarely paved and turn into muddy quagmires in the wet. Most dwellings are extremely poor quality, very crowded and often without running water. Unemployment is more than 90 percent. The provision of schooling is patchy and often resented by parents who are more interested in sending their children to work in a trade, or worse as beggars, thieves and prostitutes.

The Bulgarians like to think of themselves as a nation of almost unique tolerance in the Balkans. But they cannot abide gypsies and the result is massive discrimination. They may have refused to send their Jews to Hitler's death camps (There was a genuine national revulsion against this idea). They may have reached a political accommodation with the Turkish minority, avoiding Yugoslavian type strife in the immediate post-communist years. But gypsies have been ruthlessly excluded from Bulgarian society. They are hated because they are dirty, untrustworthy, clannish and all to frequently involved in crime. But for many gypsies, living in slums with no facilities, no education and no jobs, there is no choice. It is an appalling catch-22.

This is an ever growing problem. Literally. The official census says that 370,908 gypsies were living in Bulgaria in 2001. Their number increased by one-fifth in ten years. There may, in fact, be even more than this. An unofficial census carried out by the government in 1989 said there were more than 570,000 gypsies. Some anthropologists estimate that the number of people of gypsy origin could be as many as 800,000 or more than ten percent of the population.

While the number of gypsies is growing, the ethnically Bulgarian part of the population is shrinking rapidly. Overall the country suffers from a negative birthrate, compounded by massive emigration (an estimated 750,000 have left the country over the past ten years. The population is one million less than it was in 1985). These figures only make Bulgarians more worried about gypsies. No one has any idea how to solve the problem.

• • •

A few weeks before Yana introduced me to Spas, I had been arrested. It was the only time I was ever arrested in Bulgaria. The only reason was because I was in the company of a gypsy. I had gone to Stara Zagora to a Roma pop folk festival and was staying at the home of Petko Emilov, the mayor of Lozenec, the town's gypsy quarter.

The first thing I noticed when he met me off the train in Stara Zagora was that he carried a stubby black pistol in a little brown leather holster on his belt.

"I am tsiganin. I have to look after myself and my family," he said when I ask him about it.

He drove me round the city in his blue Lada. Half of its insides were stripped out. The windows were jammed shut. At the top of every hill he would turn off the engine and free-wheel down the bumpy streets until he ran out of momentum. When it got too hot, he opened his door for ventilation.

At the bottom of one hill, we were stopped by a pair of policemen.

"*Kakvo?*" demanded one of them, gesturing with one hand. The one word enquiry said it all.

"What?"

In other words, explain yourself and what you are doing. Justify your presence here and your existence. What is a gypsy doing driving around with a foreigner in his car?

The policeman snapped his fingers:

"*Documenti?*"

I handed over my passport for inspection. But Petko had left his identity papers at home. We were taken to the police station. That day at lunch we had argued about this very thing.

"In Britain we enjoy great liberty," I had told him, proudly. "We don't need to carry identity cards. Everyone has the right to go about their business unhindered."

Petko could not understand this.

"So how do you prove who you are?"

"I don't need to."

"But say the police think you have committed a crime. How do you prove they have got the wrong man?"

His question had opened a different perspective on the issue for me. In Bulgaria, gypsies are automatically regarded as criminals (As is anyone in their company, regardless of origin.) Petko thought he needed his card to safeguard his civil liberties, not to undermine them.

"My identity card is the only proof that I am a good citizen," he told me as we sat on the hard bench in the lock-up. "I don't know why I left it at home today. It's something I normally never do."

He telephoned his wife from the police station and we waited for one of his sons to bring the documents down the hill. I could see the force of his argument even if I could not get rid of the idea that an identity card was an instrument of repression.

Nearly a decade into the era of democracy and still everyone carried their old communist documents with them. This was because the parliament could not decide on a new national emblem to replace the communist symbol of a lion standing on a cog wheel. The old passport contained information not only where you lived but where you worked. The most sinister fact of all was that gypsies were identified by a tiny dot next to the 2 on page number 12.

Petko's son brought his papers and after an examination, the police let us go. As we walk out of the police station, the mayor showed me his passport. I turned to the page 12. He still had the little dot just by the number.

As we went up to the Roma neighbourhood, the sound of a clarinet led us down the unpaved street into the heart of the quarter. The houses were scrappy and basic. Outside one of them a wedding was being celebrated. Half a dozen plump musicians sat under an awning. Up close, their music was deafening. There is a guitarist, a pianist on a synthesiser, a drummer and two clarinetists and a singer.

The singer warbled with syrupy emotion and the clarinets wailed and shrieked. Sounds of drinking and revelry could be heard from within the house.

"The men are indoors. They let the women dance during the hottest part of the day," Petko told me.

The horo was led by the most unlikely glamorous looking woman to be found amidst the yellow mud and dust. I guessed she was the sister of the bride. Her black glossy hair was piled on her head in an elaborate coiffure that exposed her neck and shoulders, and cleavage, which were spangled liberally with silver glitter. Her body was encased in a clinging crimson dress, almost too tight to dance in. But she managed it gracefully picking her way over the uneven baked mud of the road in a pair of impossibly high and sharp stilettos whose heels were filigreed with a pattern of gold. No one paid any attention to the bride, who danced beside her dressed in demure white flounces.

The other residents of the street (only the men) who had not been invited to the celebration, stood with their backs to the wall and watched. They looked at me curiously.

"Don't stare too hard," said Petko tugging my arm.

We walked back up the street.

The "town hall" was a tiny office up the hill. A crowd of people had gathered outside, waiting for Petko to open up. I sat on the old sofa and listened to complaints of corruption and embezzlement.

"Doesn't the government give you any social support?"

"There is European money that has been allocated for pensioners. But it never get this far. We have no schools, no transport, no drains, no electricity," Petko explained.

Evidence of this was all around. When amenities did exist, they were primitive. Petko's house was perched on the edge of a rubbish dump. But it was grand for the gypsy quarter, fairly new and built of breeze blocks and red air-bricks. Everything inside was spotless, almost as if it were never used. There was a TV, a hi-fi, a foam-stuffed three piece suite. This physical evidence of success was not to be touched. Life was mostly lived in the concrete back yard, where there was a plain wooden table, some benches and a sink with a tap, the only running water in the house.

• • •

Following my Stara Zagora experience, I decided to investigate the lives of the Roma street children in Sofia. I started with the Faith, Hope and Love children's home that had been set up by Dimi Panitsa, one of the first Bulgarians I ever met. My mother had known him in the 1960s when he was managing editor of Reader's Digest in Paris. When I told her that I was going to live in Bulgaria, she had sent me over to see him. My passport was in the Bulgarian Embassy in London, awaiting a visa, so I had borrowed my twin brother's and hopped on the train.

I was to discover that his name opened doors all over the country. He had fled Bulgaria with his family, at the time of the Soviet invasion but had returned as soon as the communist regime fell. Now he was one of the country's leading philanthropists.

The home he created for Sofia's street children was perhaps his greatest project. It provided fresh meals, medical care, clothing and first aid for acute infections diseases. Only children under 16 could stay there over night but those who were too old or who didn't want to stay could wash and get clean clothes.

The centre opened in autumn 1995. Since then more than 400 children up to the age of 16 had passed through its doors. Many more still lived on the streets.

I met up with Angel, an outreach worker, employed by Faith Hope and Love. His job was to visit all the places round the city where the street children lived and slept. He tried to get them to attend the home or at least to visit it to get clean clothes and proper food. The next step was to persuade the children to attend school regularly.

"Some are in the city on their own. Other have parents who don't want them in school. They come to the home and complain that we have kidnapped their children. They want them to be on the streets, begging, bringing in money," he told me.

One of the main homeless camps was just outside the city centre near the central railway station and the international bus station. Angel took me there and as we walked he told me about the homeless problem in the city.

"Look at that building."

He pointed to the collapsing ruin of a town house surrounded by metal fences near the socialist party headquarters.

"Some Roma youths were living there until a month ago when a band of skinheads attacked them while they were sleeping. They smashed bottles on the heads of some of the boys and killed another by throwing him out of window. That's where he landed."

He pointed to a spot on the road.

"People hate the tsigani because they steal. But they have not other choice. Anyway the people who have stolen most from Bulgaria are not the tsigani, but the mutri who are all ethnically Bulgarian."

About 30 people were living by the hot air vents outside the train station. They had formed an extended family led by Ivan, who, in his late 20s, had been living on the streets for ten years.

"We want to work and to have a home," he told us. It was a simple request, but one unlikely to be granted. The ground was strewn with empty flattened tubes of glue, empty bottles, waste paper, and discarded plastic bags. A small baby scrabbled around in the dust playing with an old glue container while her mother looked on disinterestedly and sniffed from a plastic bag.

We found an extremely grubby young man with the dirt of months caked on his skin lounging under a tree in an overgrown empty lot. He was reading a book. This marked him out. Most of the street children are illiterate. Lack of education is one of their main problems. The boy looked up and greeted Angel lazily, not shifting from his comfortable position under the tree.

"What's the book?"

He lifted it so I could see the cover. It was a translation of Melville's Moby Dick.

"This one isn't a thief," Angel told me. "One of his brothers has been convicted of thieving and is in jail but this one is honest."

A third brother lay in the grass on the other side of the tree. He was inhaling deeply from a plastic bag. Amongst the debris of plastic bags, rags and junk lying around I noticed squeezed out tubes of glue.

"After another hour or of that he will be incoherent and probably aggressive. That's why I do my rounds in the morning."

Angel prodded the inhaling youth with his foot.

"Hey, we haven't seen you in the home for a while. You promised me you would come."

The glue sniffer waved him away sulkily.

"Yeah, yeah, I'll come. I said I would."

Then he put his face back in his bag.

A slatternly looking girl nearby was also sniffing glue. She was the girlfriend of the boy who was reading. She worked as a prostitute and was most probably infected with syphilis.

This trio was part of a larger group of about a dozen teenagers who had been living under a tree near the public lavatories at the bus station behind the Novotel Evropa Hotel for the past couple of years. Originally they had come from the town of Lom, a deadbeat place on the banks of the River Danube. Having staked out their territory in Sofia, other homeless people would not come on their patch – at least, not without risking a fight. They made money by working in a couple of nearby cafés where the owners paid them tiny amounts for clearing tables and performing other menial tasks.

Angel had built up a relation of trust with them. So now if he was having trouble making contact with a particular kid, who might be hiding from him or distrustful for some reason, the others would pass messages along for him and try and persuade their unwilling companion to take some good advice.

Crossing the Luvov Most heading back to the centre, Angel plucked a skinny little boy in dirty clothes out of the crowd moving in the other direction and gave him a swift interrogation: where was he working? Where was he sleeping? Was he safe and healthy?

Still holding onto the boy's shoulder, he turned to me.

"Meet Petyo. He's just ten years old. We did not know who his mother was until last year. He ran away from home at the age of five and since then has been homeless and looking after himself. He won't go into the home because he is used to his independence and he wants to have his own money."

Petyo looked at me curiously. Angel squeezed his shoulder and asked him some more questions about his welfare. The little boy meekly answered all the questions and then ran off back towards the train station clutching a bundle of cellophane bags. He had been collecting them all morning and would sell them for a handful of stotinki.

At least he had a job.

Kutso Magare

Limping donkey, ma-le-leee!
Limping donkey, ma-le-le
Four little legs, ma-le-le
And a spare! O-le-le!

Turn and jig, go!
Give a jig, give a jig
Swing your arse, go!
Hey to the left hey to the right.

Blonde madami, ma-le-leee!
Black limousines, ma-le-le
Sofia number plates, o-le-le

Who will drive them, ma-le-le?
Those limousines, ma-le-le
With blonde madami, o-le-le!

An early chalga hit, by the Priest from Hisar

Disappointing a Hermit

CHERRIES herald the Bulgarian summer. I associate them with everything that is best about the country. I associate them with plenty and with love. Yana and I had gone to the mountains for *Chereshova Zadushnitsa* –- summertime All Souls' Day (literally Cherry All Souls). This is one of the three days in the year when Bulgarians remember the souls of the dead. Families tend the graves and leave food offerings. In the winter, All Soul's coincides with our own Hallowe'en. On that day every type of food is left, but mostly sweet things and boiled, sugary wheat. On Cherry All Souls, which happens in early June, mourners simply make offerings of cherries.

It was one of those hot Saturdays when everyone seemed to have resigned themselves to shade and topor. Only a few small figures in the distant fields appeared to be still bent over their work. An old woman hobbled towards us along the verge of the dusty and empty highway leading out of the town in the direction of the cemetery.

"Turn round my dears, you don't want to go there," she said when I told her where we was headed. "That's a place just for old people. Not youngsters like you."

We told her about wanting to see if people still put cherries on the graves. Perhaps she thought we planned to collect them because she made an offer.

"I have left the cherries I had with me at the graveyard. But come to my house and I will give you some from our trees. I'll give you as many as you like. Just go to the *mahala* by the church and ask where Baba Maria lives."

We promised to do this.

The graveyard was a wilderness of flowers. The gravestones sprouted from a rampant meadow of sweet long grass dotted with pink, yellow, powder-blue and tiny white wild flowers. Roses clambered over the white monuments. Most were angular and uncompromisingly modernistic, in that brutal socialist way. They were etched with deliberately clumsy block writing and five pointed stars instead of crosses. The faces of stern angular men, who looked as uncompromising as the pale marble of the monuments, stared fixedly from little black and white photographs, embedded in little oval frames.

Pathetically, even many of these "atheist" graves were stained with sooty wax and not a few had little offerings of cherries on them. The orthodox church has an ambivalent attitude towards this ritual. A religious pamphlet entitled "How to look after our departed" tries to convince readers that there is no need to leave food on a grave so that the dead person won't get hungry in the next world. It points out that:

"Food left on graves will not be eaten by the deceased, but by stray dogs."

But then it is amazing how flexible people can be on matters of belief. Throughout the entire 50-year regime, the communist state repressed and discriminated against people who chose to practice religion. But this did not stop the dictator Todor Zhivkov consulting blind Baba Vanga, one of the most famous soothsayers in the Balkans. As soon as the regime fell, many senior party figures rushed to be seen back in the cathedral, self-consciously crossing themselves in front of the TV cameras. This trend has not slackened.*

Later we went in search of cherries. Baba Maria's house was surrounded by a rich orchard, dripping with red and pink and black cherries. The garden was reverting to wilderness. The grass already at knee height, brambles scaling the walls. I walked round the corner

---

* When Pope John Paul II visited Bulgaria and toured the cathedral, there were, amongst the inevitable crowd of toadies who pushed forwards to kiss his hand, a number of well-known former Party *apparatchiks*, and their wives. One can only assume they were working on the assumption that any authority is worth sucking up to even, or perhaps particularly, when he had led a crushing moral and political victory over their own system. This is one of the most depressing features of Bulgarian and east European society in general. I saw it again and again. It is not just hypocrisy but *slavish* hypocrisy, mixed with appalling self-satisfaction. These people were actually *pleased* with themselves.

of the house to the door. Walking past the window I caught a brief flash of a great fat woman, getting dressed. I darted back in embarrassment but the door flew open. The woman was there, pulling at her skirt.

"What do you want?"

Baba Maria was not in, she explained, when she heard our story and gave us an old saucepan from inside the house. Pick as many as you like, she said. Some of the cherries were pale pink, slightly sharp and very refreshing, others almost black. We picked and picked filling the saucepan and then we ate until we collapsed, sated in the long summer-smelling grass.

We lay replete, hidden amid the wild flowers Yana threw cherries which I caught in my mouth. Bored of "Tinker, tailor, soldier, sailor..." with the cherry stones (I game that I had taught her), Yana tickled me on the nose with a piece of grass. I pretended to sleep. She picked off the ears from the grass, counting: "Happiness, Unhappiness, Letter, Journey, Love, Kiss."

• • •

Later that summer, Matei Brunwasser suggested an exploration of the Strandzha in South east Bulgaria. This is the wildest and most remote part of the country. Any person who wanted to escape the law could flee into its huge forests of beech and oak and never be found again.

The two of us set off in a hired car. It didn't take long before we were completely isolated, in the midst of a lonely wilderness. As the crumbling tarmac coiled and divided through this untended forest our map became less and less useful. Matei pointed at an expanse of blank green between two lines denoting roads that the cartographer had actually noticed and told me:

"We are somewhere here."

From this point our navigation was a question of hunch and reckoning by the sun. Trees carpeted the rolling hills as far as the eye could see. Very occasionally the woods opened into glades or meadows, where families of wild pigs roamed through the trees. The grass was thick and long, ungrazed and unmown, scattered with bright flowers.

In communist times a colonisation programme "Strandja – the Republic of Youth!" had offered financial bounties to anyone who settled there. It was a complete failure. In the few villages that we passed, linked sometimes by nothing more than a dirt track, the only people we saw were aged peasants.

In half an hour of driving we had not seen any sign of human habitation, when we passed a wooden sign nailed to a tree. In crude letters someone had written Trakitsi, the name of a village. The dirt track led intriguingly into the forest. We couldn't let it pass.

Shortly after the turn off we made our first acquaintance in this benighted region. A shepherd was tending some goats by the path. He struck an anachronistic figure as he was wearing a sort of up-dated version of national dress. His baggy trousers and leggings looked home made. His jacket was an ancient and faded army issue. His hair was close cropped and he spoke a dialect that we could scarcely understand.

He pointed us down the path with friendly advice about which paths to take and which not. But in moments we were lost again. It was impossible to tell what was "road" and what woodman's track. For a region seemingly devoid of life and habitation there were a great many directions to travel in. We pushed on out of bloody-mindedness, but every bend revealed just more trees.

At the point of giving up and going back we saw the ruined roof of a large building in the distance. Then just short of this ruin we drew up outside an iron gate with a smart modern sign outside it proclaiming that we had arrived at the Monastery of the Holy Lifegiving Spring. There could surely be no more remote spot in the whole country.

An old man in a faded grey cassock was tending his garden on the other side of the gate. He put down his mattock on our arrival and walked slowly down his garden – a woodland glade and spoke to us.

"Why don't you come in? What are you waiting for?"

The little compound was a self sufficient paradise, cut out of the woods. On one side there was a small house covered in bright acryllic murals of biblical scenes. The garden was bright with flowers and rich in vegetables. In the middle of it, incongruously, was a kitch little model village of tiny houses constructed in the 19th century national revival style. At the far end of the glade was a small white-washed church.

The monk's name was Archimandrite Evtimii. He stared at us intently with luminous speckled eyes as we stared at him. The hands he stretched out to greet us were calloused and grimy with the earth of his garden, the nails cracked and worn, the fingers knotted and traced with the dark lines of ingrained dirt. They were the hands of a gardener or a peasant. At first glance it seemed he must be more than sixty. He was remarkably thin. His long white hair was gathered into a bun at the back of his head and his snowy beard fell to his waist. His long narrow face seemed longer and narrower thanks to the beard. He looked like he as just stepped down from a mediaeval church wall painting -- one of the hermit saints.

We followed him back through his glade towards the church. Here we could see how the monastery got its unusual name. From its very foundations gushed a powerful spring of sweet soft water. Evtimii told us it had healing qualities.

Soon we were drinking little cups of muddy coffee at a small table under a venerable walnut tree, from which hung the brass monastery bell. Evtimii was overjoyed to have company. From alarming way that our conversation rambled from the historical to the contemporary and from the spiritual subjects to worldly and then to, let's say, very worldly subjects for a monk, it seemed that he can't have had much practice with conversations for quite a while.

"So you are bachelors?" he enquired as he served us more coffee.

"I am too and, man, is it difficult!" He shook his head in disbelief.

"But you are a monk. You have to be a bachelor."

I had always assumed that after a certain age most clerics overcame the problem of sex. Evidently not.

Evtimii shrugged his shoulders and we lapsed into an embarrassed silence. I hadn't expected to be discussing the difficulties of celibacy with a hermit in the middle of the wilderness. It was hard to know what to say.

Evtimii broke the silence in a sensational fashion.

"Sex!" he blurted out.

We stared at him in bemusement. Was this a statement or a question?

"Sex!" he repeated more definitely, as if we had been slow on the uptake. "How is it in your countries?"

I looked at Matei. He at me. We both looked Evtimii.
"Oh...err..normal?" I suggested.

"Yes. Normal. Quite normal," added Matei, nodding emphati-
cally. What else can you say to a monk on this subject? Again the
conversation lulled and I tried to steer us back to safer waters by asking Evtimii about the history of the monastery.

Our attention turned to the ruins behind us and the little church
from which the water streamed so beautifully. The old building that
we saw from the road was the remains of a monastery that had been
destroyed during the 1912-1913 Balkan wars. From the time of its
destruction until Evtimii came here to rebuild it, there had been
nothing. The previous monastery had been built in the 19th century
on the site of a still older mediaeval monastery, destroyed by the Ottoman Turks in the 14th century.

Somewhere in this region, Saint Gregory of Sinai had founded
the monastery of Praoria in the 13th century. St. Gregory was one
of the most influential mediaeval monks. He brought the mystical
Christian cult of hesychasm to Bulgaria. Followers of this cult believed they could achieve a vision of the Almighty through media-
tion and prayer. Gregory's followers were responsible for the last
great flowering of Bulgarian monasticism, one of those lost moments in Bulgarian history when the political and cultural and intellectual environment seemed ripe for great developments. The few
works of literature and art which have survived from that time show
signs of an artistic flowering that could have led to great works
comparable to the Italian renaissance. But the Ottomans invaded,
conquered and either destroyed or suborned the aristocracy. It is
one of the great "what ifs" that litter the disappointments of Bulgarian history.

Could this have been the birthplace of all that? I hoped so.
Archimandrite Evtimii seemed a worthy inheritor of the tradition of
Gregory, and his pupils Theodosius and Patriarch Euthemius (Greek
for Evtimii). At least so far as appearances went.

The monk's history was a troubled one. Evtimii had worked in
the Bourgas copper mines before he took holy orders. He had even
been married, but his wife had gone off with his best friend. He had
been ordained in 1981 – a strange time to go into the church, which
was suffering great repression. Almost straight away he moved to
this hermitage, in spite of the opposition of his bishop. To start with

it had been little more than an archaeological dig but after the archaeologists had left he had stayed, founded the church and become its abbot. So for nearly 20 years he had lived with no neighbours, no telephone, no company or assistants.

"When you get back to Sofia get the mobile telephone company to put one of their aerials up near here. Then at least I could have telephone," he begged.

But what were we doing in this remote spot, he wanted to know. We told him that we were on our way to the Black Sea.

"Ah! The Black Sea. Its always best when you are with another woman!"

The monk's face illuminated with a flood of happy memories. As he enlarged on the theme his grin grew wider and more manic. Other tourists had passed through here, hiking to the seaside.

"This is a good place to take a girl, in these woods no one can hear you," he told us. He laughed excitedly.

Later Matei told me that he had also detected bitterness in this expression of the enjoyment which a visitor could find there, but that he, eeking his life out day by day, could never do.

This was anyway the beginning of a conversation of great confusion.

"I am a *muzhkar*," the monk announced with decision.

What did he mean by that? I couldn't tell exactly. Or rather I hoped he didn't mean what he seemed to. The linguistic root of the word is *muzh*, the Bulgarian word for man. It literally means a male animal, or a sexually mature beast. But there is another Bulgarian word *zhenkar*, which comes from *zhena*, meaning woman. But *zhenkar* doesn't mean a female animal or sexually mature woman. It means a man who fucks a lot of women.

Before there was any chance to think out the implication of this linguistic puzzle he continued, confirming my worst suspicions.

"In Bulgarian we have a word for sex which is *ebane* (fucking)".

What to say? We assured him that there is a similar word in English too.

"Do you like to fuck?"

Even after everything he said before I was not sure if I had heard him right. Perhaps my embarrassment and confusion at having an elderly monk quiz me on this subject had made me forget my grammar. I asked him to repeat what he just said.

For a second this jolted his composure. Perhaps this was as hard for him as for us. But from here there could be no going back. He took a deep breath and started again. Matei and I glanced at one another. I think we both knew what was coming. There was nothing to do but to see if we had guessed right, hoping against hope that the ghastly suspicion was wrong.

"There are some people who fuck and some people who are fucked. I am a *muzhkar*. I fuck. Are you amongst those who fuck or those who get fucked?" asked the monk.

"Like a woman" he added for further clarity.

Ahhh. I had hoped it wouldn't be this that he was getting at. In retrospect it seemed obvious.

"We are both of the former persuasion. We are fuckers too."

Matei nodded in firm agreement.

"We fuck."

The monk is crestfallen. Having let him get this far down the line we had raised his hopes.

"So we can't have sex then?" he asked, making doubly sure.

"No."

"No?"

"No. Definitely no." He shrugged and sighed.

"What a shame." The air of manic excitement that had glazed his eyes as this surreal conversation progressed fell away from him as he stood up from the table.

"Well, I'll get some of the goats' milk yoghurt which I promised you, we'll drink some more. We'll chat and be friends," he said matter-of-factly.

He went into his house and brought out a tray of drinks showing no hint of embarassment. It was as if the conversation had never happened. Matei reported later that Evtimii did spend quite a lot of time looking at his crotch but that might just have been self-consciousness.

With ideas of sex banished for the time being, Evtimii began to encourage us to write newspaper stories to get donors to help the reconstruction of the monastery, for which he had ambitious plans. He mentioned a rich Bulgarian who had been outed in *Shock*, Bulgaria's most unreliable and salacious tabloid.

I don't know what was more odd, that a monk would read *Shock* or that he could get hold of it in the middle of the wilderness. Nothing could surprise me about him any more.

We lit candles in his church and he accompanied us back to our car. At the gate he turned on us for the last time.

"Come on!" he cried. "Are you sure you won't?"

"Give it a break. We are not that type," I retorted.

"Ah you are brave! But Matei why don't you have courage Matei? Are you sure that you don't want to?"

"It is not a question of courage," said Matei. "It's a question of personal preference. Some people like strawberries, others like raspberries."

We set off into the wilderness again. Matei had one last simple comment on the whole adventure.

"To fuck or to be fucked. It shows how important grammar is. You have to know which form of the verb is being used."

Kako e i taya chasha

Even as this cup, my son
Is brimming with red wine
So also is my heart, my child
Brimming with poison.

Drink it up, my faithful son
Drink it to get drunk
The bitterness, my only son
Thus to overcome.

Listen to me, O my son,
Your mother's words now hear
Even if you drink, Stoyane
It will be no use.

You must go, must take yourself
High up in the hills
And there find, my only son
Your true fatherland

Macedonian folk song

Red Wine, Black Earth

THAT autumn I went to Macedonia. Not the Republic that is, but the bit of that chopped up land that Bulgarians like to call Macedonia.

"I have found something for you," said Aglaya, draping her arm around my shoulder and pulling me into a conspiratorial huddle, the fingers of her free hand bunched as if to grasp the special essence of what she was telling me.

"This is something which you must see. You must! Very few people know about it."

Aglaya had wild black curly hair with traces of grey, and spectacles that flashed. When I first arrived in Bulgaria she had deliberately undertaken the task of making sure that I understood her country. That was when her battered white Fiat used to double as her mobile office while she was a roving reporter for Radio *Deutsche Welle*. Later she ran the news desk at the independent national TV station.

She guided me through the networks of influence that so quickly grew up around the new government. At the same time she had introduced me to the most beautiful villages in the Rhodope mountains, to the Islamic holy places of the Alievi cult, to my friend Hristo Stoyanov, the ruffian author.

Aglaya had taught me which meze went best with rakia, and which with wine. It was with Aglaya that I had stayed up late on balmy summer nights, each of us reclined on a narrow settle in the deep veranda of a village house, engrossed in conversations about life. She had taught me the lexicon of words, all borrowed from Turkish, which describe all the best pleasures of Bulgarian life.

Aglaya didn't have the same curiosity about the seamy side of existence as Matei – my other regular travelling companion. Nor did she understand his readiness to shack up in the lowest budget accommodation he could find. Instead she commandeered and orchestrated her travels in quest of ideal experiences. The destinations she took me to were always special in some way. Her invitations to travel often prefaced with a conspiratorial flourish.

What gem had she come up with this time?

"Did you know that Winston Churchill liked Melnik wine?"

I could tell that she has been waiting for a suitable moment to spring this bit of information on me. Gratified, by my surprise, she continued.

"Yes, and I know the man who can tell you all about it."

"Let's go." It was all I had to say.

• • •

The road that wound southwards towards the Greek border follows the valley of the River Struma. Scrubby yellow fields stretch to the dusky mountains looming in the distance like grey shadows in the haze. Grizzled men in faded blue jackets lean on sticks and gaze stonily at half a dozen goats or a few cows which forage on the dry grass by the road side or bite off the leaves from scraggy trees which are just showing the tinges of autumn at their edges. A couple of shaggy little horses are tethered in a patch of bright green by the stony riffling river. Fishermen fish, women hoe half an acre of brown earth and young boys perch on overflowing piles of greeny grey forage hauled on rubber wheeled carts by plodding horses.

Where the hills are not covered with vines they are often marked with lines of blackened twisted stumps, the remnants of dead vineyards. We are approaching the border area.

This is a strip of land two or three miles wide that extends northwards from the actual frontier with Greece. It has a claim to be one of the most forsaken spots in the Balkans. Until 1913 these villages were the scene of bitter rivalry between those Greek and Bulgarian proselytisers eager to establish national claims to the region. Macedonian revolutionary *cheta* (armed bands) played cat and mouse with the Turkish authorities through these villages.

At that time, at least, they were on a route which led from the towns of Bansko and Melnik southwards to the ports of Kavala and

Salonika. As well as the main roads, a network of sheep tracks and donkey paths, like miniature blood vessels, spread over the mountain passes and led down to the Aegean coast. This was a legacy of a time before borders and national rivalry. Now, for more than nine decades they have wilted under the shadow of the border that was erected after the Balkan Wars.

During Bulgaria's communist era this border became the southern iron curtain of the Warsaw Pact. A double row of great iron chain link fences was guarded with watch-towers, military patrols and dogs. They were there to prevent people from leaving as much as to warn against possible attack from Greece. Unreliable people living inside the fenced area were dispossessed and relocated to other towns. Other inhabitants soon followed them and the area gradually depopulated.

Nothing has been rebuilt or replaced for decades. The few remaining inhabitants fend off the encroaching forest and wait for the European Union to reopen the ways to villages on the Greek side of the border, in some cases less than a mile away but – officially at least – completely unreachable.

It is no wonder that the villages are so wild and desolate. Their history is one of unremitting conflict and isolation. Only one thing has redeemed life for people there. It is the location of the best Melnik vines, in fact some of the finest vines in Bulgaria. It only comes into its own in the hottest of years. Then they produce a fantastic dark wine and potent rakia.

At the first of two checkpoints a confused young conscript examines our documents slowly and minutely. He turns over my Bulgarian identity card, a sky-blue minature passport, many times. Probably he has never seen one before. He hands it back reluctantly and waves us through.

At the next gate, the guard is lying on the grass outside his shelter with a half full bottle of dubious brown liquid at his side. He waves at us laconically without getting up.

The road winds through a thick and luscious wood. Another bunch of soldiers saunters past us back along the road with their guns propped upside down on their shoulders. Their leader flags me to stop.

"Where are you from?"

"Sofia."

Aglaya chuckles.

The soldier stares with puzzlement and suspicion, mulling over the seeming lie, but he can't decide on any action. My papers are in order. He lets me drive on.

The village is utterly isolated. Its large old houses must have once been very fine. But now, like the inhabitants, they are decrepit. Many of them are deserted. Weeds sprout luxuriantly from the windows. In the unkempt village square square an a group of ancient men sit cracking walnuts at the base of an angular revolutionary statue.

"We've come to find Metodi Shterev," we tell him.

"Go and ask the priest."

The church is perched on a ridge at the top of the village. Like everyone else the priest is very old. We find him performing the daily service. He mumbles through the prayers and an old woman, the *popadia*, his wife, is the only congregation. She sings the responses at the same time as she bustles around with her straw broom sweeping the messes left by the birds that roost in the rafters into a short bent shovel.

When the short observance is over we sit with them on the low wooden bench outside the church. The priest tells us his story.

"My name is Father Angel. I have been the priest here for 52 years. There were once 1000 people living here. Now? Oh, less than 100. Grandfathers and grandmothers. Why should people stay here? There is nothing for them. They began to leave many, many years ago. Most left in 1950 when they put up the fences. But I stayed, yes, I stayed. This is my village."

"It was difficult. Particularly when I wanted to cross the check points to go in and out. When I left, I worried, perhaps they will not let me back in again."

Father Angel is not bitter or angry. Instead he is just sad about the miserable fate of the lovely village he was born in but which is now nearly dead.

He tells us where to find Metodii's vineyard.

Our path takes us through a maze of vines. In contrast to the village's decay, the hills surrounding it are luxuriant. They are reputed to be the best vines in the region.

In every one of them people are working. Many of them come from villages far outside the border zone. These vines have just been returned to them. At every place we enquire for Metodii.

We have a Bulgarian saying," Aglaya tells me. "You can get to Tsarigrad by asking."

Tsarigrad is the Bulgarian name for Istanbul.

Eventually we find Metodii amongst his vines. He is wearing a pith helmet and holds a stubby pruning knife in one stained hand. He looks like a sweet-faced old adventurer in a tame jungle.

"Ahhh, Aglaya, you have come to see my vines."

He greets her warmly and we settle down in their shade on the dry yellow earth.

"They say now that it is possible to make good wine from rubbish grapes. My grandfather old Diado Shtero wouldn't have agreed. He always said that if you are greedy and don't prune your vines properly you will not get good grapes. Why should we make wine which tastes like it comes from Australia when Bulgarian wine is so delicious?"

We nod in agreement as he launches into a kind of panygeric to grapes.

"Think of a hot day, like today, a beautiful baking hot day, such as is needed for the grapes to ripen. You can look at a vine of the *Shiroka Melnishka Loza*, like this one." He uses his knife to cut down a large bunch.

"Look. Its broad leaves and huge bunches of grapes seem to smile. The whole vine seems to laugh like a person. In the evening it becomes cooler and the breeze brings down the pine-scented air fresh from Pirin so that it blows over the vines. The next morning the breeze will be faintly scented with iodine, with salt from the White Sea, that has blown through the passes..."

Aglaya interrupts him gently. Metodii, we wanted to ask you about Winston Churchill.

"Ah yes, that story," he sighs. "I never asked my father exactly how Churchill fell in love with Melnik wine. But the connection must have been made through his restaurant in Sofia. The menu was roast pork and Melnik wine, which my father made himself. The restaurant sent demijohns to the British Embassy for several years. Someone must have taken some back to London. However the connection was made, my father sent a barrel of wine every year to Winston Churchill from the mid-1930's to the outbreak of the Second World War. He had a letter of thanks from from Mr Churchill himself. I saw it when I was young. It said that of all wines, he drank Melnik wine with greatest pleasure. He said it was good for his health."

Where was the letter, we wondered.

"The letter? Ah, it is sad. It was lost or destroyed during the Communist take over. You know they hated anything to do with the British and imperialism." *

• • •

I first came down to this region when I had not been living in Bulgaria for even a year. Aglaya had invited me to take part in the grape harvest. This was more than just an introduction to a way of life. It was also how I cam to understand what Macedonia means to Bulgarians.

We took the bus. It smelt of sweat and ingrained dust, axle grease, old workshops, sun-baked plastic, sweet straw, sour animals and good cooking. It smelt like the smell of life. A fastidious person might gag on it, like on an overripe cheese. But really it was a comfortable smell, unpretentious and honest: a smell that welcomed, a smell that you could relax into. In a strange way it prepared me for what was to come.

We disembarked at dusk on a wide bend of the narrow tarmac road, just outside the sandy, sunbaked, semi-ghost town of Melnik. A steep stony path led up the hill to a neat modern villa. A cheery red-faced man wearing old wine-stained tracksuit and a dusty baseball cap, from under which poke white wisps of hair, was loading sacks of grapes into the back of a battered Russian car.

He welcomed us with unshaved all-welcoming expansiveness as if we had known each other for ever.

"*Dobre dushul.* You are welcome."

---

* Unfortunately I have not been able to verify this story. The cellar archives at Chartwell have no record of Bulgarian wine. Nor does the Churchill Archive in Cambridge. His daughter, Mary Soames has no recollection. But then, as she says, she was probably too young at the time to be interested in wine. Meanwhile, Metodii Shterev still makes wine according to his father's recipe. But it is for private consumption only. However, the vast Damianitza wine factory down the road, now a thriving private enterprises, has started to trade on the old legend and markets Churchill's wine for sale in the UK.

"Dobre zavaril. I have arrived well." This polite, if slightly archaic response is what guests traditionally use in Bulgaria.

The man was delighted.

"An Englishman who speaks Bulgarian!"

"He's a surprise. I hope there is space..." Aglaya explained to
him.

"An extra guest means an extra hand for the work. We'll worry
about sleeping arrangements later." He stretched out a hand towards
me:

"I am Chicho Kolyo. Everyone calls me chicho (uncle). You are
ready for the grape picking, eh? Well, you are welcome. Grape-pick-
ing is not a holiday, like some people think, it is back-breaking work
and I need every hand I can get to complete the harvest this year. The
rains will come soon. Everything must be picked by Sunday. My two
rows are there."

He pointed to the other side of the valley, where a green and gold
criss-crossed pattern of vines spread over pale sandy hills away from
the Pirin Mountain down to the River Struma. As the crow flies it
was only perhaps 70 miles to the bay of Salonika and the White Sea
as the Bulgarians call the Aegean.

The other members of the household had gathered round the
table in the shady grape arbour outside the door. A plump old woman with dark curly hair, and a cheerful smiling face laid out cups of
coffee, plates of white cheese and tomatoes, thick soft doorstops of
white bread and a dark green bottle, that might have once contained
sunflower oil.

"My wife," said Kolyo.

He poured out glasses of strong, purple wine, the last bottle from
the previous harvest. Then he pointed round the table:

7"My daughter Katya, my son-in-law Luidmil, my niece, her husband, my daughter's friends."

At each introduction a glass was raised in greeting. I raised mine
back, toasting each person again in turn. Then we drank. Kolyo
poured more from the green bottle into my cup.

"They come down every year to help me pick the grapes. There
is no money to pay workers. So I pay in kind," he chuckled.

Kolyo's full name was Nikola Shavulov. He was a retired officer
from the Bulgarian army, now living the life of a semi-peasant. During the winter months he and his wife stayed close to the comforts of

civilisation in their Sofia flat, with central heating and nearby shops. But from the spring until the autumn, they lived off the land.

The scene was modern-bucolic, almost mediaeval, but with a few amendments. Everyone was at work. Old and young, men, women and children moved slowly down the lines of vines, filling wicker baskets, old crates and plastic sacks with the large bunches of small dark grapes. Mules with twin baskets on their backs and creaking donkey carts vied with small tractors and dented old Ladas, to climb the dusty yellow tracks towards the asphalt road. Everyone and everything was over-laden with mounds of grapes, destined for the cellars of the village.

There was something satisfying about plucking the heavy bunches from the vines, snapping the stems with the nail of the thumb and dumping them in the plastic sacks which each of us dragged along. With each bunch a tiny residue of sap and wood pushed into the soft flesh under the thumbnail. It was not long before my undernail was black and sore and the pad of my thumb was bruised. My hands were sticky with juice. Vine leaves and dry earth clung to them.

I was given the job of porter. I relieved the pickers of their sacks when they became too heavy to hoof along. At the top of the row I hefted them into the trailer dragged by Kolyo's car and then into the boot, and onto the back seat, and onto the roof. The pickers shouted my name when their sacks were full.

"Jon-aaaay! Jon-cho!" Aglaya had Bulgarized my name (I was christened John), adding vocative and diminutive endings. It was a pleasing joke because of its incongruity. Non-Bulgarian names do not take these endings. Sticking them on sounds a bit odd.

"*Haide bei* Joncho! Come on now. My sack is full. Give me another."

Sometime in the course of the afternoon the call changed. Once again it was Aglaya who started off shouting:

"Ivan-eee! Vancho!"

For the afternoon, at least, I had been completely Bulgarized. I marched up and down the rows with the big bags of grapes on my back. There was nothing but the fresh taste of grapes in my mouth, the tart skins and bitterness of crunched pips. Their stain was on my skin and under my nails. Their jammy smell and sticky feel was in my clothes and hair. Purple grape juice trickled down my shirt and seeped into my trousers.

For the first time since I had been in the country I felt a part of something, rather than an observer looking on. All around the golden green hills, tarnished with haze crept with little figures slowly picking at the vines. Kolyo creaked away in his car, laden to overflowing. There were sacks piled on the passenger seat beside him.

Back at his villa, Aglaya and I helped pile handfuls of grapes through the square holes cut in the top of two 500-litre wooden barrels that occupied most of the space in his garage. Kolyo kept more than half of his harvest for himself. It would ferment here for the next two months. By Christmas the fresh dark wine would be ready for drinking. Some of it would be sold but most Kolyo would serve at his own table or give away.

"The best grapes I make into wine, the next best into rakia. Only the worst go to Vinprom," he chuckled.

Vinprom was the large wine factory near the main road to Greece. It was built to satisfy the Russian demand for large quantities of cheap plonk.

That evening more than a dozen people crammed round the long narrow table in the villa's small front room. On two sides a bench was fixed to the wall. At the far end a fire crackled, frowsting the air with sweet pale smoke.

Space was found for me on the bench. A bowl of *shkembe chorba*, literally "belly soup" was put in front of me. Strips of tender furry tripe floated in a thick milky broth. It is a Bulgarian classic.

Almost before I could start on that I was given another plate with tomatoes, cucumbers and white cheese. Chicho Kolyo leant over with an earthenware pitcher and poured a clear liquid into a small pottery beaker.

"Rakia! Drink! *Nazdrave!* Your health!"

Everyone raised their glasses, and leaning forwards clinked them together, making direct eye contact with every other person. In Bulgarian drinking etiquette it is deeply uncouth to start drinking without raising a toast and equally bad manners not to look straight into the eyes of every person you are toasting with.

"Nazdrave! Nazdrave! Nazdrave!" The rakia was home-made, grapey and potent. It burnt my mouth and throat, making me gasp.

My beaker was replenished. Kolyo's wife appeared from some other room with more food, put it on the table. She put wood on the fire and sat on a low stool near the other end of the table, surveying her work with a look of satisfaction.

"Why is the boy not eating? Tell him to eat, Kolyo! Eat! Eat!" she called to me.

I had been doing nothing else since I sat down. I was in a daze, like a blessed fool accepting all good things without question.

It is confusing to land up in a house where everyone speaks a foreign language and who are mostly related to one another. Being plied with over-large slugs of rakia doesn't help. Every time Kolyo drank, I drank also. Then he topped up my beaker again. After the rakia came the wine.

"That is not a good combination," Aglaya muttered under her breath. "Melnik wine and Melnik rakia. You will not be up to much tomorrow."

I ignored her warning.

Both the wine and the brandy in this region are famous not just for their strength but also for their debilitating properties when drunk together. They induce mammoth hangovers. They are, however, too good to refuse.

"Nazdrave!" said Kolyo. We chinked glasses.

The conversation revolved around the day's events, told and retold and embellished amidst interruptions and laughter and digressions like the epics of mythology. I cut serious figure at the table with my pocket dictionary and notebook attempting to grasp the threads of political gossip and the punchlines of jokes as they whizzed by. The stories branched off in directions that I had ever growing difficulties in following. Eventually they merged into pure sound: hard sounds, round vowels, repetitive choppy rhythms and endings:

"*Tototo... deteto... momchetata... momichetata... mamamustara... datigonachukam!*" *.

I leant back against the wall and let the words wash over me, no longer paying attention to their meaning. Then someone called for a song. The talk died momentarily in a moment of hesitation and decision.

---

* These words mean: "The Tote... the child... the lads... the lasses... his old mother... up yours!"

Another voice filled the silence. For the first phrase, Chicho Kolyo's deep baritone alone set the tone:

"*Nazad! Nazad! Mome Kalino, ne moi da hodish podir men!* Go back! Go back! Kalino my lass, you cannot follow me!"

Slowly other voices joined in. Firstly, those who could sing but could not lead, followed by those who didn't quite know the words, and finally those who thought they could not sing, but when everyone was singing anything was better than keeping silent.

The song owed nothing to any other sort of music I had ever heard. It contained a hint of the east – a plangent Turkish lilt embellished with strange semitones and quartertones. But it was harsher and wilder, both melancholy and defiant. It was sung in Macedonian dialect and thrilled with tragedy and sorrow.

It was an exchange between a man and a woman. The man was attempting to turn back the woman who was following him.

"Before us rears a great mountain, you cannot climb it," he told her. But she wouldn't be turned back.

"I shall become a hawk, and I'll come after you. I'll fly over the mountain. I'll come back to you. I shall be yours for ever."

The pattern of the song repeated. Each time the man presented his lover with some new barrier that she would not be able to overcome, a river and then a vast plain. Each time she swore to cross the barrier in the form of another animal: a fish or a snake, and vowed:

"I'll come back to you and be yours for ever."

Finally in the last verse the man revealed the truth.

> *Go back! Go back Kalino, my lass*
> *You cannot follow me.*
> *At home I have a beautiful wife*
> *And some tiny little children.*

But he had not reckoned with the fury and determination of the Macedonian lass.

> *I shall turn into the black death*
> *And I'll come after you.*
> *I shall kill your woman,*
> *I shall care for your children*
> *I shall be yours for ever.*

It was a spine tingling climax. I looked at Aglaya across the table. Her eyes were wet with emotion.

"A true Macedonian song! This is what our past is all about."

I was fascinated by this culture that could express love in such deathly terms. Every song seemed to be about love or death, and often both. More specifically they were about unrequited love and sacrifice for the national cause. They spoke of a time when arranged marriages were the norm and love affairs doomed to failure.

Certain plots recurred again and again. Fearsome mothers intervened against every incipient attraction. One of the sweetest laments simply ended with the hopeless line: "Your mother, my darling, won't let you come to me."

But then, in even more pathetic songs, those previously adamantine mothers wailed copiously over their dead or dying sons.

"Where is my son, Kostadin Voivoda?" pleaded one bereft woman.

There was only one answer to such a question. There was only one marriage that these heroes of song could make.

"Your son, mother is married to an enslaved Macedonia!"

This theme repeated itself again and again in different songs, the dying hero was wedded to "the black earth" of his grave.

It was so beautiful, it was so sad. These thoughts, mingling with the refrains of more songs and the wine and the rakia swirled through my head. I stumbled off to bed.

Slusham kak shumat shumite

The sighing beech leaves sigh, hark their sighing
The sighing leaves they sigh
They are crying for our leader, the Captain.

Comrades, O loyal comrades, my comrades
When the village you pass by
Let not your horses strike
And your rifles do not fire.

Let me not hear you, mother mine, old and frail
Let me not year you, mother mine
He will ask you for me, O for me.

Where is my son, my Kostadin, Kostadin
Where is my son, my Kostadin
Kostadin Voivodata, the Captain.

Your son, O mother married is, he's married
Your son, O mother married is
He is married to Macedonia, enslaved.

Macedonian revolutionary song

The Macedonian Question

THE town of Melnik on the southern slopes of Pirin is a good spot to understand what Macedonia meant to the Bulgarians and still means to them. It is a place haunted by eerie destruction. Its fine stone houses cluster at the far end of a sandy gulch. In the summer it is unbearably hot. The sun's heat is reflected from the valley walls, which shimmer like unglazed clay just plucked from the kiln. In the winter there are floods. Only now, in the autumn evening is it cool and pleasant.

The buildings, which climb up the sheer crumbly cliffs, seem in perpetual danger of being utterly engulfed by sand, which is washed down from the hills surrounding the town on all sides. Every rain storm shaves the crags and pinnacles of the crazy yellow gulch to a more extreme thinness. They are as sharp and angular as old Russian bayonets.

Melnik is an ideal place to understand the tragedy of the Macedonian question. By the dawn of the last century, the town had become inextricably enmeshed in this terrible puzzle. One hundred years ago, everyone in Western Europe was asking themselves what was the answer to this question. But no one knew the answer.

It was the same sort of riddle that the Kosovo question is today. In fact, during the 1900s, Bulgarians regarded the territory of Macedonia with much the same resentment and jealousy with which Serbians now looks at Kosovo. It was not just that the land belong to them and that the inhabitants spoke their language and shared their culture. Macedonia was part of their national idea too. And it had been torn, they said, unjustly from their grasp. They would do anything to get it back.

Melnik was in the part of Macedonia that Bulgaria most wanted. Its only trouble was that within the ethnic patchwork of the country, it wasn't particularly Bulgarian. In the late 18th to mid-19th century it was one of the region's richest towns, thanks to the commercial success of its predominantly Greek merchant traders, who had built fortunes as vinters. They bought in these grapes from the surrounding vineyards and made wine in their dark cool cellars. Long mule trains laden with wineskins travelled over the mountains southwards to Salonika and northwards to Prague, Vienna and Budapest. In its heyday it was a town of 10,000 people with 74 churches.

This prosperity and most of the town was destroyed in the destroyed in the two Balkan Wars. In the first war in 1912, Serbia, Greece and Bulgaria united to expel the Turks from Macedonia. In the second War, a year later Serbia and Greece defeated Bulgaria and took the lion's share of Macedonia for themselves.

Melnik was cut off in a box of borders. The remainder of the Greek population fled or were chased out. Until this day, the old Turkish quarter, although the most pleasant and most shady part of the town, has never been repopulated. In 1915, Dr Bogdan Filov, director of the national Archeological Museum (and later Prime Minister of Bulgaria) noted in his diary that:

"The town is almost entirely destroyed with the exception of its central part. Earlier there were about 4000 inhabitants, very well to do people and almost exclusively Greeks, Armenians and Turks. Now there are scarcely 1000 people, all of them refugees."

Was this an early example of ethnic cleansing? At least partly it must have been.

It took a century of political and military calamity to wean Bulgaria off its Macedonian obsession. In 1992, when Macedonia declared its independence from Yugoslavia, Bulgaria was the first country to recognise it. A few years later, after much public debate and anguish the government abandoned the last vestige of nationalist policy, by recognising Macedonian as a separate language. Finally, after more than a century, the Macedonian Question, that famously unanswerable diplomatic puzzle, was solved.

But too late for Melnik. The town is still mostly a ruin. Narrow stone paths and stairways meander between venerable stone houses and lush vegetable plots, heavy with red tomatoes and peppers. One

of them leads to a open space at the top of a cliff, where a few up-
ended logs have been draped in cheerful red cloths and turned into a
little taverna. There is no house here, although there might have been
once. Now there is just an opening in the hillside leading to a network of cool cellars. From the mouth of the cave one can look down
on the roofs of half the town. Traces of past glory still remain. Several grand mid-19th century houses, built in the Bulgarian revivalist-
style, with the upper stories overhanging the lower, still crowd in the
lower part of the valley.

This is the bodega of Mitko Shestaka "Six-fingered Mitko", so-
called because he has an extra digit on his left hand. Inside the cellars, barrels line the walls. Mitko taps one of them and pours me
some dark red wine. It tastes heavy and resinous from the barrel. I
sit at a low wooden table and he tells me about the greatest of the local heroes, or perhaps the greatest villain.

"Yane Sandanski was a mafiot, a bandit," he begins. "He used to
team up with bashibozouks, Turkish irregulars, in high Pirin." At this
Mitko gestures in the direction of the vast limestone mountain range
that sits beyond the sandstone hills of the town.

"The Bashibozuks would terrorise a village. Sandanski and his
cheta would appear and drive the Turks away. They would earn
themselves a fine feast for their bravery. The villagers would kill a
sheep, or two or three. 'Give us some food to take away,' the cheta
would ask. 'We get very hungry high in the mountains.' So the
grateful villagers would give them what they could. The well-fed
fighters then retired into the hills laden with presents and victuals,
that they would share with the Turkish bandits at their hidden ren-
dezvous."

"I thought Sandanski was a friend of the poor?"

"He was a tyrant/. My great grandmother was one of his mis-
tresses. She was one of three or four girls kept by him at his mountain retreat for cleaning, cooking and other duties... you know, bed.
When a girl became too old, or pregnant, Sandanski would order
some village boy to marry her. That's what happened to my great
grandmother. At the age of 25 Sandanski brought her down here to
Melnik. He found a 15-year old shepherd. 'Hey you!' He said. 'This is
your wife.'"

"Was it a happy marriage? She obviously had children."

"They had three children. My great grandmother was very content. She died recently at the age of 98."

Sandanski must have been quite a vain man in some ways. There are many photographs that show a tall, burly, unsmiling man with a dark spade-shaped "old Slavonic" beard. According to one of his comrades he had: "big black eyes, as kind and merry and gentle as they were severe, sharp and peircing, and – to his enemies –terrible. He only had to look at a person to freeze them to the spot."

Other eyewitness accounts describe a "weird wild look of the eyes which...seemed almost insane".

He had one of the longest and most colourful careers of any Bulgarian revolutionary. His most famous exploit was the kidnapping of an American missionary Miss Ellen Stone in the autumn of 1901. He asked a ransom of 25,000 Turkish pounds from the authorities. It took them six months to pay up. For the whole of that bitter winter, Sandanski and his band dodged the police while hiding in the Pirin mountains. The job was made even more difficult by the fact that Miss Stone's companion, a Mrs Tsilka, was five months pregnant at the time of the kidnapping. Miss Stone became one of the first recorded cases of what has now become known as Stockholm syndrome. After her release she devoted her life to extolling the cause of an independent Macedonia and raising money for Sandanski's revolutionary efforts.

In 1915, three years after he saw his dream of independent Macedonia destroyed by the Balkan Wars, Sandanski was assassinated by his own side. Seven men with rifles, sent from Sofia, ambushed him as he rode his horse over a pass in the Pirin Mountain. His body was discovered riddled with bullets. His death seemed to coincide with the death of old Melnik.

Today, the question of exactly what happened in the town is never talked about. The local museum mentions the town's glorious past without ever saying how it was lost. The 300 people who still live there are equally reticent. Even Mitko Shestaka can't say exactly what happened.

"That's war for you," he shrugs vaguely and pours more wine which I drink as the sun sets over the jagged crumbling peaks and the shadows swallow up the roofs of the houses below.

Many ethnologers are of the opinion that the... kukeri inherited a tradition which, in part at least, goes back to the Dionysian festivals.

Bulgarian Folk Customs,
Mercia MacDermott

The Good Spirits

I AM squashed with Chicho Som, Lelya Somka, their sons Lalyo and Pavel and my friend Itso, who works for the secret service, around a table in the central room of a cosy house in a village 100 miles east of Sofia. The name of the village is Turia. It is a simple agricultural place in the heart of the Rose Valley, which is really a narrow plain between the Balkans and the Central Highlands. A small river weaves its way along its length. It is sheltered, and lush and fruitful, surrounded on all sides by rolling hills that in early summer are heavy with the scent of roses.

But now, in early spring, the hills are barren and the life of the village is more indoors rather than out. We are crammed around the table so tight, I feel like I'm in the cabin of a boat. This room is a friendly place on a chilly night, frowsty with the heat from the stove. It is a living room in the literal sense of the word. Everything happens here: cooking, eating, sleeping and celebrating.

The table is cluttered with glasses and bottles of *rakia*, although that is not what the labels on the bottle say. There are whisky bottles and gin bottle and Coca Cola bottles. But they all contain the powerful rakia that I had seen distilled in the primitive village still. The technology of its production was so basic that the only way of controlling the temperature was to douse the fire or stoke it up. It seemed impossible that it would not be the sort of poison to make one blind after a couple of glasses. But experience told me that it was extremely pure. I had drunk it all night and not suffered a hangover the next morning.

Between our glasses, Lelya Somka has put out lates of *meze* – snack-like accompaniments for serious drinking. There are bowls of glistening red peppers, gherkins and cauliflower, chunks of clean-tasting white goats cheese and thin slivers of *slanina*, salted bacon fat that is a highly prized meze for rakia, perhaps because of its stomach-lining properties. This gathering does not count as a meal. It is just that there is a taboo against serving alcohol without something to eat alongside it. With a good supply of such hospitality, the recounting of favourite jokes, the telling of stories, arguing over politics and mulling over of problems can go on late into the night.

A big double bed takes up one-third of the room and another single bed is ranged at right angles to it. They are both covered in furry blankets. They double as benches. On the wall opposite the window there is a sink, a cooker and a dresser with plates and cutlery. Next to the small bed a door leads out into the yard. Another door leads to a storeroom at the back.

Pavel, the eldest son lies on top of the double bed in his pyjamas. He is recovering from burns after prank with gunpowder went wrong and so creates a strange, almost sinister picture. Both his hands are wrapped in bandages. His round face, puffed up to a nearly spherical ball, glistens with a dark brown ointment. His features seem on the verge of disappearing into a blank muddy slick. The only thing bringing some humanity back to this expressionless mask is a white cigarette that dangles from the slit of his mouth.

Every so often Somka, a broad and powerful woman, deeply suntanned, with straight jet black hair. lights another cigarette for her son, which he holds clumsily in his bandaged paw. From time to time, he stands and leans heavily against the door frame, his brown face shining in the chiarosucuro of the room lit only by a couple of small lamps.

"They were drunk of course," says Somka. "In that pub all bloody night. Then one of his friends throw a bag of gunpowder on to the fire to see what would happen, as if it wasn't obvious."

The gunpowder was doubtlessly lifted from the Arsenal weapons factory up the road, one of Europe's main production centres for Kalashnikov AK-47 assault rifles. Until recently this was where most of the village had work but the factory is now in trouble. The Bulgarian military is moving to the NATO standard and it has become harder and harder for Bulgarian companies to flog weapons to African warlords as they used to do so lucratively.

The flames had engulfed Pavel completely, for a moment he had been like a human torch. His friends had pulled off his clothes and extinguished the flames. But in their drunkeness they had decided not to disturb his family in the middle of the night. Perhaps they didn't realise how badly hurt he was. Nor did Pavel himself, because they all slept in the bar, crashed out just where they were.

The next day was Sunday. A doctor had to be called from the nearby town, but he had gone fishing. Pavel had to suffer a day of pain before he could get treatment.

"You are a fool. No nous," Somka tells him, tenderly lighting his cigarette. She is a striking woman. Years of backbreaking work have worn into her. She has a tough, almost masculine air as if she is capable of anything. I can't imagine anything knocking her down, but she is still beautiful. Her face, framed with straight black hair, is brown and deeply lined. Her eyes are bright. They still retain the dancing light of the slim lively beauty she must have been in her youth, when she played netball semi-professionally for the town of Haskovo.

Now she is fat, her short body slightly lop-sided thanks to a mastectomy. At rest her face speaks of hardship and sorrow but when she speaks it changes. Her smile is irresistible and is followed regularly by an infectious wheezing, rumbling laugh. It is impossible to feel uncomfortable around her.

Her husband is a quiet man with an easy laid-back expression and wild curly hair. Chicho Som means Uncle Catfish in Bulgarian. Lelya Somka is Aunt Catfish. The family acquired this nick-name because Som used to sport large droopy whiskers. Although the facial hair has gone, the nickname has stuck.

Everyone in the village has a nick-name.

"You are now on the lowest branch," Som tells me with a wink. "That's because you are the junior monkey. If you are staying with the *maimuni*, you must be one too."

The Maimuni are the "Monkeys". This is the nick-name given to Itso's family, apparently because Itso's grandfather used to be fond of climbing trees. Itso's sons are also called by this name. It has already served four generations.

Itso, a burly middle-aged man with a round face and thick grey walrus moustache, chuckles delightedly at this and I am toasted as the new monkey with fiery draughts of the rakia. We are all quite drunk.

It is hard to imagine at this moment that the man at my side is a secret policeman, albeit rather a junior one. Once or twice a week, he completes a 24-hour shift in the communications room at the top of the Ministry of the Interior, across the square from where I live. He tells me he spends all day transcribing morse code but I'm not sure if I believe him. I suspect he is tapping people's phones. But he can't be drawn on that subject and after a while I stop asking him.

At the end of his shift, or whenever he is bored, which is often, Itso rings me up and we go out to drink fake brand-name vodka in one of the little cheap bars in the narrow streets behind my flat.

"I'm not ashamed of my job. It's honourable being a cop," Itso told me during one of these day-time drinking sessions. "But it's much more boring than you would imagine. People don't know what we do. They think it is all corruption and dirty money. Ohh! I wish someone would try to bribe me! Where are all these bribes that officials are supposed to be getting?"

It is obvious that he hasn't been supplementing his meagre salary. He lives with his family in a small bare flat in a tower block in the suburb of Liulin, a forest of grey tenements. The flat is on the fifth floor. You have to go up in a smelly lift. Someone has melted all the plastic buttons with the end of his cigarette. The front door is covered with a padlocked steel grill. The whole area looks grey and dead even on sunny days. When Sofia is shrouded in the clammy winter fogs that sometimes lodge for days on the enclosed plain that surrounds the city it is one of the most depressing places on earth.

Itso would much prefer to live here in the village like a peasant, scraping by on a virtually non-existent pension. Unfortunately for him, his wife, who has a much better job than he does (she works in one of the recently privatised banks), is in love with the city. Peasant life bores her as much as it pleases him.

So like many Bulgarians, he is a weekend peasant. It is a way of life he goes back to whenever he can, replacing the grim of the city with the more wholesome real dirt of the village. Although on this trip he has been in the village for only a few days, his cheeks are thick with stubble, and his clothes are old and ragged. He looks like a different person.

He raises his glass to me and winks with moist, inebriated eyes.

• • •

I first met Somka and her family the previous June. In early summer, life in the village revolves around just one subject: roses. June is harvest time. In the rose gardens the scent of millions of roses just coming into flower hangs at the sunrise like a half-remembered promise. The smell is everything, everywhere, it permeates the dew and the damp earth.

I helped Somka with her harvest. We had to struggle out of bed at four o'clock to pick the blossoms before the sun evaporated the night-time dews from them. It was a calm and ethereal experience. As we moved silently between the rows of prickly bushes, the silhouetted hills acquired ever sharper definition and colour in the growing early midsummer light. The greyness of pre-dawn dissolved into fresh pale morning revealing the lines of bushes running away from us towards the far woods, which were still as dark as night.

Rain during the night had made the flowers heavy with moisture. The air was also heavy and sweet. (In the rose oil distilleries this smell is multiplied so many times that it becomes overpowering, an almost chemical stench. Here it was pervasive but beautiful.)

Somka showed me how to pick the flowers, plucking the soft buds between thumb and forefinger gently so the petals did not fall away. These were not the great intricate roses of English gardens, nor the sculpted, deep-coloured roses from bouquets. They were simple, delicate, almost undecorative pale pink flowers which looked more like wild dog roses or briars.

Somka had been a child during the early years of communism. Rose picking then had seemed like a sort of idyll. When it was muddy she would go bare-foot between the rows, sinking up to her knees in the soft reddish mud. The rows were so carefully tended then, that there was not a single blade of grass let along a thistle to tread on. If it was dry she sometimes fell asleep under the bushes. I imagined her using a sack of petals as a pillow and dreaming youthful dreams of feather beds and luxury.

In 1990, when they denationalised the land, they gave Somka back four rows from the village collective close to where her grandparent's rose fields had once been. She maintained her bushes separately from the old collective. Beyond her few lines of bushes, the signs of slow impending ruin stretched over the field. Weeds and brambles choked the straggly unpruned bushes, many of which were dying back to a few twisted black twigs.

Why spend the extra time on pruning and weeding? Why spend money on fertilizers, and weedkillers when you could not afford to employ extra hands to pick the flowers?

My apron grew heavy with the damp blossoms, the dew soaked through my trousers. My clothes, hair and skin were gradually impregnated with the scent of roses. I imagined going back to Sofia surrounded by an aura of flowers. But the reality of the situation was revealed when we took our morning's work to the village weighing machine to be sold. Our gross takings for the day were 20 levs, approximately seven pounds.

I can't imagine how I shall spend it all, joked Somka. The gross for the entire harvest would be approximately 200-300 levs, or less than £100 pounds sterling. Anything not immediately spent on household costs would go towards Pavel's wedding, an event which would swallow up all her other savings too.

But it was part of Somka's strength that she would carry on anyway. She put the small handful of notes carefully away in the inside pocket of her coat, clapped me on the shoulders and suggested that we go mushroom hunting if I wasn't tired. There had been some good rain the night before.

• • •

A whole summer, autumn and winter has passed. As I sit with my friends around their table, we are eating pickled mushrooms made from the ones we picked back then. Pavel is going to be married as soon as he has recovered from his burns. Life somehow, miraculously, is continuing, the money from the rose harvest has gone, but more has been earned somehow, elsewhere.

We are celebrating the success of a minor escapade. I had helped Somka intimidate the mayor of the next door village into giving her sister Gergana a telephone. Gergana's husband had suffered a stroke. Whenever he had a seizure in the night she had to run half way through the village to call a doctor.

I don't know why the mayor wouldn't write the simple letter telling the telephone company to install a line into her house. But we had paid him a visit and I had waved my journalist accreditation in his face threatened to publicise his meanness in the international press. It seemed like a ridiculous threat, but incredibly it had worked. A telephone line would be installed.

"Oh! Did you see that mayor's face? He went quite green when he saw your car drive up and we stepped out. And you with your camera."

Somka chuckles hoarsely and then seized by an idea, suddenly bustles into the back room. A short while later she comes back hauling a huge pile of heavy clothing on the floor behind her.

"They belonged to my grandfather," she explains, as she holds out a pair of baggy *poturi* made from thick heavy brown wool. They are jodhpur-like trousers, tight around the calves but with a vast baggy gusset. I had seen similar items depicted in romantic 19th century prints of wild Balkan figures. They are traditional shepherd clothes, but not work clothes. They are intricately designed national costume. The seams are encrusted with coils of black filigree embroidery. Somka flings them towards where I am sitting on the little bed. The trousers are followed by a low square waistcoat and a short bumfreezer jacket of the same material all decorated in a similar fashion.

"I'm giving them to you."

For a moment I'm dumbstruck, then I protest.

"I can't take them!"

"Rubbish," says Itso, "Put it on and see if it fits."

The waistcoat fits but the jacket is too small. Itso arranges it over my shoulders. Somka by this time has pulled from the pile a cummerbund, a shirt and a pair of intricately patterned socks. At her insistence I wind the cummberund around my waist. I try to refuse again.

"I can't take it. These are your family things."

"They are no use to me. In any case, you have helped me and my sister. This is a way of saying thank you."

"It was nothing."

"You'll offend me if you don't accept."

I bow as graciously as I can from the bed, feeling a bit like Errol Flynn with my shepherd's jacket draped on my shoulders.

It is nearly midnight when Itso grabs me by the sleeve.

"We should go. We still haven't been to the krutchma. The *kukeri* will be there."

We leave Som and Somka's hospitality behind us and head down through the winding, unlit streets, stumbling over the loose stones, heading towards the village centre. I carry Somka's gift to me in a large bundle, all except the jacket which is still on my shoulders.

We stumble along the village's narrow streets in darkness. There is no moon. All the early spring constellations are clearly visible in the clear sky: Orion, Gemini, Leo, the Great Bear, Cassiopea, Cepheus, Perseus and Andromeda. In the distance we can hear music. There is a barely suppressed sense of madness in the village this evening. It is the eve of *Kukovden*, one of the many coincidences of Pagan and Christian rites that litter Bulgarian rural tradition.

In the Orthodox Christian calendar it is the eve of *Crni Zagovezni*, when pious folk give up meat, eggs and milk products until Easter. This year it coincides with another traditional festival: *Zadushnitsa*, a day when the dead are remembered and the living beg forgiveness from each other.

But there is nothing Christian about Kukovden, nor about the Kukeri who are already roaming the village and who tomorrow will make it their own. They are part of Turia's ancient pagan past, probably a 2000-year old legacy from the era of the Thracians.

We round the corner of the church and an awful clashing of bells suddenly breaks out of the darkness.

"Ahh, the kukeri are coming," says Itso.

The noise gets louder and louder. It is a rhythmical bashing. It sounds like metal being smashed, the advance of some terrible machine or the tramp of iron boots. Eventually it coalesces into shadowy forms on the edge of the square. A troupe of men, bare-chested and girded with what appear to be dull brass fustanellas, burst into the dim light of the square. They each have a dozen huge bulbous cowbells attached to wide leather belts around their waists. With each ponderous leap, the bells crash together like the pleats of a heavy metal skirt. The men seem completely unaware of the cold as they dance by us and disappear into the early March night.

"Every year we do this," Itso tells me. "Since a time before anyone can remember. The young men of the village dress up like devils to drive the bad spirits away. I remember doing it a long time ago. It's a good excuse for getting very drunk."

I ask him what kukeri means but he doesn't know.

Both of the village bars are crowded this evening. We catch up with another group of kukeri at a temporary *krutchma* more like a canvas shelter, where they are selling home-made wine flavoured with wormwood. The wine is called *pelin*. It would be intolerably sweet without the bitter herb pelin, also known in Slavic languages as *cherni bil* (black herb). In English it is artemesia or wormwood.

This is the same herb that flavours absinthe and which is mentioned in the book of Revelation as one of the seven seals which are opened before the Apocalypse. (This little fact explains why the Chernobyl nuclear accident in Ukraine was seized upon so eagerly by doomsdayers as evidence of the approaching end of the world.)

But we are not really thinking about doomsday this evening. The insistent rhythm of the traditional folk music thumps out of a very untraditional hi-fi system. The catchy beat is like a magnet. Most of the clientele are already very drunk.

One of the dancers has taken off his bells and invites me to fasten the thick leather belt round my waist. We link arms and dance a ring dance on to the street.

Soon a long string of people from local lads, grizzled mechanics and fashionably dressed students from Sofia have linked hands and are nimbly tripping through the steps of the horo.

This is Bulgaria's intricate version of the *horo* or ring-dance that is danced all through the Balkans. The style of the dance, like the music which accompanies it, encapsulates the different characters of the Balkan races. Greek dances are most lively, capturing the irrepressible gaiety of the Greek spirit, while the Macedonian heavy horo, which is only ever danced by men, is almost menacing in its slowness. I saw it being danced by red shirted VMRO (Internal Macedonian Revolutionary Organisation) activists on top of a mountain near Krushevo, where the Macedonian Republic celebrates its independence day and the anniversary of a terrible uprising against the Turks in 1903. The men grasp each others arms at the biceps forming a solid wall and move round slowly first crouching low then leaping up. To perform this dance for any length of time requires phenomenally strong thigh muscles. It is a macho dance that sums up the entire ethos of Macedonian revolutionary brotherhood.

Some people say that Bulgarian dances are gloomy. This is an easy mistake to make. The rhythms are extremely intricate and difficult to understand. Bulgaria is home to a great number of different *hora*, each typical to its own region. There is the easy and ubiquitous 2/4 time and more estoteric dances in 5/8, 9/16 or even a devilish 11/16 time. Whatever the rhythm, the dancers turn in a great circle and match their steps to those of the leader.

This particular horo, in the bar at Turia the night before Kukovden, is thankfully quite an easy one. But as we whirl around the
outside of the bar in a crazy chain, it seems to be a good symbol
of Bulgarian society. At one end of the line is the village drunkard
clutching his bottle, some bare-chested kukeri with their bells, a few
youths in leather jackets, their girlfriends in designer-ware, a few old
men and Itso and myself. And so the revelry continues far into the
night and into the next day.

Itso wakes me the next morning. "Soon they will be here."

I pull on my clothes and go down to the yard via the outside
staircase from the upper veranda. Itso's house is an old building tht
presents noting but a façade of crumbly mud-coloured bricks onto
the narrow street outside. From the inside the place has an entirely
different aspect. There is a large yard, given over to vegetables. In one
corner is a wooden privy. Round the corner of the house though an
iron gate is a chicken run and a barn. In the summer an old vine would
spreads its shade over the front of the house. Now it is nothing but
twigs and frame. Outside the front door there is a collection of ancient galoshes, wooden clogs, slippers and broken shoes. Every has
been mended many times because there is no money. The door opens
into the kitchen where Itso's mother, Baba Maria is boiling fresh goats
milk and preparing golden omelettes from new laid eggs. We rush
through our breakfast to be ready for when the festival arrives.

We hear them coming down the street and then they are upon
us.

"Ohhh ho! Here are the tsigani!"

Itso's cry is drowned by the great riot which explodes into the yard.
The tsigani are the bad spirits, who with crude village sterotyping are
dressed up as Turks and Roma gypsies. Their association with evil
spirits is scarcely questioned. They arrive with a cannonade of musketry from a wicked-looking arsenal of ancient rifles and long barrel-
led pistols that belch vast explosions of black smoke and wadding.

Their leader is the prostitute mother of evil. She is a vast, slut-
tish rolling woman in a shabby floral headscarf, baggy pyjamas and
aprons. She carries a baby doll carelessly under her arm and swigs
from a bottle.

This role has been taken by the biggest man in the village – a
powerful rotund man, from a family made only of powerful, rotund
men and women. In ordinary life he goes by the nick-name of Vozh-

da – leader. His round stubbly cheeks have been grotesquely rouged, his lips painted red and eyes shadowed with green. Behind him his minions, whoop and roar, waving their weapons like pantomime pirates. They are dressed in colourful patterned pantaloons, gaudy shirts and jackets with gold tassels and fringes. Their bodies are entirely painted with black soot.

Then the noise gets even louder. The dancers we saw the night before burst into the yard. The dark shiny cow-bells make twice the noise in the enclosed space. Today their faces are also covered with horrifying mask, each of which is about three-foot high made of hairy goat skin stretched on a light wooden frame. The frame tapers to a point, topped with a white-dressed doll like a bride. Each mask has a staring face of wild eyes and sharp teeth, cut from black and red felt. The kukeri are bare-chested and wear flowery waistcoats. Every limb is tied with coloured ribbons and bows. They carry phallus-like wooden swords also tied with ribbons.

These creatures throw themselves into the ritual with frenetic energy. They look like another set of devils, but in fact they represent the good spirits, who will drive out the bad from the village. Bell ringing, according to old Bulgarian tradition, increases fertility and drives away demons. This is both a cleansing and a fertility ritual. Each yard in the village is being ritually exorcised of bad luck and blessed with fecundity for the year.

In an inkling, the black-painted imps are all over the place. One rushes up to me and smears a sweaty, sooty hand across my face. A masked kuker chases him away brandishing his wooden sword, and pretends to shave the evil away from my cheeks.

Black figures are dancing and singing and rummaging through the store rooms. They come out clutching fistfuls of potatoes. Heavy reports of musketry echo off the straw and mud plastered walls.

"Ours, ours!" they cry. Potatoes and eggs are their traditional bounty. The old village idiot   trundles in with a barrow. The fresh loot is added.

Itso makes his way between the revellers holding out a large bowl of home-made wine, from which everyone is drinking. It is a refreshing fruity rosé, less than one year old and tastes so mellow and fresh that it is like nothing which has ever seen the inside of a bottle.

It is fuel for the madness. The combination of religion, superstition, anarchic noise and hard drinking creates a scene which must be as close to a Bachannalian revel as the modern world is capable of producing.

I have done some research on these celebrations in the library in Sofia. But little in the academic tone of the collections of ethnology has prepared me for the intensity of this celebration. One clue comes from the writings of Mercia Macdermott, who probably knows more about Bulgaria than any other writer in the English language. She says that the kukeri festival is probably linked to the cults of the Thracians. These were the uproarious Dionysian cults made famous by Herodotus in his history.

Another book told me that in the 19th century real fights used to break out between the kukeri. People even died. But under communism the celebration seems to have gone to the other extreme. In many places it became little more than a dutifully colourful, officially sanctioned folkloric show in the town square.

Thankfully, Turia, being a small and out of the way village, has preserved its ritual rough around the edges. The meaning of it, the ritual cleansing and driving away of bad luck and bad spirits from every house, still exists. As if to prove that it is a living tradition, new innovations have arrived too. Next to the many traditional costumes, some of them passed down through families for generations, there an modern innovations, most of them linked to some theme of cross dressing. One boy, heavily made up and wearing a bright bikini, brandishes an umbrella. There is a girl dressed as a Chicago hoodlum.

Just as suddenly as they arrive, the revellers depart, charging down the street to the next house. I follow them. The ritual is repeated again and again with increasing drunken intensity until late in the afternoon the village gathers in its main square to witness the finale.

The tsigani charge wildly into the square like an army bent on destruction. They are followed closely by the kukeri. Mock fights break out between the two sides. Soon there are figures rolling and yelling all over the square. It is chaos. Meanwhile to one side, the final piece of mummery is being played out. The Vozdh, playing the evil bride, has crawled into a little straw shelter with a few of his acolytes around him. With gross distortions he pretends to give birth to the plastic doll that he has been carrying under his arm all day.

The hubbub reaches a climax as the kukeri grab the doll, and set the straw house on fire. The symbolism is obvious. This is the birth and destruction of the new evil. Various Bulgarian enthusiasts, looking for closer links with the Thracian past believe that the burning of the baby could represent the death and rebirth of Dionysus or Orpheus.

But such speculation can never be proved and the revel is nearly at an end. In a final spasm of drunken enthusiasm the entire company: kukeri, turks, roma and bride leap from the main bridge into the river that has been specially dammed for the occasion.

It is the end. Evil has been banished, burnt and washed away. Winter is over and spring is coming. Once again the villagers link arms in the horo. Soaking wet youths, hold the hands of dyed blonde teenagers in platform boots and the huge ring of people slowly revolves around the village square.

An incantation against a devil

Sar'sar! Far'far' Seeing sweat. Sadragasi. Adraga.
Gasigdefa. Mer'gari. Far'gatere. Gel'me. Zelime. Amesamidik!
Koraga. Semast! Sabbath. Having created heaven and earth,
always, now and for ever and for ages to come.

Translated by Thomas Butler

The Witch's Cup

I SHOULD not have been surprised at the connection between Todor Zhivkov, the brutal, atheist dictator, and Baba Vanga, the most famous witch in the Balkans.

Baba Vanga died in 1996 aged 84 just before I arrived in Bulgaria. Her death was mourned with the sorrow normally reserved for major national heroes, or even for a saint. One of the oddest facts mentioned in her obituaries, alongside tales of uncanny visions, was that Zhivkov used to consult her.

I have tried to imagine the scene. The dictator's black and shiny limousine must have looked incongruous next to the mud, the chickens and the simple little whitewashed cottage where she lived all her life. I can't quite picture his round fleshy face, heavy with power, next to her blank, staring features. Was she in awe or him or was it the other way round? What did Zhivkov ask her about? Was he worried about his rebellious, eccentric daughter, Lyudmilla, who died from a mysterious illness in 1981? It was her enthusiasm for spiritualism and folkloric cults that probably secured official favour for Vanga in the first place. Did Vanga reassure the dictator that he would die peacefully in his bed, or warn him that his 35-year long rule would end in failure and disgrace? Or was it just a matter of one creator of a powerful cult of personality paying homage to another?

It is amazing that the regime, normally so heavy handed about matters of belief, tolerated the witch. But it had done more than that. It had given her official sanction and had awarded her, bizarrely, a research fellowship at the Bulgarian Academy of Sciences. A state official was appointed to sell tickets to anyone who wanted to see her.

Over the whole course of her life, more than one million people may have consulted Vanga. The legend of her power began when aged 12, she was swept up by a tornado which carried her for more than a mile. Probably she should have died. If not from the physical shock, then, according to folklore, because whirlwinds are created by *"samodivi"* – fairies or sylphs. Anything which is picked up by them belongs to the fairy world. For a person this means death or madness.

Although she survived, the experience did damage her in some way. She began to lose her sight. By the time she was 14, she was completely blind. This gave birth to other legends. One said that she was given the choice between physical sight or second sight. She chose the latter. But her blindness also caused her to be venerated as the living incarnation or descendent of Sveta Petka Paraskeva, a potent Bulgarian female saint, patron to women and blind people. Vanga herself did a great deal to foster this idea. Sveta Petka was the aunt of Sveti Dimitur, another powerful saint in the region. She deliberately surrounded herself with men named Dimitur and even stipulated that her coffin should be born by six men of that name.

Towards the end of her life, after the end of communism, she requested that a church dedicated to Sveta Petka, be built close to the cottage where she lived her whole life in the village of Rupite in south-west Bulgaria. The money was raised in record time. The murals inside were painted by one of the most fashionable communist-era artists, who abandoned traditional iconography in favour of potraits of his lover, himself and, of course, Vanga. The Orthodox Church hated it, and still does. But in this story the Church as an organisation is almost irrelevant.

Vanga's personal chapel stands near her cottage in the lush garden where every day hundreds of people would patiently wait for a chance to consult the famous witch. The whole complex, now a tourist site, is located in the crater of an extinct volcano, believed by hippy types to be a source of natural energy. It is a place of pilgrimage, redolent with the inventive semi-pagan, semi-Christian superstition which seems to come more naturally to many Bulgarians than orthodoxy of any sort: Christian, Muslim or Marxist.

When I started to look into fortune-telling and the many other superstitious traditions which fill Bulgarian life, I thought that communism itself was probably to blame for undermining the country's religious orthodoxy, making a space for other stranger beliefs to flourish. But the further I looked back in history, the more it seemed that

Bulgarians have always had a flexible attitude to these things. The country is, after all, the spiritual home of the White Brotherhood*, one of the handful of 20th century cults to have become established as a world religion alongside the Moonies and the Scientologists. It was also the spiritual home of the Bogomils, the most feared of all mediaeval Christian heresies. And diving even further back into the past, it was home to the ancient Thracian cult of Orpheus and the bacchanalian mysteries with which he is associated.

None of these things have been remotely forgotten, neither in the less educated, rural parts of the country, nor in the cities. The White Brotherhood still gathers every summer to worship the sun on the highest peaks of Rila. Historians argue that the Bulgarian Muslims who live in the Rhodopes are probably descendants of the Bogomils. Serious academics are more than happy to discuss the influence of Orpheus, not only on traditional Bulgarian music and folklore but on the whole of the national culture.

In some cases they might be right. One evening, walking home through the narrow streets near my apartment, a middle-aged woman stopped me and invited me to eat a meal at her house. It was the anniversary of her husband's death, she told me. Every year she honoured his soul by giving a meal to a complete stranger.

This is indeed an ancient, probably pre-Christian custom. A similar thing happened in a village on the banks of the Danube. I passed a funeral party outside the church. A gypsy brass band was wheezing out sorrowful tunes. The coffin had just been interred. A young man, a relative of the deceased offered me a spoonful of sweetened boiled wheat from a large bowl and then a ladle of wine. It was an obligation.

And if you want to consult a fortune-teller, it isn't hard to find one. Newspapers are full of advertisements for "Extra-senses" and *vrachki* (soothsayers). Several of my friends in Sofia, journalists sceptical to the point of cynicism about most things, consult vrachki as a matter of course, before making big decisions.

But it was some friends in the village of Breznitsa high on the eastern slopes of the Pirin mountains who introduced me to a witch who told my fortune by stirring at an egg yolk in a bowl of water.

---

* Founded by Petur Dunov, who had been dictator Georgi Dimitrov's next-door neighbour.

"Go to Shukra," my village friends had told me. "A month ago she found our calf, which had been lost on the mountain for a whole week."

They had taken her an egg and the beast's spare bridle. It was enough for her to tell them exactly which glade the animal could be found in.

So I went to her house and placed a present of money, not in her palm but on the bed – a gift, not a transaction.

Lelya Shukra was an old woman. Her shiny black eyes were sunk deep in an old face as sharp and thin as a baby bird's. Her head was wrapped in a white scarf so that no hair could be seen. She was a Pomak, an ethnically Bulgarian Muslim. She wore the traditional Muslim clothing for the region: a long pale blue smock and a pair of baggy striped pyjamas.

More than fifty years ago Shukra's mother-in-law, herself a famous witch, had felt her powers ebbing together with her bodily strength. She had placed her mouth over Shukra's and breathed into her the gift of second sight. Since then the witch had achieved renown in the region around the Mesta valley as a finder of lost things.

She crouched on the floor of a one room cottage at the lower end of the village. The air in the dim frowsy room was close and aromatically scented with the smoke that escaped from a flimsy metal stove. The walls and ceilings might formerly have been white-washed. The tiles around the sink in the corner also must have been white. But smoke and age had given every surface a sepia wash that had seeped also into the once colourful rugs and bed coverings.

Before she began the seance, she was happy to talk about her art. She waved her long bony fingers and told me about good and bad luck, while I sat before her on a tiny wooden chair that must have belonged to a child.

"If a person is sick in their heart I can divine their trouble through the molten lead of a bullet. The lead must have passed through the barrel of a gun. I pour it into cold water. The shape it makes tells me where the evil lies." Remedies for these bad spirits might lie with the doctor, the Muslim *hodzha* or the priest. There are no denominations in Shukra's magic.

"What if there is no remedy?"

"The person dies. Some things cannot be changed or prevented."

Then, very slowly Lelya Shukra began the ritual that would provide the answer to my question. First she looked at me for a short
while as if trying to work something out from my expression or manner. Then she nodded, almost imperceptibly. Her demeanour subtly
changed as if she had come to a decision about me.

"What would you like to know about, sonny? What is troubling
you? Love? Work? Health? Have you lost something?" she asked in
an almost whisper, but matter-of-factly. For all the mystery and mys-
ticism of her profession she was a person who dealt with the every
day questions of people's lives.

"Tell Shukra," she rasped.

I hesitated before I asked my question. What was I getting into
here, I wondered. I had never consulted a fortune-teller before. Back
in England it was something I would never have even considered. It
had always seemed to me a foolhardy thing to do, like putting one's
full weight on a bridge that is not obviously supported. But I could
not restrain my curiosity. I had to find out about this facet of Bulgarian life. I leant forwards and whispered my question in her ear.

"Give me threads from your clothing," she asked. I pulled two
threads from my jeans and handed them to her. She twisted them
together deftly, mumbling as she did so. Then she reached out from
where she was squatting on the floor and took the egg that I held out
to her, still warm from the hen. She wiped the twisted threads on
the egg and the bowl, muttering charms, rocking backwards and forwards with the insistent repetitiveness of the mentally ill (although
she was far from being that).

Tap, tap, tap, tap. She knocked the egg four times against the rim
of a simple clay bowl filled with water. North, south, east and west
– the shape of the cross. Then she cracked it. The liquid insides slid
effortlessly, whole, into the water. She placed the cleanly halved shell
to one side and mumbled again, peering and poking at the floating
golden yolk, surrounded by cirrus wisps of albumen.

I sat in nervous silence, oppressed by the gloom and fascinated
by the twitching of the witch's bright red finger nails, ten spots of
colour flickering around the bowl. It was almost too dark for any
reflection to escape from it.

After what seemed a long time, although it was only a few minutes, she looked up at me from her dirty rug and her deeply lined face
creased into a reassuring smile.

"Ne se boi! Ne se boi Don't fret! Don't fret!" she cackled. The egg and the threads had behaved well.

After she had told me the answer to my question, Shukra's sharp face lost the trance-like blankness of a seer. She laughed again.

"So you are writing a book about us, eh? If you want to write something true, write about how much a loaf of bread now costs in Bulgaria. For us, that is our life and death."

The cost of bread. The ability to live. The soothsayer was right. For most Bulgarians that still was the most important thing.

Red Ferrari

If I had God's telephone number
If I had it for myself
I'd call him
and we'd make a deal
I with him and he with me.
We'd find an understanding.
And when he asked me
What I wanted
I would tell him – just like this:

Only just one red Ferrari
One for you and one for me
That is all a man needs...
And just for luck a tanned blonde girly
One for you and one for me
That is all any man needs...

Don't you have a mobile phone,
Don't you have one Lord my God
That I can call you on?
For you to ask my holy Lord
What I dream of, what I want.
Whatever, God, that you grant me
We will split it evenly
One for you and one for me.

A chalga hit by Slavi Trifonov

Saving my Soul

I BALANCED my experiences of Bulgarian paganism by visiting Bulgarian monasteries. A friend had told me about one that was more spiritual than any other. It was like a fortress, but high in the Balkan Range, miles and miles from anywhere. Stranger still, it was inhabited by a single solitary monk, a young man but a recluse, almost a hermit, with wild hair and eyes and strange stories to tell. You like the strange things of Bulgaria, so perhaps you will like this place, my friend told me.

Evening was falling as I pushed my heavily laden bicycle up the last steep slope towards the monastery gate. I had pedalled half way across the mountains to get there. The final road had given me tantalising glances of my destination through the trees for the past hour: a tower, a ragged grey wall swirling in mist, rickety wooden buildings overhanging a great cliff. The monastery perched on the forested shoulder of Mount Lisets, overlooking the valley of the Beli Vit River which cascaded from the heart of the Balkan Range and drained eventually into the River Danube many miles to the north.

Even though night was falling fast, the windows high in the stark wall gave off not a glimmer of light. The place might even have been completely deserted. It was too late to turn back. In any case, I had nowhere to turn back to. So I trudged onwards.

Having almost convinced myself that I would find the place empty, it was a shock to turn the last corner and find a dark young man with a wispy black beard, dark eyes and pallid skin standing outside the tall wrought iron gates. He stood in silence as I approached, showing neither surprise nor great curiosity. It was as if he was expecting me. I wondered if he had heard the sound of my tyres on the surface of the track.

"You've come on a visit?" he asked me.

"Yes."

"Follow me." He turned and led me through the gate which he carefully shut behind us and locked with a padlock. I shouldered my bicycle and followed him up the steep stone steps, overgrown by grass and weeds, which led to a small archway in the tall outer wall. A crazy wattle and daub upper story with crooked windows and twisted wooden joists jutted out above us. He beckoned at me and entered.

I ducked into a stone-lined tunnel, 20 foot long with scarcely enough room for two to walk abreast. It opened into the cramped monastery courtyard. Looking around I understood that we had walked underneath the church built on the highest part of the crag. It was a long thin space. A few paces ahead of me another door had a battered notice above it reading "The kitchen". A simple cobbled cloister, bordered by a rustic veranda on two sides, opened to my right. Some faded cassocks and a couple of pairs of many times washed pink long johns hung from the rickety wooden balustrade in front of what I took to be the monk's own quarters.

To my left were some broad stone stairs descending to another building. There was a stone basin cluttered with implements for washing dishes and clothes. Wooden steps led up to a large open second storey, only a little higher than the level on which I now stood. A large plain table stood on this *chardak*. Several doors opened from it, leading, I later learned, to the guest quarters.

My host invited me to enter first into the small bare kitchen. The windows were open. Through the bars I could see a sea of green and coppery leaves rising up on the other side of the valley. The monk grinned at my appreciation of the view and set about making coffee for us both.

"I am Father Nektari," he told me.

He was a prototype hermit, a thin, bony-faced aesthetic with dark, longing eyes and straggling beard. His unbrushed, uncut hair coiled and sprouted in every direction. His purple cassock hung from his bony frame. He seemed to have been consumed by his passion for the monastic life (or perhaps the struggle of it).

He refused to eat any of the simple meal that I unpacked from my rucksack, saying that he had already supped. Later, when I put the food I had brought with me away in the fridge, I saw that he had nothing to eat there but some crumbly white cheese, half a loaf of bread and a few tomatoes.

While I ate, he kept me company, playing selections from a large collection of new age music, battered cassettes that he pulled out of an old cardboard box.

He had been at the seminary in Sofia for three years and but had left before completing his studies. He had volunteered to come to Glozhene, what must be one of the most remote, lonely and least comfortable monastic retreats. This decision had not been met with approval by his religious master but he had secured the support of the abbot, who was, unusually, not himself a monk but instead was the local priest from the village of Maluk Isvor, that I had passed ten miles back along the road. The abbot mostly stayed in the village with his family.

"Its best in winter. So beautiful. And so solitary. After the snows it is sometimes impossible to get in or out. I see no one for days or weeks," Nektari told me.

I was not surprised that he had decided to adopt a hermit like existence to escape the jealousies, politicking and in-fighting of his clerical colleagues. The Bulgarian Orthodox Church is one of the most discredited institutions in a country where corruption is the norm.

There was, said Nektari, no point in having any contact with other monasteries or monks as all they did was play games with politics and money. If he wanted contact with worldly people he had his friends in Sofia who were not in the church. They were, he assured me, very worldly people.

It was time to go to bed. Nektari lit one of the slim orange candles from the church and took me up a flight of stairs and along the wooden balcony to a large bare room. I washed quickly in the freezing water and rolled myself into bed in all my clothes. The time was just after 8.30pm.

I spent an uneasy night. Perhaps my exhaustion and the strange dark silence of the place conspired to unsettle me. My first shock was to wake in the darkness with an unpleasant sensation that something was tickling my lips. All kinds of fancies immediately sprang into my sleep-drugged mind. Was someone attempting to slyly introduce some evil thing into my mouth; the antennae of some unpleasant insect come to drink at my lips; attracted by the smell of fruit juice on my lips some bewhiskered rat or bat or urghhh! I threw off my bedclothes and sat up fumbling for my flashlight in the gloom. A minute search of my bed and the whole room revealed nothing. But my lower lip felt sore as if something had indeed bitten it. Sure enough an examination in the bathroom mirror revealed a tiny incision just below my lower lip. All kinds of gothic speculations began to crowd in on my over-tired mind. Vampire bats? Mice? Insects? Who or what had been attracted to my sweet sleeping breath? Why had I been placed in such a remote room? I struggled to dismiss my fears as childish superstition. But the lack of any sign of my attacker disquieted rather than consoled me. I re-lit the candle and drifted off to sleep again only to jump awake again convinced that I had felt the weight of a small animal jump on my leg. Again I could find no sign of anything. It was still scarcely past midnight. I despaired to think how many hours lay before me until sunrise would banish my fears.

It was the healthy upsurge of annoyance that saved me from an awful sleepless night. I was damned if I would let nonsense of this sort keep me from my rest. I banished my creepy speculations to the realm of fancy. This return of sensibility enabled me to think and I soon convinced myself that I had been tickled on the lip by the edge of my blanket or some hairs of my moustache, which at that stage I had been allowing to grow long. The shifting of a piled up fold in the blanket, dislodged by an involuntary twitch or spasm in my leg must have awoken me for the second time. I settled myself down and awoke for the third time only when the pale silver light of early morning was already lightening my room.

A whole year passed before I went back to Glozhene again. The news I had gathered about Nektari in the meantime was not good. Aglaya, my dear old friend, who was by now running the newsroom of a large television station, had sent a crew to film him in the snowbound monastery as part of the Bulgarian TV Christmas broadcast. He had taken the opportunity to put his sharply critical views of the church heirarchy on record. Stories about him started to appear in the newspapers. Members of his family appeared, claiming tearfully that they had believed him to be dead for three years not having heard anything from him.

One newspaper reported that he had been a more than unusually ugly child and had been rejected by his mother. By the time she repented of this harsh treatment it was too late and he had already become estranged. His brothers travelled to the monastery and brought him back home to spend Christmas with his family.

By the spring, I got reports that he was no longer at Glozhene. The friend who had originally introduced me to the monastery claimed to have seen him selling books from a stall in the city. But when I asked, no one at the book square claimed to have heard from him. I went back to Glozhene in the summer. Nektari was there.

Most of what I had heard was nonsense, he said.

"My family knew very well that I was here. They were just embarrassed because they had treated me badly and wanted to make some publicity."

He denied ever selling books.

"I did leave the monastery for a while. I tried to make a living in the city as a Herbalife agent."

I tried to imagine this wild crazy-eyed figure door-stopping housewives in the Sofia suburbs. Surely a disaster? But apparently not.

"I was quite successful," he told me. But in the end he had decided to come back to the monastery.

There was a new Abbot, so life at the monastery was much more regular than on my first visit. In the early morning, Nektari hammered on the wooden plank suspended under the cloister, that served the monastery instead of a bell. The morning service lasted for several hours. I emerged from my little cell into the cobbled courtyard when it was already half way through and sat at a small table outside the church, whose door was open. The shadow of the church receded from the table until I was enveloped in a warm comfortable glow of sunlight and my head was soothed almost to drowsiness by the repetive chanting of the monks.

Nektari came out out of the church and joined me at the table. He was followed by Abbot Pankrati. We ate some breakfast and gossiped about the church. The abbot cut a different figure from any of the other monks I had met in Bulgaria. He was a compact, energetic man in middle age, with a carefully trimmed salt and pepper beard. He was talkative, but practical, with ideas, plans and ambitions. His only concession to flamboyance was a tall black velvet skullcap that he wore instead of the more usual black "pillar box".

At Troyan there had been a miracle, Pankrati told me. Tsar Simeon (warming up for his political come-back) had attended the monastery's feast day: the Assumption of the Virgin Mary, during which he had carried an icon of the Virgin with three silver hands. A few days later, some drops of myrrh had appeared on the glass. The newspapers had reported that cupfuls had been collected. Pankrati thought that the secretary of the monastery had probably put the myrrh onto the icon.

Many monks in the church are fervent monarchists and hoped that the return of the Tsar would boost the church's influence. Unfortunately for the church, it is still more associated in the public mind with communist oppression, rather than the glory days of monarchy. Nektari rattled out a list of bishops that he thought were former KGB agents. Some had strong contacts with the Moscow patriarch Alexei II. Some were also in league with *mutri* and other dubious businesses.

• • •

As soon as Russia gets into the equation, everything in Bulgaria gets a sinister spin. Whether we are talking about religious, political, mafia or former secret service influence, the connections all run along the same tracks. One link implies all the others.

The Bulgarian church was never very strong. Even before the communists took power and began their campaign to atheise Bulgaria, it was probably one of the least religious countries in Europe. The church was poor. It had few estates and even after it gained autocephalous status from the Turkish Sultan in the mid-19th century it was obliged to depend on state hand-outs.

The newly independent national church played an important role in fostering the national revival, but unlike Greek Orthodoxy, it never became the lodestone of nationalist identity in the country. After independence it was relatively insignificant. So when the Communists took over, the church was in no position to resist the new restrictions that were placed on it.

To start with the regime banned religious instruction to children under 16. By the 70s, the church had been badly weakened, but it still retained the remains of its integrity. So the government adopted a policy of massive infiltration to atheise it from within. The Sofia Theological Academy was separated from the university and filled with university rejects. It became a recruiting ground for agents of the security services where were then expected to make a career in the church. DS agents were appointed to teaching posts and helped to shield young agents during their studies.

It was a successful ploy. The church was "tamed... with terror and brutalities," wrote one theologian. The regime reduced its leaders to "totally submissive robot-like lackeys." Even if only half the priests were stooges, the other half were blackened with the same suspicion. The bishops were "security colonels in cassocks".

With democracy came the need for church renewal. But instead, the first anti-Communist government declared war on the Bulgarian Orthodox Church. It used Communist era legislation to dismiss Patriarch Maxim and the Holy Synod and to appoint a new church heirarchy in its place.

But the old heirarchy refused to go. The result was schism and violent schism at that. During the summer of 1992 the country was presented with the horrifying spectacle of priests fighting each other to gain control of key church buildings. Both sides hired armed bodyguards to help them storm or retake various churches, the offices of the Holy Synod, and the religious academies and seminaries. On one occasion they used tear gas. The government and police refused to intervene.

The conflict reached its climax on the night of Aug 31 1992 when one of the leading schismatics, a certain retired professor of canon law, led a group of hired bodyguards over the walls of the Sofia seminary.

"They climbed over the walls with guns in their hands, disarmed the personnel and occupied the offices," said one report.

The "army" of the official church retook the building in the afternoon. 30 students scaled the back wall and disabled the guard posts. The gates were forced open and hundreds of supporters of the canonical synod rushed in to reoccupy the seminary for Maxim. According to one account the church bells were ringing, the seminarians were shouting victory and singing the troparion of St John of Rila.

Most people though the two patriarchs, Maxim and Pimen were each as bad as each other. Maxim, who was 87-years old in 2006, had been appointed Patriarch by the Politburo in 1971. According to popular but inaccurate belief, he was a Communist Party member, an atheist and a General in the State Security Service or perhaps even in the Russian KGB.

This same gossip had branded his usurper, the "anti-communist" Patriarch Pimen, as a KGB Colonel. Ironically there was more evidence to support the allegation against Pimen than against Maxim. Maxim was obsequious to the communists. In the words of one observer, he was "mediocre and submissive". He never publicly protested about the treatment that the regime was dealing out to his church. But Pimen was worse. In the 1950s, the Synod briefly suspected him of being a security agent. One US-based observer accused him of being behind the arrest and disappearance of a senior monk. As a senior official in the church, he was described as being "unequalled in his servility". He even wrote a panegyric to Stalin.

The squabble between the rival synods finally ended with the death of Pimen. But the church had lost the last vestiges of its authority.

• • •

I was to get a closer look at the Bulgarian ecclesiastical heirarchy that evening. The monastery was hosting a feast.

"Hey, *Protestantche* (Little Protestant!) what are you drinking?"

The man who shouted this at me across the crowded table was Archimandrite Sioni, Rector of the Sofia Theological Seminary. He was a large man, with a big head, a long reddish beard and disconcerting pale blue eyes. There was a disturbing physicality about him.

"Protestants aren't allowed to drink rakia," he rumbled. He nodded his head and stroked his thick red beard that reached down almost to the level of his plate.

I didn't like the look in his pale winking eyes and took a heavy swig from my glass.

"I had no idea."

Some of the other monks around the table chuckled. Bishop Gavrail and Abbot Pankrati listened in silence. Father Nektari, on my left, whispered support.

"Don't let him bully you!"

"We will have to make you orthodox," jested Sioni.

"If I drink enough perhaps it will make me orthodox,"

"The bottle is nearly half empty."

"Little by little then."

There were eleven of us crowded round the square table in the cosy lower refectory of Glozhenski monastery. Most of the other people there were monks. We had three hosts: Abbot Pankrati, Heiromonk Josif and young Father Nektari. Then there was the refectory servant who also sat at the table with us. His name was Petur, nicknamed "Cunning Peter" because of his cheerful yokelish simplicity.

There were six in the Bishop's delegation. Apart from Gavrail and Sioni, there was a third monk, two young seminarians and Vasco, the owner of a local factory for making halva, a kind of sticky sweet made from sugar, honey and crushed sesame seeds. I didn't understand why he was part of this religious delegation. But then again, he probably didn't understand either what an English protestant was doing on his own in one of Bulgaria's wildest and most remote monasteries.

The table was now so crowded with plates of food that you could hardly see the tablecloth. There were several types of salad, smoked mackerel, fresh trout, mushrooms, cheeses, tarator (yoghurt and cucumber soup), soft hunks of white bread in great piles. There were pickles, dark thin slivers of smoked goat meat, several types of salami. There were stuffed vine-leaves, baked peppers, bowls of mashed aubergine and garlic. And on the side, waiting for a place on the table was a vast dish containing a whole roasted lamb spilling with a rich stuffing of rice, liver, kidney and tripe. There were two brimming jugs of airan (yoghurt drink) and an array of bottles including perhaps half a dozen different types of rakia. Every person had at least one bottle in front of him. On the opposite side of the room a fire blazed in the hearth. The room smelt of pine-smoke and roasted lamb.

Until you have sung with a table of priests you haven't sung properly. Their voices are trained for the singing of prayers in church. They soar with melody and then, wonderfully they add the harmonies as well. Bishop Gavrail started the entertainment with a few jokes and then some Bulgarian and Russian folk songs in a fine baritone.

Gavrail was the complete opposite of Nektari. He was an avuncular deep-voiced man whose silver hair was pulled back neatly into a tight bun at the back of his head. His curly grey beard fanned splendidly over his broad chest and spreading belly. Slung round his neck on silver chains were a large wooden and silver cross and a small icon enclosed in a silver locket. The baubles rested comfortably on his belly, nestled in the curls of his beard and as he sang he fingered them fondly.

Nektari then brought out his cassette player and put on a cassette of Iranian music, to which he sang along, voicing no words, happy just to capture the soaring musical phrases. The entire table listened spellbound. It was music from the east with its roots in the church's old heartlands far, far away from my western concept of Christianity. No one else but me seemed to think it odd to hear it in a monastery.

Then later on still, Cunning Peter appeared at the doorway with his bagpipes. He had nearly transformed himself, with the addition of a broad red sash, embroidered waistcoat and black woollen kalpak on his head, into the classic image of a peasant from 50 years ago. But he was still wearing his blue fake Adidas track suit and rubber galoshes.

As always, the Macedonian songs were the best. They are filled with emotion and pride. Between songs, Sioni returned to the subject of my faith with greater and greater seriousness. He had a bottle of mastika (an ouzo-like drink) in front of his place. No one else was drinking it and it was nearly empty. He leant across the table towards me.

"You must become orthodox. You are too good a person to be a protestant."

I drank more rakia. This was not a subject I could get into.

The bishop retired to bed. Sioni and Vasco, the halva man began to dance. As they wheeled slowly round the room arm in arm Sioni gestured for me to join in. I cannot resist dancing *horo*. Arm in arm, shoulder to shoulder we stepped together. The large men trod lightly and I did my best to copy them. The music ended and I turned to my seat but Sioni grabbed me by both my arms.

"Let's make you orthodox. Do you want to?"

I was very drunk. For a second the idea of becoming Orthodox seemed exotically attractive. It is a beautiful religion, mysterious and ancient. I like the fact that its churches are always open. You can wander into a mass when you like, light a candle, say a prayer and leave again. It has none of the regimentation of protestantism. Perhaps I could be Orthodox here and Protestant back in England? But I knew it was idiotic.

"I am already a Christian," I said.

"But on the wrong path. You know that you are wrong." He drew me closer into an embrace.

"No one need know," he whispered into my ear. "Please! Let's do it."

The urgency of his appeal seemed to carry connotations of other kinds of seduction. His red beard rasped in my ear and I my thoughts unavoidably flew to Flanders and Swann singing "Have some Madeira m'dear". This would definitely have been the wrong moment to giggle. It was quite disgusting.

I broke free from his grasp. He glared at me and grasped my arm.

"Don't pull away. Don't be such a westerner. Let yourself become eastern. We are brothers." He caressed my face with his other hand.

I released his grasp.

"I can't help being an Englishman."

"But its heresy," he pleaded "Come to the true faith. You know that you want to."

He grabbed me again. This was not the moment for a theological discussion, or a struggle. In my drunkenness I took the first way out that appears to me.

"OK. I'll do it."

He pulled me closer into his embrace and kissed my cheek.

"Yes. Yes. You have saved yourself. When will we do it?"

I wavered. "I can't do this while I am drunk."

"You aren't drunk. You are not truly drunk. You are full of the spirit. It is better to do this now, while the feeling is strong."

He whispered hoarsely in my ear with his horrid red beard caressing my chin.

"Let's go up to the church straight away. We must lose no time."

The more insistent he became, the more he invoked our "brotherhood", the tighter he held me in his powerful bear clasp, the more suspicious I became. He is desperate to get me into the church to satisfy his own vanity of whatever kick he gets out of this. What does this ceremony entail? I wondered. I had seen young boys dipped naked into the font. This man's first concern was definitely not my soul.

"I will be your godfather," he said.

This was the last straw. Conversion is one thing but there was no way that I would give this mincing creep the pleasure of being my godfather.

"I want Pankrati to be my godfather," I said. Sioni made a sour face and let go of me.

"Pankrati!" he yelled, across the room and the music. "Jack has agreed to become orthodox. We are to christen him and you are to be his godfather."

Pankrati came over, a worried expression on his face. Evidently he was as disturbed by this as I was.

Sioni was jubilant.

"Let us go now up to the church."

"I'm drunk," I repeated. "I won't do this while I'm not in full possession of my faculties."

Sioni grumbled. He was suspicious that I am just trying to weasel out of it.

Pankrati came to my defence.

"Sioni you must stop this. He cannot go unwillingly."

"We will do it in the morning," said the Archimandrite, sulky, temporarily beaten.

"Fine."

"At what time?" He pushed forwards on the attack again.

"I don't care. So long as I am sober."

"Half past five," he suggested. In four hours time.

"Half past six," I retorted. I didn't believe he would get up at all after a whole bottle of ouzo.

I however, got up at six just in case. I didn't want to be pulled out of bed and into church without having had time to think things over. The monastery was silent, shrouded in damp grey clouds. Father Netkari was clearing the refectory table. No one else had stirred.

"Are you ready?" he asked me.

"As I'll ever be."

"Shall I wake the others?"

I told him not to bother and went with him to collect up a pillar of dirty dishes to take through to the scullery-kitchen.

Three hours later the debris of the night before had been cleared away and tea was boiling for breakfast. There was still no sign of Sioni. Abbot Pankrati was both forgiving and apologetic.*

"I am sorry for last night," he drank his coffee opposite me at the narrow table in the upstairs everyday refectory.

"I was mostly to blame," I tell him.

He shook his head, furious with Sioni. Not that he tried to convert me but the way that he set about it.

"You cannot go into church when drunk. It would have been close to satanism. There is still so much we have to do to restore the damage done to the church under communism."

He is referring to the problem that so many of its higher ranks are filled with placemen approved by the communist party.

When Archimandrite Sioni finally emerged from his cell it was to leave. He, his two oily seminarians and Vasco, his friend with the halva factory descended the steps below my window as I skulked behind the flimsy curtain.

"Where is he? Is he hiding from us? He has run away."

Sioni's rumbling mockery echoed throught the stone passage leading back into the monastery. The black robed figures passed out of my view. I heard them singing a prayer under the noise of a car engine, which faded into the distance. And then silence. I had been saved a confrontation. Perhaps Father Sioni felt the same way.

---

* He was a good man. But, also brittle as it later turned out. Shortly before sending this book to the printer I read Bulgarian newspaper reports saying that he had been arrested for trying to burn down part of the monastery after the ecclesiastical authorities launched an investigation into the management of the place. In the investigation several guns were confiscated. Truly, it is hard for monks to keep their equilibrium in these remote places.

Explorations
Under the Skin

Letter to Mr Nikolaj Canovic Cuski, 1842

*In all the world there is nothing like our Bulgarian people:
talking one way, thinking another, acting a third – declar-
ing one thing and agreeing to it, but doing the opposite and
ruining it! Why? For no other reason than their thrice-cursed
self-interest, glory and pride.*

Neofit Hilendarksi Bozveli
Translated by Thomas Butler

The Last of the True Marxist-Leninists

The newstand behind the dingy rectangular block of the social-ist party headquarters was the only place where I could find copies of Komunistichisko Delo and Rabotnichesko Delo. The kiosk also sold crossword puzzles and other strange and flimsy newspapers which looked like no one ever bought them.

They were printed on coarse porus paper, like thin blotting pa-per, and the ink came off on my hands. These used to be the biggest selling newspapers in the country. But they had become museum pieces, relics from the past that somehow, inexplicably, had managed to survive.

It was not just the red ink of the front page titles, the hammer and sickle in the corner, the generously bearded silhouettes of Marx and Dimitur Blagoev (who founded Bulgaria's original socialist work-ers' party in 1891) that made them seem anachronistic. Everything about them was from another age.

The front page of every issue of *Komunistichisko Delo* was crammed with dense columns of text about the imminent return of Marxist-Leninism and the betrayal of modern Bulgaria. The photographs were not of contemporary politicians, but of Georgi Dimitrov (Bulgaria's Lenin) and long dead partisans. The head-line of the main story in one issue was "When Will Soviet Power Return?" Page three was given over entirely to six unbroken col-umns of text under the title "Economic Problems of Socialism in the USSR", written by one J. Stalin. The article had been reprinted from 1952.

The front page of *Rabotnichesko Delo*, its sister paper, told a similar story. It was given over entirely to a piece entitled "Leninism – Flag in the Struggle of Millions of Working People", illustrated with a portrait of Lenin against a background of the red flag.

My newspaper friend Matei's theory was that the survival of these relics proved that Bulgaria exists in a kind of time warp.

"People have a completely different sense of time here. Haven't you noticed how long they will spend doing something? It takes an hour to drink a cup of coffee and smoke a cigarette," he said.

I wanted to know who was responsible for keeping the flame of totalitarian rule alive. I made some calls and a few days later travelled by tram out to the suburb of Strelbishte next to the South Park. I had made an appointment with the General Secretary of the Bulgarian Communist Party.

On the telephone the General Secretary had sounded old and croaky as he gave me the number of the tram, the location of the stop and his apartment block. Its was like all the others in the street, tall, grey and orange. Every flat had its own balcony, crammed with individual clues to its inhabitants, washing, bicycles, DIY. A few old cars were parked out front. There was a tiny convenience store on the ground floor with a few bottles of cheap booze, packets of crisps and flaky chocolate bars. The lift was smashed up, so I walked up eight floors.

A gloomy looking woman opened the door. Her skin was yellow and parchementy and she wore a permanent worried frown. She gestured for me to come in. The flat was decorated in dingy shades which in Britain would instantly evoke images of flat caps, wire milk crates, coal fires and boiled cabbage. The main difference of the Balkans is that cabbage is pickled. There was a strong smell of vinegar. The hall and corridor were cluttered with cardboard boxes and piles of newspapers tied up with string.

The remnants of the "purist" wing of one of Europe's oldest socialist revolutionary parties sat in the kitchen. An old man, faded, dull and dry-looking, with silver hair and spectacles, stooped over a manual type-writer on the kitchen table. He continued to jab at the keyboard without looking up.

The woman who opened the door gestured for me to sit on a hard wooden chair. The old man finally stopped typing and looked up. His name was Comrade Vladimir Spasov, General Secretary of the Bulgarian Communist Party and former General Secretary of the New Communist International, successor to Georgi Dimitrov and Todor Zhivkov, he told me. The small cadre of the party meant that some doubling up was necessary. Spasov was also the editor of the newspapers.

His wife, Comrade Stoika Spasova, moved to the sink to wash up some coffee cups. She was also a member of the Politburo, Secretary for Information Policy and Party Control. Class struggle had not been kind to the Spasovi in these years of defeat and old age. The couple looked like they had both squeezed every last drop of their blood into the communist struggle. I tried to imagine them as young and idealistic firebrands but I could not. Was their struggle always this hard and bitter or did they once glow with zealous, naïve optimism? Were they once comfortable and happy, part of the privileged elite? Or did the growing realisation of corruption in the decades before communism finally collapsed, already gnaw at them? It would be funny if it were not so tragic to see a pair of pensioners attempting to fend off the advance of capitalism from their cluttered kitchen.

As a strict adherent of a political philosophy which claims to be historically inevitable, the General Secretary had to start his argument from first principles. No questions could deflect him from this course. So I resigned myself to a history lesson before moving onto the complexities of the present. We started with the events of 1891, the year when Dimitur Blagoev founded the Bulgarian Social Democratic Party at a secret congress on Mount Buzluzhda, a bare and windy peak in the very centre of the Balkan Range*.

---

* This is a place full of associations in Bulgarian history. It is where Hadji Dimitur, one of the early martyrs of Bulgaria's national struggle perished in a suicidal last stand against the Ottoman army in 1861. It borders the Shipka Pass, scene of the most terrible and definitive battle in the 1877 war of liberation. The Russian army, strengthened by thousands of Bulgarian and Romanian volunteers, defeated the Turks, opening the entire Upper Thracian Plain to conquest and ending 500 years of occupation. A distinguished stone zigurrat to the Shipka victory stands on a neighbouring peak. Buzluzhda, however, is crowned with a concrete monstrosity which looks like a flying saucer next to a factory chimney. The chimney used to be topped with a red star that glowed at night. But no more. The whole edifice has been thoroughly vandalised.

For the first decades of its existence Bulgarian communism was illegal and could only exist in secret. The party endured many bitter rifts and splits. Comrade Spasov had joined the communist partisans during the Second World War. As second in command of his unit he had helped attack police stations in western Bulgaria. 1944 and the creation of Stalinist Bulgaria was a moment of political perfection. By contrast, everything that had happened since the death of Stalin in 1953 had been a betrayal. Perestroika, Glastnost, Demokratsia, Kapitalism: the words simply spelt 'kleptocracy'.

"We are the true Bulgarian Communist Party. We alone have the right to carry on the struggle to restore Bulgaria to pure Marxist-Leninism! Only we have the right to carry on the struggle and to resume the rightful position of the Party! The people who call themselves socialists are traitors and usurpers!"

There was a murmur of assent from the direction of the sink. I got the impression that Secretary for Information Policy and Party Control was well used to listening to this rhetoric.

"It was a conspiracy!" he protested as if I were a public meeting and not a young man sitting three feet away across an old table. There was, he said, a plan cooked up by the Central Committee of the Communist Party in May 1989 to manufacture an ersatz democracy or quasi-democracy in which dissent would be allowed but would still be secretly controlled.

"Andrei Lukanov – you know who he was don't you?"

I nodded. He had led the 1989 politburo coup to depose Todor Zhivkov. He was the last communist and the first "democratic" prime minister. Only he had not been all that democratic, and rumours said not that clean either. He had been assassinated in October 1996, just before I arrived in Bulgaria.

"Andrei Lukanov created the opposition parties himself. He put his own people into them so that he could keep control of the country after he had destroyed communism."

To prove this theory, he showed me a list of more than 150 people drawn up by the Durzhavna Sigornost in early 1989. It was a list of possible dissidents, one that many people would now be proud to have their name on. Spasov had printed it in full in an issue of *Komunistichisko Delo*.

"Look! Look at the names!" he jabbed with a finger. I read down the list. There were many important names. Some had become politicians or public figures. Others had withdrawn from their short careers of political protest as soon as the regime had fallen and now led private lives. It is true a few had, shamefully, turned out to have been informers for the secret police.

This was hardly surprising. But uniquely to Comrade Spasov the list was proof of a deep conspiracy. The Bulgarian people may not have realised it, but these dissidents were stooges pretending to be dissidents.

"Bulgaria's present day so-called democracy was created by the Secret Police! The whole thing was a fix up arranged by Lukanov! And it gets worse!" he shouted, spitting in anger, his voice hoarse with bitterness.

"There was a great fraud practised against the Bulgarian people by the revisionists and Zhivkovist mafia!"

"Eleven years ago a member of the Politburo was sitting opposite me. Just there," he pointed at the space opposite him on the leatherette banquette as if the impression of the man's backside might still be seen there, like the imprint of the devil.

"Do you know what this man told me as he drank my rakia and ate my meze? He said: 'Go to the Rila Hotel. Go tomorrow. Friends of ours from the Party are handing out money. If you are loyal they will give you a share. You can start a political party, a business, whatever you like.'"

Spasov repeated the conversation verbatim, reliving the outrage. I goggled at him. What was he talking about? It was crazy. The Rila Hotel was a dingy tower block in the centre of the city, with a cheap casino annex. I had never even heard of anyone staying there. It seemed the most unlikely place for a conspiracy involving large amounts of money.

"21 billion Bulgarian Levs were printed in Leningrad and stored in the Rila Hotel in the autumn of 1989," Spasov told me. I must have looked utterly incredulous. "Yes! Secret party funds, all arranged by Lukanov. They started buying everything. Everybody!"

"So what did you do?"

"I spat at him! I told him 'No!'" Spasov spat again at the space on the worn out banquette, where now there was only a pile of old newspapers. "I spat at him. I was disgusted by the suggestion."

It was one of the most extraordinary conspiracy myths that I had heard since arriving in the country. I felt a pang of guilt because not believing a word of it, I was still nodding and encouraging Spasov to go on. He did this at full tilt, desperate to tell his story to someone who was hearing it for the first time, who might believe it, who could pass it on, and give it the credibility and the publicity that he could not.

"The decision to change the name of the party was also illegal," he said.

"They had no right," murmured his wife, who had moved across from the sink into the passage and was now tying up bundles of newspapers with string and brown paper and painstakingly address-ing each bundle to a member of the party faithful to distribute them further.

"We didn't allow it. We held our own congress and voted to con-tinue with the Party. I was elected General Secretary."

"We are the true Party," came the echo from the passage.

Spasov reached across and handed me a dossier of carbon copied letters which he had written to the government and current leader of the rival socialist party. He had put them in a folder decorated with the portrait and signature of Lenin. They were mostly lists of govern-ment, municipal and party properties claimed by the true BCP and empty threats of legal action against: "artificially created anti-com-munist puppet parties of the Bulgarian Socialist Party, which have taken the Communist Party's initials with the aim of confusing and tricking Communist sympathisers."

One of the main offenders was the BCPB, nothing to do with the BCP, but in fact the Bourgeoise Capitalist Party – Bandits. Would any communist sympathiser have been so stupid as to vote for this party instead of the BCP at the last election?

Another letter contained a proposal from Comrade Spasov to the leader of the socialist party. All will be forgiven, he had written. We might even agree to join with you in a coalition. But first the socialist party must hand over one of its offices, complete with office equipment, two light automobiles and 100 million levs (30 million pounds sterling), which belongs to the true Communist Party and was taken from it by the socialists in 1989.

"Lately I have also been forced to resign my position as Secretary General of the new Communist Internationale. We didn't have the money to pay the cost of air fares to international meetings," Spasov told me. "We can't even afford to take part in elections within Bul-garia."

Georgi Dimitrov, the first Secretary General of the Bulgarian Communist Party was also, for many years head of the Comintern. Spasov saw no irony in having being asked to take his place, only bitter regret that he was not able to.

Our conversation moved on to international politics.

"Bulgaria will unite with Belorussia and Serbia. We must reassert the solidarity of our Slavic brothers!" Again Comrade Spasova murmured in agreement. I dared not ask when or how. The speech continued, hectoring, insistent, full of fury against monarcho-fascists, NATO, America, democrats, the Zhivkovist renegades.

"Did you know, Mr Hamilton, that the Masons and the Jews planned to do away with the Bulgarian people to create a new homeland for the Jews? This was a plot arranged by the government of your country."

I gulped.

"You don't know and yet you call yourself a journalist. You should write these things so people can realise what is going on. Your Margaret Thatcher is a Jew!"

"I don't think she is. But..." I wanted to ask what difference it would make if she were. There was no chance.

Stoika Spasova wagged at me wit a bony finger. Her voice cracked with emotion.

"There has been a campaign of genocide against Bulgarian pensioners. One million have died in the past ten years."

"But..."

"One million."

I shut my mouth. These were claims beyond rational enquiry or argument. When winter closed in, it was true that thousands of old and sick would perish as the temperature plummeted below freezing. Heating was an unaffordable luxury even on the highest pensions. The casualty wards would fill with grannies who had slipped on the ice-piled pavements. But genocide?

"The Prime Minister is a *tsiganin*," interjected Spasov. This was a fresh tack. "You only have to look at him to tell. The president is too. That is where this country has got to. It is being run by gypsies."

"They are not capable."

"The current government is made up from the drop outs and failures from the Communist Party."

"They were either active members of the BCP or they are the sons of members."

"But the ones who weren't good enough to get anywhere."

"Failures."

"Now they are in charge."

"We were betrayed by the revisionist Zhivkovite mafia."

"A catastrophe."

"A crime."

"Time will tell. We are ready to re-establish a pure Marxist-Leninist state. The workers will not be betrayed for ever."

"You will see that we are right."

It was time to go. Spasov pressed a pair of green cloth bound books into my hands.

"Read them, you will see." It was the Green Book of Libyan leader Colonel Ghadaffi translated into Bulgarian – more conspiracy theories from a world champion.

Two weeks later I walked through the brass rimmed double doors of the café of the Grand Hotel Bulgaria. Its huge plate glass windows look out across the yellow brick pavement of Boulevard Tsar Osvoboditel (formerly Boulevard Lenin) towards a shadowy corner of the small park by the old royal palace. A plump middle-aged man wearing a dogtooth check sports jacket was waiting for me in one of the booths.

He introduced himself quietly. His name was Kalin Todorov, son of a communist era chairman of the National Assembly. He had been the editor of a national newspaper during "The Time" (a popular euphemism for the communist era). Now he worked for a manufacturer of fridges, whose owner happened to make a lot of money during the Yugoslav oil embargo in the early 90s. (How convenient it must have been at that time to own the first petrol station across the border from Serbia!)

Svetlana, the girl who sold me my weekly copy of *The Economist* from the dark-green cylindrical kiosk in Battenburg Square had introduced me to Todorov.

Sometimes I would sit and drink beer with her while she told me about the passers-by. She commanded an esoteric network of friends and acquaintances, from her vantage point, and loved making connections. She had divined a possible common interest between Todorov and me and had set up this meeting as an experiment.

"He knows lots of things that could help you," she had told me. "Secret things."

Todorov looked well cut out for cloak and dagger stuff. The aura of a by-gone era hung around him like the wistful self-importance of lost privilege. It was as tangible as the polished pale brown marble and well-stuffed sofas, which decorated the café. Todorov was not one of the nomenklatura who had obviously done well under democracy. Perhaps he just hid it better than most. He gave the impression of being stranded after a flood tide, nostalgic for the great waters which had lifted him up before leaving him dry.

Our discussion did not start easily. The unspoken question of money floated between us. I was certainly not going to raise it before he did.

"I've worked with other English journalists," he told me. "But never very successfully. I tried publishing this book. But we had to withdraw it at the last moment." Was he in the disinformation business? He was clearly a broker. I wondered what he would try to sell me.

"If you want anything from me it will have to be cash up front. I don't trust English journalists any more."

Quite right! I didn't trust him either. The only question was how much I could get for free, seeing as it would be totally unreliable anyway.

Fortunately for me, Todorov was at heart a purveyor of rumours and theories. His large balding head was bursting with plots and scandal. But there were not that many people with whom he can share his stories. Bulgarians had long since grown cynical through mulling over the embers of their unsatisfactory democratisation.

Todorov pined for his old profession. But only a handful of senior journalists from the old regime had managed to continue their careers, and none of them so closely related to the rulers as he was.

Even so, he wanted me to believe that his family connection was useful to him. While barring him from the media, it had given him access to the centre of the old network. He was an inhabitant of the twilight world of the sons of the former regime and was eager to stress that the old influence had not waned. And so we talked and as we talked our voices dropped lower and lower, to near whispers.

"There are people," he told me darkly, "who know what is going on. Telephones are still tapped, of course. Sources are exploited.

Every week an unofficial intelligence bulletin is circulated within a secretive private group. I'm one of the subscribers. You would be amazed at what is reported there."

"Freelance spies? Really?"

The Durzhavna Sigornost never really went away, he explained. It was officially disbanded in 1990 and recreated as an intelligence service more or less on western lines. The Intelligence and Counter-Intelligence departments continued to exist but they were drastically cut back. The other four departments, including the political depart-ment, were disbanded. But some of it still operates in secret. The ex-personnel found new loyalties, aligning themselves with various new business groups – the *groupirovki*, or oligarchs. Most of the struggles, shooting and chaos of the early and mid 90s could be in-terpreted as a civil war between these groups.

Todorov almost seemed to ache with nostalgia for those days in the early 90s when the *mutri* swaggered around Sofia like they owned it and protection rackets were a fact of life. By the time I arrived in Bulgaria these ostentatious displays of muscle had become some-thing of a bitter joke – thoroughly despised by ordinary people. Now they were moving onto the next step.

But even so, the past was still hidden. No one had been found to take responsibility for crimes committed in the last years of commu-nism and the early years of democracy. Every year that went by "truth and reconciliation" was becoming an ever more distant goal.

Todorov was eager to build on the mysteries of the past.

"Don't try and work out who got the money from the Party before 1989. 60 percent of the killings in Bulgaria since 1990 are linked to that conspiracy. It's the most likely motive for the assassination of Andrei Lukanov. As chief architect of the conspiracy, he simply knew too much."

Here was old Lukanov again. I decided to tell Todorov about my meeting with Comrade Spasov and all the money in the Rila Hotel. He sniggered when I mention the General Secretary, a schoolboy mo-ment. But then, to my surprise, he supported Spasov's story.

"Yes, yes, it's true. Lukanov was the brains behind the operation. His aim was to create a false democracy with no power. He would transfer control of the economy to his own people over a period of two or three years. Then he would be ready to surrender political power without losing control of the money."

The plot had started when some people in the senior reaches of the Party had seen what was happening in Poland. They heard the rumblings of Glasnost in Russia and realised that Bulgaria had to adapt. They realised they had to adapt themselves. This was an opportunity they could seize. Elements in the security apparatus began secretly channelling party funds to their own people who were already posted in Western Europe, particularly Vienna.*

The problem with Lukanov's plan was that the only glue holding it together was the authority and power of the Party. Up until the very last moment, nobody expected the communist system to implode. When it did all the Party's former operatives went freelance overnight. Suddenly they were working on their own account. There were no records to bring them to book.

"Lukanov made two great mistakes. The first was not to realise that without the authority of the party, he could not command. The second was that he failed to understand the real power of money. Capital has its own rules," said Todorov. "Those apparatchiks in Vienna were never going to follow the dictats of central planning. Why would they? Suddenly they were rich!"

Our conversation had taken a surprising turn. I hadn't expected this washed up nomenklatura to support the allegations of his fellow conspiracy theorist.

But the question remained. Could I believe any of it? There was too much speculation. If only some proper account could be made, then the country could move on. But without verifiable facts, it was not possible. The truth had been corrupted. Stories had become a commodity available for trade.

"Now, what sort of information can I help you with?" asked Todorov. "You can buy whatever you like. I have information on stolen secret police dossiers. Lots of them are stored in foreign bank vaults,

---

* Todorov was not the only person I spoke to who pointed to 1985 as a year of signs and changes. According to one journalist, all investment in infrastructure had stopped by 1986 . He was first alerted to this in a conversation with the mayor of a small town. The party had stopped disbursing money for any kind of building project. Why? Answers are hard to come by. Col Serafim Stoikov, head of the information and archive department at the Minstry of the Interior, told me that the State Security archive in the ministry stops in 1985. "After that we have no memory", he said. It is both suggestive and terribly frustrating that the secret records of those final years are hidden.

you know. Then there are the business connections of today's politicians. They are a bit more expensive. How about information on
the involvement of Russian organised crime bosses in the Bulgarian
economy?"

He was warming to his theme.

"If you want genuine bank documents it can be arranged, but
they come at an extra charge. I can introduce you to former State Se-
cuirty officers and people who can give eye-witness accounts of how
the politiburo had decided to create an artificial opposition. Proof
of these things is a question of money."

I didn't want any of it. No that's not true. I did want it, but I
knew it would be fool's gold, unreliable, ambiguous and unpublish-
able. What would I do with it? Who would be interested?

Todorov pulled out a hardback copy of *The Umbrella Murder, a*
book about the assassination of Georgi Markov, the Bulgarian defec-
tor who in 1978 was assassinated in broad daylight as he waited for a
bus on Waterloo Bridge Todorov had written this book himself.

"Markov was murdered by the British. He was a double agent, a
spy for the Bulgarian Secret Service, you know..."

I was not in the market.

"I don't have any budget," I told him apologetically.

"Ah well." The hands were spread in regret. "You would need a
lot to persuade anyone to speak about these things."

President Petur Stoyanov announcing the resignation of the socialist government to cheering crowds outside the Presidency building on 17 February 1997.

A tromp l'oeil image of the Ivan Vazov National Theatre as it would be reflected in the water of the fountain that had been drained for the winter.

The church of Sveti Sedmochislenitsi on Graf Ignatiev Street, formerly a mosque.

Rooftops of Sofia with the domes of the Alexander Nevsky Cathedral and the ridge of the Balkan Range in the far distance.

The square outside the National Palace of Culture with the hideous 1981 monument marking 1300 years of Bulgarian history in the background.

Old women reading the nek-rolog death notices.

The famously tough gran-nies of the Bulgaro-Mace-donian town of Bansko

Archimandrit Evtimii, abbot of the Holy Life Giving Spring Monastery in Strandzha mountain.

Matei Brunwasser, Bulgarian scrabble champion. He beat me in this game, in spite of my seven-letter word "поминъка" meaning the livelihood.

Cross-dressing is an important part of the kukeri festival. This man plays the part of the mother of evil.

A villager of Turia taking part in the pagan spring-time kukeri festival.

Lelya Somka at the early morning rose harvest in the Valley of the Roses.

Target practice with Itso Detchev

A village witch
telling a fortune.

Father Nektari at
Glozhenski Monastery.

The first unsuccessful attempt to demolish the mausoleum of Bulgaria's
first communist leader Georgi Dimitrov

Stefan Grunchev entertaining passers by on his favourite
bench outside my flat on Sofia's
Graf Ingatiev Street.

X

Bai Angel and Zhorro, the last dancing bear in Sofia, shortly
before Zhorro was retired to a mountain refuge.

The Roma inhabitants of Kremikovtsi village, a collection of huts on the road up to
Kovachevitsa.

The author Hristo Stoyanov fishing at a lake above the town of Smolyan in the heart of the Rhodopes.

Father Boyan Saraev and his wife at his church in Kurdjali, headquarters of his attempt to convert Bulgaria's Pomaks from Islam to Christianity.

Many think that Kovachevitsa in the south-west Rhodopes is the most beautiful village in Bulgaria.

The Bulgarian Muslim inhabitants of Breznitsa
dancing one of their complex horo ring dances.

The female guests watching the dancing at Adije's wedding in Draginovo

Adije receiving guests at her wedding in the village of Draginovo, attended by her younger sisters.

Adije, with her face painted with gold on her wedding day

From Hadji Dimitur

Whoever falls in freedom's fight
He does not die. All things mourn him,
Earth and creatures, day and night.
Singers sing of him.

Hristo Botev

Zhivkov, Markov and the Poisoned Umbrella

GEORGI Markov was the victim of the so-called "Bulgarian Umbrella Murder", an assassination so unlikely that if it was presented in a film it would seen stupidly far-fetched. From the public's point of view the murder contained everything: an unsolved crime, spies, terror, Cold War conflict, unpleasant villains in the shape of the dictator Todor Zhivkov and his henchmen, and pathos in the bereavement of Markov's widow and young daughter. It also had an unbelievable murder weapon: a KBG-adapted umbrella and one of the most deadly poisons known to man.

For me the Markov case is all of these things, but it is also a brief glimpse into the black heart of an unforgiving, self-serving regime. Since I have become involved with the case I have wanted to lend my efforts to that of the many other investigators and journalists who have fought against the stone-walling refusal of the Bulgarian State to admit its crimes.

Georgi Markov's story begins in the dingy world of post-Stalinist Sofia. Markov was a handsome, dissatisfied, boastful and immensely talented writer, who had laid his skill and ambition at the service of the regime and won himself a charmed life. He had a government villa and a grey BMW. He dated beautiful actresses and even married one. He played poker with influential State Security officers and went hunting with the dictator himself, Todor Zhivkov.

The best description of the whole system is Markov's own. In one essay broadcast on *Radio Free Europe*, he said:

"We were all paid *not* to write."

He described the corrupt system that he himself had benefited from perfectly.

Seen from a distance, Zhivkov's flirtation with the intelligentsia brought magnificent holiday homes, well endowed arts funds, a profusion of medals and titles, increased salaries, consumer satisfaction and the gratification of vain ambition for posts and privileges. But in fact all this was part of the means which the First Party Secretary used generously to halt and undermine the independence without which no creative spirit can exist, to isolate the intelligentsia from any real contact with the ordinary people, and to keep it in the position of a spoilt Party creature.

It was a brilliant strategy. Apart from in the Turkish areas there was no organised dissident movement until 1988, and even then it was deeply infiltrated with informers.

For a while Markov stood at the very pinnacle of this successful, loyal elite. He was the most richly rewarded writer in the country. Most people would have been satisfied with this – a fact which explains the general mediocrity of modern Bulgarian literature, which is perhaps only now recovering from this institutionalised intellectual corruption. But Markov was too vain and ambitious to be happy. He knew he was good, but he also knew that he could be better, and believed he could be richer and more well-known too. He felt sure that outside Bulgaria he could write whatever he wanted, while at home they were beginning to stop his plays.

So he fled. One day in June 1969, the day after his satirical play *The Man Who Was Me* was taken off the stage after a single performance, he drove in his treasured BMW across the border to Belgrade and then to Italy. And eventually he arrived at London and the BBC.

Some people say he was a dissident, and perhaps that is what he had become by the end of his life. But he didn't leave Bulgaria because he hated communism. He didn't leave for any principle, but simply because he wanted more. He wanted worldwide fame. Well he got that eventually, though he paid an excruciating price.

Markov spoke about his decision to emigrate in a radio interview, for *My Kind of Music*, a BBC World Service programme not dissimilar to *Desert Island Discs*. It is the only record of him speaking English: grammatically precise but heavily accented. His voice is intelligent but penetrating. It would cut across any discussion, however boisterous, demanding to be heard. It is a voice you can easily imagine raised in anger, dispute, mockery or fun.

"I tried to compromise as much as I can, and it was eventually too much. The whole atmosphere was in deep disagreement with myself. I don't want to say that I am braver or more honest than other people. Perhaps if I were more honest I should be have been there, because if you are honest you should stay there and fight the battle there, rather than be here. I think in a way it was kind of free irresponsibility. When, you say in England, 'I am fed up' and just go away."

By the year of his death, the shine had truly worn off any romantic hopes that Markov may have had. To be sure he was married and had a young daughter. Pictures from the time show an attractive man, straight silver-grey hair parted on the left, dark eyebrows, sharp eyes. The most touching photograph has him wearing blue suit and holding his daughter in his arms. It hints at contentment.

But he had begun to hate the BBC Bulgarian Service for its bureaucratic attitude which asked so little of his talents. He had a poor relationship with most of his BBC colleagues and spent his days writing mundane news articles. The Home Office had inexplicably refused his passport application, something which had happened to no other Bulgarian Service employee. It was not exactly the exciting new future he had been hoping for.

This was why he was thinking of moving to Munich, where he would establish an émigré literary magazine in partnership with his friend Mitko Botchev. Botchev ran the cultural programme on the CIA-funded Radio Free Europe's Bulgarian service. He had been broacasting Markov's incisive damaging essays on the inside nature of Zhivkov's regime, culminating with *Meetings with Todor Zhivkov*, not aggressively slanted critiques but crystal clear, satirically humorous portraits, which described a polite and sociable man who at the same time was a despot at the head of a sycophantic oriental regime. Most devastatingly he identified and laid bare the calculation, the dishonesty and hypocrisy which lay behind Zhivkov's cult of personality and which oiled the central wheel of the Party machine.

In all honesty, I must say that in those years Zhivkov did not order anyone to worship him; he did not sent out a Party directive asking people to admire him nor did he select quotations from his pronouncements for them to cite. All this came from below quite spontaneously, in line with the corrupt nature of the Party and the regime.

These careful revelations enraged Zhivkov. They undermined the very basis of his authority. They v. ere a betrayal.

Apologists for the Bulgarian regime still insist to this day that these essays were not sufficient motive for Zhivkov to order Markov's death. This in spite of the fact that the writer had received several credible death threats warning him to stop work for RFE.

Thankfully, we no longer need to listen to these arguments. In June 2005, 27 years after Markov's death a Bulgarian journalist at the daily newspaper *Dnevnik* named Hristo Hristov published a book which reopened the whole Markov case to the world. After six years of work he published almost every document and detail currently available about the assassination, including incontrovertible evidence that Markov was the number one enemy of the regime. Documents revealed by Hristov for the first time also illustrated the chain of events leading up to the murder, and Scotland Yard's frustrated near-miss attempts to bring the killer to justice*. The book was called *Kill Skitnik. Skitnik* means Tramp. This was the code-name the DS gave Markov after his defection.

Emboldened by the publication of Hristov's book, important figures in the investigation of the Markov case in Bulgaria began to speak out about what the police had discovered and why the case had never been solved. In January 2006, I came to Sofia as a consult-ant for a documentary team for *Channel Five* that was looking at the story anew. Mark Radice, the producer of *The Umbrella Assassin:*

---

* Some of the facts in the book, including the name and agent identity of the Scotland Yard's prime suspect had been revealed in *The Umbrella Murder*, published in 1994 by Kalin Todorov, my strange acquaintance from the world of Bulgarian conspiracies. To-dorov had gone some way to explaining what happened, but he had become diverted into thickets of double and triple agents, strange ideas which put everything he wrote into question. Unfortunately for him, this book had also breached copyrights held by Markov's English widow Annabel, who obtained a court injunction to stop its publica-tion.

Revealed, was deservedly nominated for an Emmy for his documentary in 2007.

One of our most important interviews was with Bogdan Karayotov, who had led the Bulgarian police investigation from 1991 to 1999. Karayotov was a slow-moving, slow-talking solid old copper with a voice so gravelly he sounded like a car trying to start on a winter's morning. He hunched his shoulders and smoked cigarettes continuously. The smoke went in but never came out. Many people had told me he was honest and dedicated.

Karayotov told us that in 1991 he had been given special access to the still top secret archives of the Foreign Intelligence Service – formerly the First Main Directorate of the State Security – Bulgaria's version of MI6.

"There we found plans where it was written that Georgi Markov had to be neutralised, it was written exactly like that," Karayotov rumbled. He and his colleagues had spent a long time discussing what "neutralisation" might mean.

"Clearly it has a lot of meanings," he said. "But for us we understood that under this term they meant his physical removal."

Karayotov told us that these investigations had also produced the name of an agent and evidence linking him to the murder. He said the police had found the agent's file in the archives. He was code-named Picadilly, but his real name was Franceso Gullino. He was an Italian petty criminal, who had been arrested on drugs and currency offences when entering Bulgaria overland from Greece. After a week in solitary in Sofia jail, the DS had approached him. Gullino signed a collaboration agreement. The accusations against him for were suspended and he was sent for training.

The details of Gullino's recruitment were published for the first time in *Kill Skitnik*. The book quotes excerpts from Gullino's personal file from this time. It describes him as being "clever with good and quick thinking. He does not feel fear." The file also contains four false passports: two Swiss and two Bulgarian, one of them a diplomatic passport in the name of Ivan Gulinov.

To start with he spied on foreigners in Sofia. Later on the DS gave him a cover of permanent residency in Denmark. Intially he opened a souvenir shop, and after that a picture framing business. Then he began to trade in antiques. There is evidence that he became involved in the sale of forged pictures. He travelled Europe in an

Austrian registered caravan, selling antiques and carrying out tasks for the Bulgarian State Security.

Meanwhile, in England Markov continued to enrage the Bulgarian high powers with his broadcasts and essays. In 1977, they decided to deal with him once and for all. The plan was fixed at a meeting of five senior members of the DS including the Minister of Internal Affairs, Dimitur Stoyanov. Of the two men at this meeting who are still alive, one was the deputy chief of Foreign Intelligence General Vladimir Todorov and the second was the chief of the 04 Counter Intelligence Unit with special responsibility for anti-regime émigrés whose name is Colonel Micho Genkovski. (In 1992, Todorov was jailed by a military court for his part in destroying Markov's dossier from the archives.)

The record of this meeting is one of the most important documents sourced by Hristov from the police investigation and published in his book. It points to three men, all still living, and directly implicates them in what happened to Markov.

> In the first place the plan of action forsaw the selection of an agent suitable for the task. The search was concentrated on the agents of the 04KRO. They selected Piccadilly. Genkovski, also his handling officer, was detailed to visit him to check him out. Before his departure he was given detailed instructions by General Todorov. In his report of the meeting to Todorov he said that the agent accepted the task 'in good heart'

Gullino's dossier notes that he was taken off all other tasks and given the exclusive task of neutralising Markov.

Gullino visited London three times. He spent 40 days in autumn 1977 living in South Clapham, close to where Markov lived. He returned in spring 1978. The police investigation found correspondence in the DS archives in which Gullino informed his bosses that he was ready to carry out their plan. The message came via a coded telegramme sent to a cover company. He asked for the equivalent of £38000 "for the development of business." The DS refused to pay that much, but an agreement was eventually reached.

Gullino visited London for the last time in September 1978. The 7th September was Party Secretary Todor Zhivkov's 67th birthday. He was about to receive an unusual present. But for Markov it was just another day. He had driven into work by car from South Clapham.

Half way through his shift at Bush House, he took a break to re-park it in a more convenient place on the south side of Waterloo Bridge. He then climbed the stone stairway from the River Thames embankment to catch one of the north-bound buses back across the river towards the Strand. He was at the bus stop on top of the bridge when he felt a sharp prick in the back of his left thigh. Later, in hospital, he told his wife how he turned in time to see a man picking up an umbrella from the ground. The man apologised and ran across the road, hailed a passing taxi, gave it instructions in a heavy foreign accent.

Was Gullino this man? We know Gullino was sent to neutralise Markov. Markov had been neutralised. But without more information from the Bulgarian DS archives, there may never be enough evidence to answer this question beyond doubt. There is no doubt however that a murder had just taken place in broad daylight.

It seemed odd to Markov for a man to wait for a bus travelling in one direction, but to take a taxi in another. But did he suspect anything? He had received several credible death threats in the previous months and was taking care not to eat or drink in restaurants and to hide his travel plans. The prick on his thigh discomfited him enough that he thought it worth pulling down his jeans to show the tiny wound to Teodor Lirkov, his close friend and work colleague back at the Bulgarian Service. Lirkov said later that they thought it might be an insect bite.

Markov didn't feel like going to drink beer with Lirkov that evening. At home he complained of nausea. But it was not until late that night that Annabel called an ambulance. The poison was in his blood. Nothing could now save Markov.

The very next day, according to the *Kill Skitnik* files, Gullino arrived in Rome on a plane from London. He made visual contact with another officer from 04KRO, the anti-regime emigrant department of the DS. He had completed his job.

Meanwhile, back in the St James Hospital in Streatham, south London, no one took the Markov's claims of a secret police assassination plot seriously.

"They've poisoned me the brutes," he told his Lirkov, as his vital systems began to inexorably fail. Eventually, the doctors begin to suspect that he might be telling the truth. By then it was way too late.

The present day Bulgarian investigators use this delay to justify the almost comically unconvincing claim that Markov may have died as a result of medical error. This is not the only unlikely theory that they have grasped. It is almost as if they were hunting out reasons not to bring the investigation to a close. In Sofia, the chief investigator told me that 80% of the evidence points to the fact that Markov was killed by a State Security operative. He said that without 100% it was impossible to proceed.

But the medical error theory is absurd. The fact that the doctors didn't know what was happening doesn't absolve the murderer. Even if the doctors had guessed correctly at the beginning, there is little they could have done. There is no antidote to ricin. It destroys the operations of the vital organs by consuming cells. If a pacemaker is fitted early enough, this sometimes can keep the heart beating until the crisis has passed. The extremity of Markov's organ failure made that an unlikely possibility. On 11th September Markov's heart finally stopped beating. It was not a good death.

In the following weeks, the forensic pathologists extracted a hollow titanium-iridium pellet from his thigh. This was exactly the same as a pellet extracted from the back of a former Bulgarian State Security officer, who had defected in Paris and received a death sentence from a court in Sofia. This man had been injected with the pellet as he exited the Paris Metro a couple of weeks before the Markov incident. But perhaps the pellet did not enter his body deeply enough. He suffered similar symptoms of nausea to those that initially affected Markov, but he survived.

Each pellet contained two tiny channels, which the doctors deduced had contained ricin, a poison with no antidote and which leaves no trace. If these pellets had not been found, there would have been no way of telling that Markov had been murdered.

• • •

Why did Markov have to die? He was not a politician or a leader of a great counter-revolutionary movement. He was just a writer who had decided to speak the truth. In the words of one Bulgarian writer, he wrote what everyone else was thinking but did not dare express. But was this really enough reason for the regime to bend all the evil force at its command to murder him in this risky and bizarre fashion in a far away country?

I got a rare chance to question one of the only people who could have told the truth about Markov's murder when I had been in Bulgaria for just six months. In September 1997, Todor Zhivkov, First Secretary of the Bulgarian Communist Party for 35 years, was let out of house arrest. He was 85-years old and for the previous eight years had been confined to his grand-daughter's villa on the outskirts of Sofia. In the early 90s a court had found him guilty of financial impropriety and abuse of power. However, the most important charges had been dropped. The closed court had found no evidence that he had ordered a campaign of ethnic cleansing against the Turkish minority. It had been a whitewash. The idea of trying him for ordering Markov's murder had probably not even crossed anyone's mind.

He celebrated his release with a press conference at a large grey hotel on a hill just south of the centre. It was known as the Japanese Hotel because of the slick semi-oriental gloss to its décor. A great crowd of gossiping journalists packed into the banqueting hall to see the former dictator. There must have been a couple of hundred of us. It was as if he was a circus freak-show. When he walked in there was a sudden hush. He was short and wrinkled, a shaky grandfather in a grey suit. He wore thick glasses and had a wide mouth with full lips. There was something vaguely clownish about his features that made him look curiously vulnerable and innocent, almost like a caricature of himself – Bai Tosho – the simple old fellow from the village, rather than the great tyrant. When he spoke, his voice was whiny and full of self-justification.

"Ts...ts...ts... He speaks like a peasant," tutted a journalist standing next to me.

This may have been true, but he still retained an air of authority. When he spoke, everyone listened. He lectured us as if we were the plenum of the old Communist Party and he was still the leader. When he had assumed power Bulgaria was a simple agricultural country. He had turned it into a modern industrial state, he told us. Now these so-called democrats are undoing everything that he had achieved. As he spoke, he carefully identified and criticised all the undeniable failings of democracy:

"Corruption... incompetence... criminal privatisation... theft of state assets... economic collapse..."

When he had finished speaking he took questions. I had never asked a question in Bulgarian at a press conference. I didn't feel prepared to start but I realised that I must. I scribbled the words on a piece of paper to see how they came out. I was ready. I put up my hand, but it was some time the ex-dictator's minder picked me out.

"You."

I looked behind me to make sure he was not pointing at someone else. He wasn't. I stepped up to the microphone and read my question. I was so terrified that on the first attempt no one could understand what I said. I tried again, enunciating more clearly.

"*Koi e ubil Georgi Markov s Bulgarskia chadar?* Who killed Georgi Markov with the Bulgarian umbrella?"

The question was greeted with a buzz around the hall. It was a piece of bravado. What could he possibly answer? Zhivkov paused a moment before he answered.

"You have answered your own question. You shouldn't have said 'the Bulgarian umbrella'. That was never proved. You should have asked: 'Who killed Georgi Markov with the umbrella?'" He sat back and smiled smugly as a titter of laughter went around the hall.

Standing at the microphone I saw red. How dare he make a joke about this of all things? The ex-dictator's minder had already pointed out the next questioner but I interrupted.

"In that case, who killed Georgi Markov?" I called out. "Who did it?"

The dictator spread his hands in regret.

"You should ask your own secret services. All that I know is that Georgi Markov, the friend with whom I used to go hunting, came to me one day and said that he was leaving for the west. I tried to dissuade him, but he was determined. Eventually I let him go."

Nearly 30 years after the murder, with Bulgaria on the verge of joining the European Union and coming in from the long cold of its communist past, the Bulgarian authorities are still content to provide the same answer to questions about Markov as their former tyrant gave me. They shrug their shoulders and say they don't know.

It is outrageous that the State has never acknowledged its guilt for this crime. Not only this, but the Bulgarian authorities continue to blankly insist that there is no more evidence about the case in their files. This has never been demonstrated and cannot be accepted as truth. It is true that thousands of files went missing in the chaotic disbandment of the DS in 1990. Markov's huge nine volume dossier was one of the most notorious.

In 1990, General Stoyan Savov, the Deputy Interior Minister with special responsibility for State Security ordered its illegal incineration. He committed suicide in 1992, shortly before the opening of his trial for this crime. Eventually General Vlado Todorov, Francesco Gullino's ultimate boss, was imprisoned for his role in its destruction.

But as one interior ministry official once observed to me, "the secret archives are like a flour sack. So long as you shake it well you will always be able to get a bit more out of it".

This is the reason that the authorities do not want to fully investigate the Markov files. The potential for embarrassing revelations is too huge. If they investigate Markov, why not other crimes too? There are many possibilities.

Meanwhile, every year another few top public figures are exposed as having collaborated with the State Security. In 2006, President Georgi Purvanov admitted that he had worked as an agent. His code name was *Gotse*. A few years earlier a superficial and short-lived investigation had come up with the fact that two prime ministers, 121 ministers and 129 deputies had been former agents. Does this sound like a lot?

Ten years after the end of communism, there were approximately 70,000 people still living who had worked as informers. This is a part of Bulgarian history in which many people have a lot to lose. Even the former Tsar Simeon II was against opening the files. When he became Prime Minister, he almost succeeded in passing a law which would have consigned the entire painful and embarrassing history of the DS to oblivion, by incinerating it.

So, perhaps it is not surprising that Scotland Yard got nowhere when it was working against this culture of institutionalised silence. The closest the Yard ever came to solving the case was in 1993 when they tracked down the prime suspect, Francesco Gullino in Copenhagen. He was detained by the Danish police. Two British detectives went to interview him and so did Karayotov. This was the moment when the crime could have been solved definitively and completely.

Gullino admitted nothing.

What followed next has never been made explicit. It was clear that Gullino at the very least was connected in some way to Markov's death and that he was involved in espionage. Yet the Danish Police let him go. Conspiracy theorists, of whom there are many still looking at this case, say that this was because Gullino was protected – for some reason – by Western intelligence services. Maybe he had also worked for them, they suggest. That would certainly be embarrassing if it were true.

There is however more than a hint of cock-up in the muddle that followed, and that has followed ever since. Painstaking research in *Kill Skitnik* reveals that the Danes needed official copies of the Bulgarian documents which implicated Gullino in the case. The British police had brought with them copies (or perhaps only transcripts?) which had been handed to them by the Bulgarian investigators.

We know that the Danes badly needed these official documents because a request for judicial cooperation from the chief of the Copehagen Police was sent to the Bulgarian authorities via an urgent diplomatic note. The Bulgarians ignored the request, which was amazing as official diplomatic requests are sometimes refused, but very rarely ignored. Somewhere deep in the Bulgarian bureaucracy the DS was protecting its own, even at the expense of an international row. There was nothing the detectives in Copenhagen could do. In the meantime Gullino, who had been released after his interrogation, had sold his house and left the country.

The Bulgarian authorities never produced the files which the Danes had requested. Nor was any official attempt was made to find out where Gullino had gone. No Interpol warrant was put out for his arrest. Eventually the detectives who had managed the case moved onto other investigations, and then retired, leaving behind them vast piles of paper in English and in Bulgarian – a puzzle that no one would ever have the time, the skill or the patience to unwind. And lying at the heart of it the certain knowledge that progress could only come if the Bulgarians ever decided to release files which the government does not even admit to possessing.

In January 2006, I visited Copenhagen with the *Channel Five* documentary team. Most of the people we spoke to about Gullino, who knew him during his time in Denmark were too intimidated to speak about him, even off the record. One art dealer admitted to seeing him within the space of two or three years. We found references to his arrest on the Czech-German border with a forged painting in 2002.

Finally we tracked down a source who had met Gullino when he was running the picture framing business and kept in touch with him off and on for 15 years. He had last seen him as recently as two years previously. Although he was scared to talk, we persuaded this source to speak to us on camera, under condition of complete anonymity.

He told us that when the news about Gullino's link to Markov's murder first leaked out in 1993 he had been shocked. So he had approached his friend, who diverted his questions with a sort of denial.

"Of course I asked him about it. He couldn't understand how a secret service could do a thing like that, because he was only a small man, a little man. And we didn't speak any more about it."

Our source was clearly nervous talking about Gullino, anxious in what he told us not to reveal any tell-tale fact by which Gullino could learn who he was. Many of his answers were frustratingly vague. But he made it clear that Gullino had not disappeared at all, but was moving around Europe following the life of a traveller, "a nomad" as he put it.

"He doesn't need anyone... he has no fears. He isn't running away from the police."

Our source also believed that Gullino still visits Copenhagen from time to time with no apparent fear of arrest:

"Common friends meet him sometimes. He still lives here and comes and goes goes"

Here the revelations stopped.

"I don't want to have any trouble," he concluded nervously.

So much for the "finger", as Gullino was dismissively referred to by Luben Markov cousin to the writer, who still wages a determined and passionate campaign to get justice for Georgi against massive official indifference.

We had visited Luben, a thin and mournful individual, at the simple two-room peasant house where Georgi was born and brought up on the outskirts of Sofia. The black and white photographs of the writer and his mother hung on the otherwise bare walls – perpetual symbols of mourning.

"The finger who did it isn't important," Luben told us. "The important thing is the mind who thought it up."

That mind and the evidence of its workings is still hidden and those who served it are still protected. While we were in Sofia we had tried to speak to Gullino's former State Security bosses. Both his handling officer Col. Genkovski and Gen. Todorov, deputy head of Foreign Intelligence are still alive. According to the documents of the police investigation, they were both in the room when the decision was taken to "neutralise" Markov. We tracked them both down to the "Association of Retired Intelligence Officers", of which Todorov is the chairman – evidently he is a great hero to them.

After several calls, a woman called Mrs Dimitrov read out a statement from the association on Todorov's behalf. It was a less than convincing denial.

"The case for him and for the Association is closed definitively. Everything which there was to say he has said. He doesn't want to be disturbed any more," she said.

Todorov and Genkovski had "been crucified by these questions for many years. These are old people they don't want to deal with it any more. They are more than 80 years old... What has been said has been said."

There has never been any chance that hard men like Todorov or Genkovski will ever speak – not for them the post-Cold War career of media commentary that some Russian ex-KGB officers have taken. They will take their secrets to the grave as Zhivkov did*. The dictator, who in 1973 signed a politburo decision allowing the DS to assassinate opponents of the regime outside its borders, died in 1998. The corrupt and evil regime that Markov satirised and described and undermined with his writing, and in whose name he was killed no longer exists either. But the archives still remain, and even after the Markov case has been solved they will still contain many other truths that killed.

---

* In 2008, Scotland Yard interviewed these men again. And as the 30-year Bulgarian statute of limitations passed in September 2008, the journalist Hristo Hristov finally won access to the most secret state security archives and published further documents proving Bulgaria's responsibility for the murder. But in spite of this renewed interest and activity, the case is far from being closed.

A biography of the regime

I don't know how many descriptions I have read of the heroic death of Malchika and the slogans he is said to have shouted. In fact, when I came upon the rather pedantic report of the police officer who was present at his execution, I was overwhelmed by the simple human truth. To the prosecutor's question as to whether he has a last wish, Malchika replies: "A glass of water please!" They give him a glass of water. Then the prosecutor asks him again: "Is that your final wish?" Malchika replies: "Another glass of water please!" They give him the second glass of water. Then they shoot him. There is no "Long live the Red Army"; nothing of the kind.

Georgi Markov

Burying the Past

VLADIMIR was a Russian poet-artist-tramp, who slept under the bushes behind the Military Club. My friend Hristo Stoyanov, an author, former alcoholic hell-raiser and six-pack a day smoker had introduced me to him. I had bought a picture from him.

One day as I walked by the bench where he spent his days, he called out to me in his thick booze-slurred accent.

"The bastards are going to blow up my house!"

Vladimir was in self-imposed exile from Moscow. He used to be quite successful and had several books of poetry published. But he took to drink when his Bulgarian wife left him. (Or perhaps it was the other way round. It is hard to get the story straight.) Since then he had mostly loitered in the little garden next to where the artists hawked their canvasses.

Occasionally, he still produced strikingly colourful but disturbed Kandinsky-esque daubs in crayon on the back of old calendars and bits of scrap paper. He could also write you a poem to order, though unlike his pictures not a very good one. Mostly he would give them away or sell them for enough money to buy another bottle or two. But for one glorious week a little earlier in the summer he had been master of the great white Dimitrov mausoleum that squatted like a temple to a sinister god opposite the former royal palace on the edge of Battenburg Square.

"The door was open just a bit and I was curious so I nipped inside. It was dark down there, I tell you, but I found my way alright. I slept in the chamber where they had put old man's casket."

He pulled a solemn frown onto his dirty face in comic imitation of official mourning.

"He was much shorter than the news films showed him," he said, stretching out awkwardly on the collapsing park bench under which he stores his piles of cardboard and plastic bags filled with whatever it is that tramps collect in their plastic bags.

"I couldn't fit on the plinth."

He shot his legs and arms out from the bench to demonstrate the lack of comfort he had suffered.

"I explored too," he added darkly. "There were many other rooms and underground passages, but I couldn't follow them. It was dirty down there. Syringes, rubbish... Lots of other people must have used it."

So, the burial place of "Bulgaria's Lenin" had become a home for the problems of democracy: drug use and vagrancy.

Perhaps that is why it had to go. On a sweltering furnace-like Saturday afternoon n the middle of August 1999, the Bulgarian army moved into the centre of the city with its sandbags and explosives. Anyone with half an excuse or opportunity had left the city for the mountains or the sea. If not, they were sitting at home with the curtains closed and the windows shut. Opening the windows didn't help when it was that hot. There was no cooling breeze in the centre of the city, only slabs of roasted air.

An urgent deadline had kept me in the city. I had been grumpily grinding over my word processor all morning. Then, after lunch, I came out on the baking streets with the other fools, loungers, rubber-neckers and journalists.

For weeks, Sofia's newspapers had been debating whether or not the demolition was a good idea. Some thought that historical monuments should be preserved even when they were symbols of an evil past. Others felt that this powerful monument of communist tyranny should be removed at all costs.

I was sorry to see it go. Not that I liked it. But it seemed wrong to destroy something for the sake of destruction, without any idea of what should replace it. Bulgaria has seen too much of that since the end of communism, and perhaps all through its history. All too often the replacements have been no better than what was there before. I would have liked to see the mausoleum reopened to the public, adapted, put to some constructive use, turned into a museum.

There had been attempts. When the film of 101 Dalmatians came out, they covered its white facade in black spots and hundreds of dalmatian owners came to parade their pets in the garden behind it. Then the city council painted its front black and used it as a stage for a grandiose outdoor opera production. It became a popular base for the city's beer festival. For a week every year kebab stalls sprouted on the broad granite plinth. Someone wanted to turn it into a night-club.

All these uses seemed apt to me. It pleased me that the mauso-leum occasionally managed to acquire a kind of shabby utility, like Enver Xhojda's ultra-modern pyramidal tomb in the centre of Tirana, which I saw Albanian children use as a massive and terrifying slide.

But it was not to be. The mausoleum would give the small crowd of idlers and rubber-neckers one final spectacle. It would soon be forgotten.

One of the two men in the crowd front of me was clearly simple. He pointed at the pigeons still perching on the flat roof and tugged the other's sleeve.

"Why are the birds still there? Hasn't anyone told them?"

His friend patted him on the shoulder gently.

"Of course they don't know that there's going to be an explosion. They wouldn't be so stupid as to sit there otherwise."

A few people had brought beer and video cameras. One man silently held a copy of Dimitrov's biography to his chest like an icon. It had the tyrant's picture on the front.

Why did some Bulgarians still revere Dimitrov? He was Bul-garia's first communist leader. It was probably lucky for the country that he only ruled for three years. It was a period of terrifying vio-lence. The regime consolidated its power through brutal revenge on the bourgeoisie. The People's Courts sentenced to death more than 3000 members of the monarchist elite. Tens of thousands more were imprisoned.

The man who orchestrated this violence was born in a village to the west of Sofia in 1883. At the age of 13 he got his first job in the Sofia print house of a liberal newspaper. He helped found the first printers' union and became an energetic member of the under-ground communist party.

One can still visit the humble three room semi-detached house where he lived with his mother and siblings. It looks tiny and out of place now, surrounded by large blocks. Billboards with bikini-clad women advertise car parts on the other side of the road.

It is a more interesting monument to the man than his tomb. It still contains some of his books and furniture, his spectacles, his pipe and his pen. It used to contain the manacles that he wore when imprisoned in Leipzig during the 30s. But these have been stolen. The glass is still broken in the case where they used to lie.*

Dimitrov achieved his Communist apotheosis by conducting his own defence in a show trial mounted against him by the Nazi chief prosecutor, Herman Goering in 1933. Goering falsely accused him of being responsible for burning down the Reichstag. It was a sort of David and Goliath contest, reported in detail throughout the world's media. Dimitrov was already a well known communist-in-exile. He attained heroic status within the global anti-fascist movement by running rings around the lumbering Nazi prosecutor, making him appear both dishonest and foolish. He was acquitted and went to Moscow in triumph. There he became leader of the Third Comintern and survived Stalin's purges by ruthlessly betraying anyone who stood in his way, including many other Bulgarians. In 1946, he returned to Bulgaria to become the first General Secretary of the Bulgarian Communist Party (BCP).

He died just three years later, shortly after visiting Stalin in Moscow. There followed an orgy national grief, whipped up by overwrought propaganda. His mourners built the mausoleum in six days and nights of uninterrupted work, while crowds of people stood by in floods of tears. Several soldiers perished in the manic haste of the construction. Dimitrov was embalmed to lie in state for ever like the relics of a saint.

Or a martyr. Matei Brunwasser, who was by now reporting on Bulgaria for US National Public Radio and the San Fransisco Chroni-

---

* By strange coincidence Dimitrov's next door neighbour was a man called Petur Dunov. He was one of the few people to have successfully founded his own religion during the 20th century. In 1895, when Dimitrov the print worker was establishing his radical credentials by making unauthorised political changes to editorials that he was supposed to be typesetting, his next door neighbour was establishing the White Brotherhood. This was a theosophic religious community, combining Orthodox Christianity, sun-worship, yoga and vegetarianism. Legend says that when the police came searching for Dimitrov, Dunov used to hide him or lend him his clothes for disguise. This kindness was not repaid. By 1944 the White Brotherhood had acquired some 40 000 adherents. But the communists banned it along with all other religions. Even so it is still actively followed today.

cle, told me that he once met the doctor who had the job of looking after Dimitrov's corpse. He had to repickle it every 18 months. The doctor had shown Matei Dimitrov's brain.

"He has it in a glass jar in his lab. He kept it to do tests on, to see if Stalin had poisoned him."

The tests were not conclusive but many people still believe Dimitrov to be another Bulgarian mystery assassination victim (alongside Tsar Boris III secretly poisoned by Hitler; Lyudmilla, daughter of dictator Todor Zhivkov, supposedly killed by the Russians; and of course Georgi Markov.)

When democracy came they took Dimitrov's preserved remains and reinterred them in the city graveyard next to his wife. Now the temple of the false god was to be torn down and this whole story consigned to the forgotten past.

The crowd hushed. A boom shook the air and a cloud of thick orange smoke obliterated the view. From the side streets, car alarms wailed in unison, like a cacophonic last post. The smoke hung for some moments and we waited in silent expectation of the destruction that it must hide. Slowly it thinned revealing the mausoleum again, still standing, its pillars intact. The whole edifice leant slightly towards one corner. Nothing more. There was a moment of silence after the explosion as we waited. Then everyone laughed. It was like a shout, a simultaneous guffaw, a hoot of derision. It seemed to say:

"We knew it! You fools! We knew you could not so easily get rid of something which has been with us for so long!"

I didn't wait to see the next explosions. They tried twice more that day, with little more impact and the next day and the next. In the end it took a whole week to level the tomb. Apparently it had been built strong enough to withstand nuclear attack. Its rubble was transported to a secret location and buried to deter souvenir hunters.

"Typical, eh," said Johnny when he and Tanya returned to the city some weeks later, cool and refreshed after a summer spent in their mountain cottage.

"We failed to destroy communism properly. Now the government can't even knock down the mausoleum."

A problem that can't be solved with money
can be solved with more money

Popular saying

The Rise and Fall of a National Capitalist

F ROM the era of the Macedonian Question to the present day, assassinations have been one of the constants of Bulgarian history. Few ever get solved. Between 2001 and 2006, not one person was brought to justice for more than 150 gangster executions.

The most dramatic of these killings happened at 7.50pm on 7th March 2003. Ilya Pavlov, the founder and owner of Multigroup Corporation, left his offices in the suburbs of Sofia. As he stepped out of the glass electric door with his bodyguards at his side, he was shot in the heart with a single bullet fired by a sniper, who had been hiding in some bushes opposite the main entrance. He died instantaneously.

By the time the police arrived on the scene, the assassin had fled. There is still no clue to his identity, nor to who might have ordered the hit. There is no doubt that the killer was a professional, but apart from that there are almost too many theories.

The threat of assassination may well have been on Pavlov's mind that evening. He lived in a world where the threat of professional killing was real and present. He was the biggest oligarch in Bulgaria and without doubt the country's most feared and richest man. That is why he always had bodyguards, although in the event they were unable to protect him. And in a curious twist of fate, on the day before his death, the 43-year old had appeared as a witness in the trial of five men accused of the other definitive assassination in the history of Bulgaria's transition.

Ex-Prime Minister Andrei Lukanov, once regarded as Pavlov's mentor, (the self-same Lukanov who was the subject of the Stalinist Spasovi's crazy theories) was assassinated in October 1996. His murder sent a shock wave of speculation and fear throughout the country. It seemed to confirm that the country's attempts at democracy had failed, that something evil had come in alongside political freedom. As with Pavlov's death, there were far too many theories who might have killed the ex-PM and why.

At the time, no one expected that the perpetrator of that earlier crime would ever be captured. For a long while, the Multigroup boss was himself one of the names mentioned by ordinary Bulgarians as the most likely suspect. But, as if to confound conspiracy theorists, Lukanov's murderers were found. Moreover, in a further irony, the chief defendant in the dock of the Sofia central court, whose trial became Pavlov's last public appearance, was a nobody. He wasn't former KBG, or its Bulgarian equivalent the Durzhavna Sigournost. He wasn't Russian mafia. He had not wanted to prevent Lukanov from revealing secrets of "red money" and how the most ruthless part of the Communist Party had managed to seize control of Bulgaria's economic assets even as totalitarian power was slipping from its grasp. He was the owner of a construction company, who had fallen out with the ex-PM over some business in their home town of Lovech, and hired a pair of Ukrainian hitmen to solve the problem.

So for Pavlov, appearing in the witness box at this trial was a demonstration of his innocence. It was an attempt to show that everything was really normal, that the conspiracies about himself were also wrong. It was a small contribution to the long slow process of personal and corporate legitimisation that he had been working on for many years. Any observer seeing the confidence with which he was treading the Bulgarian and the world stage could have easily concluded that he had nearly made it.

There were many other signs to suggest that Pavlov might be getting clear of his past. Two years earlier, in June 2001, the billionaire had welcomed former Tsar Simeon II to the Grand Hotel Varna, the most luxurious destination on the Bulgarian Black Sea coast. The king had just won a sensational election victory and his first public appearance as Prime Minister Saxcoburggotski was as guest of honour at Pavlov's sumptuous 41ᵗʰ birthday party. Since then Pavlov had been awarded a green card by the USA, an achievement of which he was greatly proud, regarding it as an endorsement of his honesty. (He showed it to me when I went to interview him – like a child with a new toy.)

In the court, the day before his death, Pavlov's testimony was bland and uncontroversial. He appeared simply as a citizen doing his duty. He said that Lukanov, whom he had employed as chairman of Topenergy, a joint venture trading company set up with the Russian gas giant, Gazprom, had been acting nervously for about six months before his death. He did not know why, but speculated that it was to do with politics. Pavlov had sacked Lukanov from Topenergy, three months before he was shot. But the Multigroup boss was nowhere near when Lukanov died. He was in Palma de Majorca for a group management meeting. As far as he was concerned, the conspiracies were rubbish. Everything had been totally normal.

But the day after his testimony, Pavlov was shot and the illusion of normality was shattered, although no one could say why. Some people said he was still involved in crime. Others said he was going to reveal secrets from the past. Some people said he was in debt. It was wittily suggested that he might turn out to be the victim of another aggrieved builder. A year after his assassination, Multigroup started selling hotels on the Black Sea and in Croatia to pay off debts to various construction companies. Without its leader the business had begun to crumble and rivals were moving in.

But, in a way it doesn't matter exactly why he was shot. Whatever the truth about his death, Pavlov's story is the story of Bulgaria's transition. He was far and away the country's most important and the most successful oligarch. His wealth, although not extraordinary compared to the largest Russian oligarchs, was huge in Bulgarian terms. At the time of his death he had a fortune estimated at about one billion pounds or a tenth of the annual GDP of the country. He had made this money in just 15 years, while pensioners were still getting less than $50 per month. To ordinary Bulgarians, Pavlov's success symbolised everything that was wrong and unjust about the transition from communism to democracy.

Pavlov was born in the village of Gorni Bogorov, just to the east of Sofia. During the 80s he had become a champion wrestler, and probably a Durzhavna Sigournost agent, although this second accusation has never been proven. At any rate, he was a privileged member of what has been ironically referred to as the *demokratura*, the "communist aristocracy", and had translated his connections with power into economic influence before anyone else had even started thinking to do this.

In 1988, with his business partner Dimitur Ivanov, another secret policeman, he registered a business in Switzerland under the name Multiart for the export of Bulgarian artworks. This unprecedented opportunity can only have been approved at the highest level. It was given to the pair at a time when contact with the west was considered deeply suspicious and political dissidents were still in prison.

By the time I first heard Pavlov's name and the name of Multigroup, he had become the most powerful man in the country. It was 1997. People spoke of him and his business in whispers, with nervous glances towards the door, with the same apprehension that they spoke about the secret police, which officially had been disbanded in 1990. No coincidence this. In most minds the two organisations were virtually synonymous.

Several years later, in 2001, shortly before ex-Tsar Simeon II won his election victory, the ogre of Bulgarian robber-capitalism finally agreed to give me an interview. I had asked to meet him on many occasions in the past, but had never made it past the outer ring of flunkeys and anodyne spokesmen whose well-paid job it was to deflect awkward questions.

The meeting took place in his Sofia headquarters, set back from a road in an unremarkable area of the suburbs. Pavlov seemed to glow with the aura of the unfeasibly rich. It gave him a faint shimmer of unreality. His short dark hair cut en brosse was softer and finer than one would expect on such a powerful man, almost as if it might be the hair of a child. Everything about him, his skin and his nails gave the impression of a man who was manicured and expensively anointed with youthful unguents every morning.

When he turned his head I noticed another clue to his background: his small ears, pressed close to his head were crinkled and misshapen. He also had the short, broad-shouldered body of the champion wrestler he once was. But he hadn't gone to fat, although his broad oval face was fleshy. He was relaxed and easy in dark trousers and a crisp white shirt, open at his broad neck. These were the perfect, unrumpled clothes of a man who rides in the back of limos and has other people to fetch and carry for him. In spite of all this he didn't swagger like I had expected, or bluster. In fact his movements were surprisingly delicate and controlled. He greeted me warmly, ushering me into his office.

It was spacious and light and cool, with large windows and white walls. Like the man himself, it also reeked of vast wealth. One wall was lined with mint copies of Encyclopedia Britannica. Every other surface was crammed with art. Pieces of classical statuary, many of which should almost certainly have been in museums, were ranged next to formless lumps of pristine modernity.

"I am Ilya and you are Jack," he said matily. "A glass of orange juice?"

He insisted on fetching me it himself, instead of getting a secretary to do it. I was being treated to a careful presentation of chummy, if opulent, normality.

I sat opposite him at his wide desk. To the left of his leather revolving chair, in a recessed space in the wall was a massive three-foot wide chunk of lumpy brownish metal. It looked like a hide – a large rusty cowhide, perhaps a metre long and several inches thick. He was obviously more proud of it than anything else in the room. Noticing my eyes drift to it, he challenged me to guess what it was. My failure delighted him.

"It's made of gold. It's a large talent: one of the oldest and biggest pieces of money in the world! They dug it up in one of my mines."

It was an appropriate symbol of wealth for such a man. Yet, it felt very odd to be discussing this priceless artefact with the person who for the past decade had been demonised as the arch-symbol of the nexus between the Bulgarian mafia, the old *nomenklatura* and secret police and their Russian equivalents. After several years of stonewalling, refusals to grant interviews, why was he suddenly so open and keen to speak?

"All I want is for everyone to understand the truth. I want the truth about the events of the past 15 years to be told as well. There are too many lies told already."

Like the great robber barons of the American industrialisation, Pavlov had made his pile and was now in search of respectability. Perhaps the fact that he had secured US residency was making him more eager still to shed the dark cloak of his past? His Green Card was like a badge of respectability that he hoped might counter all criticism from home.

Perhaps he really had managed to put all his businesses beyond reproach. Or was it just that the change in government meant his enemies were out of power and his friend the Tsar was on the way in?

One political commentator told me that the elections that brought Tsar Simeon to power may also have delivered as many as 25 deputies to Pavlov's interest in the parliament. Also, one of the country's leading investigative journalists reported that Pavlov had been overheard in the corridors of the Privatisation Agency as he "loudly discussed" the contribution that his company had made to Simeon's election victory.

He had reportedly told the Tsar:

"We paid for the elections, and now you will sell only to us."

These accusations hark back to the era just a few years previously when one of the most corrupt governments of the transition was even known as the "Multigroup government".

Pavlov certainly knew how to exert his influence. How else could he have made so much money during the worst period of Bulgaria's transition, while the rest of his country was still so poor. He told me that he had started just as an ordinary sportsman.

"I succeeded because I was first. I am truly the father of Bulgarian capitalism. When I do well it means that Bulgaria is doing well," he said.

It is true that he was first. Multiart was the first private company to be established in Bulgaria since the introduction of communism more than 40 years earlier. Initially, it was established as a cooperative, the first kind of private enterprise that had been made legal.

"There were several of us. We each put in 500 levs. I sold my old, beaten up green Wartburg car. We didn't know we were being capitalists. We didn't know what we were doing. We specialised in video and sound imaging. We operated the son et lumiere spectacle at the old fortress in the middle of Veliko Turnovo," he recalled.

It was one of those 'can you believe it?' tales that conveniently hides a mass of unanswerable questions, summed up in the one cynical question that every Bulgarian knew to ask automatically.

"Who else but a *chenge* would have been permitted to do what he did?"

Not only was his business partner, Ivanov, a Secret Police officer but Pavlov was also the son-in-law of the then head of military intelligence. A 1995 report by Oxford Analytica, the UK-based business information publisher, explains what kind of opportunities these contacts would have created. It describes how groupirovki or "red conglomerates", like Multigroup, had grown from businesses set up in the West during the 80s as fronts for industrial espionage.

"Multigroup — which controls most of the security and protection firms in the country, staffed largely by former athletes and ex-
state security officers — for example, has its roots in the old first,
second, and sixth main directorates of the communist-era Committee for State Security (KDS)," said the OA report.

The KDS directorates from which the group emerged were responsible for respectively, intelligence, counter-intelligence and,
most sinister of all, the sixth main directorate, for political security.

The money laundering aspect of this programme had, inciden-
tally (and somewhat bizarrely) been arranged by the British rogue
financier and newspaper proprietor, Robert Maxwell*. Secret communist party funds, known as "red money", had been smuggled to the
west via the KDS, as seed capital for a massive programme of techno-
logical theft. After the collapse of the party in January 1990, these secret funds were expropriated leaving a black hole of many billions of
dollars in the state budget – but no trace where the money had gone.
Most Bulgarians assume they went to companies like Multigroup.

Pavlov's next business opportunity reeked of this sort of inside
influence. Shortly after the fall of the Warsaw Pact he secured a
sweet contract to sell several Soviet submarines for scrap. From here
he quickly moved his business into mining, metals, textiles, energy,
foodstuffs, finance, media and tourism. At the height of its power,
the visible part of Multigroup owned 150 companies and employed
25,000 people in banks, insurance companies, TV stations, mines,
trading companies, hotels, newspapers and a news agency. It turned
over a billion pounds per year. The ultimate ownership of these businesses was a holding company registered in the town of Zug, Switzerland, which has the most discreet rules on disclosure of any part
of that highly discreet country. Allegations about the invisible side of
the business included accusations of smuggling and large gambling
and prostitution businesses in South America.

This was a period when the *groupiróvki* were consuming the
country from the inside, buying state-owned enterprises cheaply,
stripping their assets, and building up vast debts which the government was left to repay. Between 1993 and 1994, Multigroup owned

---

* It is bizarre details like this which makes Bulgarian history so surreal. Sometimes you think you must be dreaming. Unfortunately for the country and its
inhabitants, the dream is all too real.

the government. It had ministers and *apparatchiks* in its employ. The corporation's influence pervaded every part of the state.

Between 1994 and 1996, even after the government had changed, its successor was powerless to prevent the group from advancing further into whichever businesses it liked. In a free market economy there might have been nothing wrong with this. But Multigroup was seizing businesses still, nominally, under state control and ownership. Most crucially it had grasped a controlling position in the transit and supply of natural gas through and to Bulgaria. With Russian help, Pavlov had put his hand on one of the country's vital life-supporting arteries.

It was this demonstration of the group's awesome power which led to its greatest battle, following the landslide election of Ivan Kostov's United Democratic Forces government in April 1997. It was only the second time in ten years that the anti-Communist parties had secured power. First time round, they had failed within a year, leaving the country worse off than when they found it. Kostov was an autocratic and fiercely ideological prime minister. He was determined not to make the same mistake and launched a campaign against Pavlov with relentless zeal, almost to the point of obsession.

Kostov went for them and managed to break them. He broke their hold on gas and on Moscow-Sofia relations. Then he went after them sector by sector: imports, banks, enterprises, hotels, the lot." This is how one local political analyst described to me what happened next.

The battle over gas was the most bitter. This is where Pavlov's story begins to entwine most tightly with that of his fellow assassination victim Andrei Lukanov. Lukanov represented above all, the Russian interest in Bulgarian politics. He had provoked the palace coup which toppled dictator Todor Zhivkov on orders from Moscow. He was the strategist who set the stage for the Party's ruthless exploitation of the chaos which came with democracy. Pavlov was his protegé. This was why Lukanov had allowed Multigroup into the lucrative and strategically vital business of gas transit and supply.

The Russian gas monopolist Gazprom wanted to sell more gas to Turkey. Bulgargaz, the domestic state-owned gas monopoly was building a second pipeline to take the gas from Romania down to Turkey. Multigroup was let in on this deal, giving it a decent percentage of a $1 billion trade, plus massive influence over Bulgarian energy policy. Much of domestic industry was completely dependent on Russian gas.

After six months of diplomatic brinkmanship and strife with the Russians, Kostov forced Multigroup out. But at huge cost. He had to sign a commercially disadvantageous gas deal with the Russians to do it. He then continued to bash Multigroup.

The Minister of the Interior at the time, a poseurish police general with grand political ambitions, launched a tub-thumping *j'accuse* against Multigroup from the parliamentary rostrum. A list of 16 indictments included accusations of running a channel for stolen cars from West Europe to Arabic countries, illegal privatisation, unpaid taxes, contraband deals, corruption of state officials and the production of pirate CDs.

That summer, Multigroup's headquarters was raided by the balaclava-wearing, automatic-weapon toting operatives of the national organised crime-fighting force. The agency was investigating a Multigroup subsidiary on charges of sugar-smuggling.

In the autumn, licenses were withdrawn from the group's insurance companies, two of its most profitable businesses. By the end of 1998, the group had also lost an oil-supply contract and suffered legal challenges over the privatisation of a couple of hotels, a ski resort and a copper smelter. It also sold its cable-television business and stakes in a local news agency and its gas-distribution joint venture with Gazprom.

In January, the financial arm of the conglomerate suffered a further blow when its bank was put into liquidation by the Bulgarian National Bank. In February 1999 Premier Kostov told Parliament that Multigroup firms were involved in an illegal cigarette-trading scam.

The group began to draw in its horns to protect its remaining businesses. The company spokesman and vice-president Stoyan Denchev, a former parlimentary deputy and professional glad-hander who had been brought in as the group's public face in August 1998, protested to me that:

"Multigroup is being used as a punching bag by a government in need of an enemy. Nothing is proved and can't be proved because none of these things is true."

He pointed out that no Multigroup personnel had ever been convicted.

"Clearly, Multigroup has not been as pure as a tear, we have made mistakes, but these monstrous crimes which we have been accused of are complete nonsense."

Protest over, he held up the white flag of surrender. The biggest mistake Multigroup made was to think it could fight with the government and win, he admitted.

"The new policy of the company, since I have been here, is that we respect the government of Bulgaria, regardless of what that government is."

The message was that the beast had been tamed. Was it true? As he took me on a tour of his office, two years before his death, Pavlov tried almost too hard to persuade me that his business was legit. He took me to every department and into every office. Door after door opened to reveal workers behind computers.

"Hi, guys!" he called.

"Hello Ilya!" the workers responded in happy unison.

He beamed at me proudly.

"It's a totally normal company isn't it? It looks totally normal."

He was telling me this. Or was he asking? We looked into another office with more cheerful waves and greetings. The money and commodities traders, the on-line travel agency, and so on...

"All totally straight forwards, don't you agree? All we do here is business, just like ordinary people..."

Even then he seemed to doubt that I would believe it. And it was perhaps already too late for him. There was no way that he could escape from his dubious origins to become "normal". Most probably, there was only ever one way that he could leave the bad world that he had helped to build. And that was the way he went.

From Bai Ganyo at the Palace

We waited there a bit and then the Prince and Princess came out. This time they put themselves out in a proper Christian manner. They gave us each an egg...

Did you kiss their hands?

And did I not? I would have kissed a hundred hands to get to that table of food. They went by and pretty quickly, so then we shifted, brother mine, straight down the stairs. You can believe me or not, as you please, but I tell you I leapt down three steps at a time, I nearly slammed into a big mirror, but no one was going to overtake me.

I dug into the caviare and once I had filled the spoon, blast my soul if it was less than a half a kilo...

I ate, I ate, I stuffed myself... I still don't know why my stomach didn't burst...

My head is still sore from that damned champagne... and when I left I crammed my overcoat pockets with cakes, but devil take it they were so soft that they dripped everywhere.

Aleko Konstantinov (April 1895)

Put Not Thy
Trust in Princes *

BY THE summer of 2006, the sense of mystery and auror of nobility which had once surrounded the figure of Simeon II, former Tsar of Bulgaria, had been destroyed. Authority was once again slipping from his hands, but his wealth was secure.

It was an unedifying conclusion to a bitter fairy tale of lost greatness that should have been a story of personal triumph and vindication. Simeon was born to rule, but he was expelled in a revolution, spent 50 years in exile, and then ruthlessly reestablished himself in power and wealth. But he became ignominiously tarnished by what he had regained.

Was this Bulgaria's fault or his? Sometimes it does seem that Simeon's life could be taken as a parable of Bulgaria's fate, as the country has lurched from fascism and monarchy through socialist dictatorship to contemporary advertising-driven democracy.

But no. He may not have written the start of his own story, but he certainly composed the end of it. It begins with the happy day in 1937 when every school child was awarded an extra grade and every army officer presented with a ceremonial pistol to celebrate the birth of an heir to Boris III, who had established a personal fascistic rule independent of parliament.

Tragedy came early to blight Simeon's life of promise and privilege. According to his own account, a military officer interrupted his play in the garden of Vrana Palace just outside Sofia and said:

---
* Psalm 146

"Your Majesty!"

These words, whose implication he understood immediately, meant that his father, who had recently returned from visiting his ally Adolf Hitler in Berlin, was dead. It was 1943 and Simeon was just six-years old.

He wore the crown for three years. In 1946, he fled into exile with his mother and sister. The communist government confiscated the crown estates, dissolved the regency, executed the regents including his uncle, Prince Kyril, and instituted the republic.

There followed 50 years of humiliating exile. It is hard to imagine the petty awfulness of being a king with no throne, no country, no money, forced to work as a business intermediary for European companies in the Middle East. By the late 60s he had given up on ambition.

One looks in vain for any public criticism of dictatorship or any sign that Simeon tried to encourage dissent or democracy or the protection of human rights in his home country. The young princes' Bulgarian lessons were stopped. They were encouraged in self-supporting professions. They made their lives in bourgeoisie, monarchist, celebrity-adoring deferential Madrid.

Then a shock. The evil empire, whose end no one could ever imagine, suddenly and completely ended. Simeon did not cheer. He did not rush back. He spent six years silently watching and observing as his country struggled to find its way.

Finally he returned, but not to contribute. Several more years past before he entered definitively into politics.

In 2001 he staged the political ambush which made him Prime Minister. It was an extraordinary triumph. In the words of Asen Oshanov, his personal factor* and one of the few people I spoke to who had no doubt about the Tsar's greatness:

"He was thrown out like the last piece of rag and came back triumphant 50 years later. He is one of the top ten politicians in the world."

Simeon himself potrayed his actions as a heroic act of self-sacrifice. An interview in *El Mundo* one year after he became Prime Minister described him reading official documents late into the night

---

* The man who writes his cheques and pays his bills (like the Queen of England, Simeon does not carry money himself)

in his office in the Vrana Palace, with only a statue of Don Quixote for company.

In the Tsar's own words his life was:

"Loneliness. Complete loneliness. Complete.... To some extent as if I am in a monastery. Completely alone."

But it is hard to reconcile these fine images with the way things happened and the way that they ended. In the tricky fractious tail-end of the 2006 parliamentary year an Italian businessman fatally slurred Simeon's reputation with allegations of corruption; unproved and hotly denied. In Bulgaria they were widely believed.

At roughly the same time, the Socialist-led *Narodno Subranie* voted not to contest the way that Simeon had reclaimed $250 million of former royal property, confiscated from his family by the Communists 60 years before. This ruled out the disagreeable suggestion the palaces, hunting lodges and forests belonged not to him personally but to the crown and therefore to the state. But the long running and grubby battle had made the Tsar appear grasping and opportunistic.

A month later, his wealth secure, the 69-year old Simeon had announced his effective retirement from politics. His party, the National Movement Simeon II, had already lost power in a general election. Now he said it would put forward no candidate for the forthcoming presidential election.

"As the leader is not going to stand, it makes sense that the party proposes no other candidate," he explained in tones of pained reasonableness.

The performance was pure Simeon from the haughty wooden manner and reserved delivery, to the prim and vacant assumption that somehow the whole question revolved around him. If he personally had no alternative to offer the voters, then none was available.

How far away this all seemed from that first slick election campaign which had brought him back to power.

I had gone to see Simeon that summer in 2001. He was touring the streets of a small provincial city called Montana, about 50 miles north of Sofia. About 100 years earlier its name had been changed to Ferdinand in honour of his grandfather the first modern Tsar. It was a pleasant worn out little place typical of northern Bulgaria with a pedestrianised main street. Most of the action took place in a few shady cafés under the trees on the edge of the main square. A few old buildings had been repainted using European Union funds.

The thin, politely-interested man dressed in a grey suit who slowly perambulated along the rutted side streets looked less like a campaigning politician than a landlord who had recently inherited a place and was going around to acquaint himself with it. A large crowd dogged his footsteps. He had a phalanx of aids and body-guards who prevented anyone from getting too close. They allowed through well-wishers. There were men who wanted to bow and shake his hand and curtseying grannies who proffered posies of meadow flowers and wild geranium leaves smelling of church incense.

I had joined a little knot of journalists, who had followed him out of the city to get a glimpse of the man in a more intimate provincial setting. We took it in turn to interview him. The bodyguards, see-ing I was foreign let me through the cordon. He liked speaking with foreigners and easily and impressively fielded questions in French, Spanish, German and English. But he didn't much like talking Bul-garian, at least not to Bulgarian journalists. They stayed outside the cordon.

I asked questions that although I didn't know it at the time, would dog his four year premiership. Who were his advisors? Who were the members of his inner court? Was he under the influence of ques-tionable businessmen, the so-called *groupirovki* who had gained con-trol of so much of the economy? How did he know who to trust?

The king said my questions were based on false rumours and *kompromati*.

"It is a type of corruption. I don't like hangers-on. I have a long enough nose and I have been in exile long enough to spot them."

It was very civilised and easy. We might have been walking in his garden except that every so often he stopped to accept a bunch of flowers or the wishes of a flustered matron. He also waved away the buzzing Bulgarian journalist flies who tried to interject questions when they could get close enough. He ticked them off like a school-master.

"Excuse me, can you not see that a colleague of yours from abroad wishes to speak with me?"

And on we walked. Simeon's visit was bound to cause a stir in a place like this, where the jaded and disappointed population was prepared to accept anything that promised change. Most who had come out to see him were middle-aged or elderly. They had lost their jobs or were eking out their meagre pensions – buying one lump of cheese every week and dividing scrupulously into seven pieces.

These people were looking for a saviour. So Simeon attended a church service. As many as possible crowded into the little 19th church dedicated to the Saints Kyril and Metodius. The Tsar stood apart, tall and distinguished in his pale suit. He bowed his head and prayed surrounded by a semi-circle of sumptuously robed priests. The candlelight glowed on his bald crown like a benediction. This was him at his best: aloof, regal and pious.

Outside the church a pensioner who had waited all morning to see him told me:

"We do not expect anything from him. We just want to see the new man. He is an aristocrat, while our current leaders are plebians. He knows that it is his duty because he was born to be king and he sees what a ridiculous situation we are in."

Later in the town square Simeon stood on a platform and gave his election speech. It was a bad speech. He didn't sound like a politician eager for a chance to grapple with problems, demanding the chance to put things right. Instead he was awkward: wooden, vague and fastidious. He didn't want to take sides, or get his hands dirty with arguments that would besmirch his royal aloofness. Instead he offered his personal guarantee like a seal. He explained why three months earlier, five years after he first returned to Bulgaria from his long exile, he had founded the National Movement Simeon II. He promised a "New Time" and a "new moral in politics".

"Believe me!" he told the crowd.

And why not? In spite of everything I was naïvely tempted to believe in him too. Perhaps royalty was capable of magic. A change was needed. Why should he not be the man?

This view infuriated my journalistic colleagues. They couldn't believe that after five years in Bulgaria I was still so wet behind the ears. I remember one impassioned conversation with a group of hacks in a leafy beer garden that had been set up in a street near the headquarters of the main private TV station.

"Simeon is slippery as a fish," said Aglaya, who had been one of the first Bulgarians to interview the Tsar after the end of communism.

"Why can't you take him at face value?"

"Poor Jack! So sweet! What a good nature. We couldn't do without your unclouded view," she teased me. "How can we take him at face value? We don't know who he is at all."

I had to admit it was true. There were too many blank areas. And true to Bulgarian form the rumour mill was filling up the spaces with gossip which ranged from the comical to the insane. Some people said that he had forgotten how to speak Bulgarian; that was why his language was so stilted and archaic. Others said that he was suffering from dementia or Alzheimer's disease. When he halted in a speech, he wasn't searching for a word, he was trying to recapture his thoughts.

He had made all his money as an arms trader. He had spent all his money gambling and had entered Bulgarian politics to pay off his debts. He was in the pay of the Russian Mafia. He was in the pay of the Bulgarian oligarchs. He was working with the Russian KGB. He had links to the Ku Klux Klan which is why all his children's names began with the letter K.

And so on and so on. There were many other rumours, all of them based on great public ignorance about Simeon's true character and the fear that perhaps he did not have the country's best interests at heart. This was the biggest question of all. Had he come back to Bulgaria for his own benefit or to satisfy his own personal destiny, no matter at what cost to the people he once ruled?

Over the next few years I hunted out people who could tell me the answer to this question. I spoke to many of former allies and advisers, parliamentary deputies and ministers, some of whom had been involved with him at the very beginning. I also did my best to interview Simeon again, pulling string after string to get through to him. One time I wrote a letter to his palace outside Sofia which began:

"Your Majesty!"

and concluded:

"I am, Sir, your most humble servant." (I left out the "obedient" – this wasn't my own monarch I was writing to.) But I didn't get a reply.

I made an official application through the government press office. This led to hours discussing a potential interview with his press secretary, but no interview. I also made contact with one of Simeon's close personal advisers, a silver-haired Bulgarian resident of London. He was much in the mould of a certain kind of rich ex-patriate who had effortlessly negotiated the switch from privileged Comsomol trusty to suave international businessman. Somewhere along the line, he had made a lot of money – none of my contacts could say how. He arrived in the foyer of the Curzon Mayfair hotel in pressed jeans and a blazer, clutching sleek logoed carrier bags of the small but expensive kind. He promised to discuss my request for an interview with Simeon that evening. Apparently, they often spoke on the telephone in the evening. He told me the Tsar knew who I was and what I was doing (by this time I had interviewed many people in Bulgaria about him).

"You are in his little black book," he told me.

Should I have been surprised? Concerned? Flattered? It didn't matter. I never got the interview.

For a while all this coyness made me grumpy. There were so many questions I burned to ask Simeon, so many puzzles that I hoped an undisturbed face-to-face interview might solve. He held the key to his country's future. Yet who was he? Why had he come back to Bulgaria? What did he want?

But then I realised I was being absurd. None of the journalists who had been granted audiences were any the wiser. I read the transcripts of their interviews. None shed more than a glimmer of light onto Simeon's central mystery, the question of why he had come back and what he hoped to achieve.

Early on in his campaign, Simeon himself had spoken about his motivation to the chief editors of the main newspapers whom he summoned to meet him at Vrana Palace.

"It isn't, as some people suggest, to do with an ambition for power because I was born with it. Nor is it for party interest, because thank God, I am free and independent, nor to do with populism, because Simeon does not know what it is to lie to the nation because he loves it greatly. The historical responsibility, which I am filled and which, if I am given the opportunity to realise in our country, will not make me more authoritative or more famous," he said.

But was he being straight? It was clear he was not interested in the restitution of the monarchy. There was never public support for this and Crown Prince Kubrat seemed to have no interest either. So perhaps he was just after the return of his property? Many people supported this theory, but to me it did not ring true either. Reclaiming his wealth was hugely important, but it didn't begin to explain his behaviour. But I did not believe what he said about loving his national greatly either. If that had been the case, he would not have stayed aloof from the country's sufferings for the first decade of its transition, during its period of greatest suffering.

After dozens of interviews with former associates of the Tsar and a close reading of his speeches it seems clear to me that Simeon was motivated by one great complex desire: the desire to fulfil his destiny had become entwined and indistinguishable from the desire for revenge on the miserable country that had rejected him. This was Simeon's story: from being an impoverished and even slightly ridiculous figure amongst the less memorable members of Europe's minor royalty, he had made himself the most powerful monarch in Europe – a monarch who actually ruled. He was driven by the quest for power and nothing else.

As I pursued my investigation, I learnt a huge amount about the manoeuvres and strategies that he had used to secure power. They combined to make a remarkable plot. His entire political movement had been assembled abroad. A series of deals had been made in various European capitals which had secured him money, expertise, media support, even a party machine. His second son, Prince Kyril Preslavski had delivered the young, wealthy, financially literate members of the London-based Bulgarian City Club. A meeting with a Bulgarian lawyer in Vienna delivered the core lobby that he would rely on in parliament. A political consultant came from France. Other meetings happened in Madrid. It had all been done in secret and sprung on the Bulgarian public as a *fait accompli*. And the people had welcomed it.

But as I interviewed his allies, supporters and helpers to find out about this scheme and the earlier schemes which had brought him back to Bulgaria in the first place, I invariably found myself also deeply involved in discussions about his personality and character. These conversations revealed a ruthless and vengeful streak, which coloured all his actions and dealings.

There are many in Bulgaria who might reflect on the words of the Psalmist:

"Put not your faith in princes".

One such is Jakov Djerassi, a Bulgarian Jew who lived most of his life in exile in the US. He had been one of the committee who stage-managed Simeon's first triumphant return in 1996, when one million people lined the road and cheered his passage from the airport into the centre of the capital. Every element had been negotiated so that there was no danger of the government refusing to allow him entry. Simeon himself had stipulated many conditions. He was not to return as a mere tourist. He had to be invited and recognized for whom he was. Djerassi had personally managed the opening up of Vrana Palace so that Simeon could go home for the first time in half a century.

As with all Simeon's plans, everything had been intricately and secretly arranged. Simeon himself had nick-named it "Plan Shipka" after the beautiful house on Sofia's Shipka Street, which served as the unofficial headquarters of the organizing committee.

This is where I went to see Djerassi. Inside the house looked much as it must have done before the Communists took over. Its faded furniture, dark wood panels and old carpets heavy with a patrician air almost impossible to find in a city that had endured so much change. It was odd to hear criticism of the former Tsar voiced within such a relic from monarchist times.

It was here that I heard how after the job had been completed, the Tsar had cut Djerassi out of his councils. Simeon had lapped up the cheers and the adulation, but had then gone back to Spain, deaf to the entreaties of those who were urging him to lend his authority in some way to solve Bulgaria's huge problems. In 1996, the banks were failing. Corruption was threatening to bankrupt the country and utterly impoverish the people. But the Tsar had nothing to offer. He had refused to risk himself in politics and had cut off those who suggested he do so.

Years later Djerassi was still trying to work out whether he had ever really known the man.

"We are subjects and subjects are disposable. We can be brought in and out. We shouldn't take it as a personal insult. This is a monarchy. It is how things are done. There is no loyalty. You are there to serve and when your service is over you just bow out," he mused.

It was a pattern I came across again and again. Sometimes it was described to me like the end of a love affair. For a while Simeon would admit someone to his closest confidence and then, having used them, would cut them out, coldly, completely and utterly.

One former deputy, who in 2000 had personally gathered the necessary parliamentary votes to get the Constitutional Court to return the Tsar his property, reminisced about the dinners he had invited the Tsar to in his own house. He pointed to the chair that Simeon had sat in and wondered why he could no longer speak to the man who would still be poor if it hadn't been for him.

Another former friend, the Constitutional Court judge who had led the decision to return the Tsar's property told me that one of the features of his character was an in-built ingratitude.

"The Tsar is a great *neblagodarnik* [ingrate]. He probably thinks that people are obliged to help him," he told me.

None of these people could quite believe what had happened to them. They had devoted themselves to the cause of the Tsar because they believed in him and the justice of his cause.

Simeon was the greatest victim of the Communist takeover of Bulgaria in 1944. So if he was allowed back to the country, if his property was returned to him, then one of the worst crimes of the Communists would be overturned. To all these people Simeon represented a political symbol. If Simeon prevailed it meant the communists and their post-communist successors would have failed.

In fact things turned o ut in precisely the opposite way. Simeon was not prepared to be a political symbol. He was the Tsar: aloof and untouchable, such concerns were beneath him. He was not to be constrained.

During his period as a courtier, Djerassi came to believe that Simeon was driven by many complexes. One was that he tended to bend over to adversaries. On his first visit to Bulgaria he was ready to agree to an audience with former dictator Todor Zhivkov who was still under house arrest at that time.

"He has always got on better with Socialists. He thinks he will be able to convince them and turn them round," Djerassi told me. Delving deeper into Simeon's psyche he speculated that "For a serious man, he is attracted to stupidity. He is attracted to something completely opposite to himself, and to questionable wealth."

Questionable wealth. Was this what attracted the Tsar to Ilya Pavlov, boss of the Multigroup conglomerate, who had made a vast fortune parlaying his former secret service and Russian KBG connections into economic and political influence and who was assassinated in 2003? One of Simeon's first public appearances after he won the 2001 election was at the grandiose celebration for Pavlov's 40th birthday at his luxury Black Sea hotel. The two men were photographed together. This would be a bit like a US President being pictured with Al Capone.

But it was not just Pavlov. Simeon had other similar friends, former Comsomol and Party figures who had emerged in the early 90s with substantial fortunes the origins of which were never explained. Once he was back in Bulgaria and back in power, these were the people who Simeon chose to associate with, rather than the supporters who had worked so hard to make his return possible. Was this what he meant by "a new moral in politics"?

It was as if Simeon found a perverse pleasure in favouring anyone with connections to the old elite. The number of former Communist Party officials, *chenge,* and their children who had important roles in Simeon's administrations infuriated the right wing and many of his former supporters. The most striking example was his chief of staff, Radi Naidenov, whose grandfather of the same name had been Minister of Justice during the period of the Stalinist Peoples' Courts in the late 40s, and who signed the death warrant of Prince Kyril, Simeon's uncle and regent. Perhaps employing the descendent of the man who killed his uncle felt like sweet revenge. Was there another reason?

Simeon himself portrayed the decision to associate with figures from the former regime as a deliberate ploy to unite the country and to remain above mere partisan affiliations. But even this could not explain the most notorious episode, which took place in autumn 2003. Simeon nominated General Brigo Asparuhov, one of the most notorious former senior officers from the State Security, as controller of the secret services. This position would have given an ex-communist spy and probable ex-officer of the Russian KGB complete control over all intelligence and the supply of intelligence to the PM and government, including privileged access to NATO intelligence. Simeon rebuffed all criticism of the appointment and only backed down after the US ambassador warned him publicly that Asparuhov's appointment would harm Bulgaria's accession to NATO.

It is deeply ironic that Simeon, an icon of pre-communist Bulgaria, should have become one of the most conflictive figures in the post-communist period. But perhaps it is inevitable. One of the things I have come to learn about the country is that very little happens the way you expect it to. The Bulgarians themselves are always looking for ulterior motives and explanations for anything that happens. To start with I thought this was absurd and over-complicated. But in their world, it is rational. Because this is the way that things happen.

So I was not surprised to be told by the chairman of the commission that was briefly allowed access to the top secret State Security archives that the DS's dossier on Simeon ends abruptly in 1963 when he was just 26-years old. The communists had given him the codename "Parasite". They had monitored him all his life, and must have found out everything worth knowing about him over this time. That such information could exist on a person of such importance is a terrifying prospect. But what is even more terrifying is that Simeon's secrets are not where they should be. Perhaps they have been destroyed. That would not be a bad thing. Or else the files are deeper in the vaults. Or they might be in Moscow, or in the private safe of the officer who ran the investigation into him. Who knows? Amongst all the rumour and speculation and ignorance, we can but guess. Does someone out there possess the DS file on Simeon, the key to the identity of this enigmatic man?

1400hrs. 23-vii-1942

The fight is pitiless and cruel,
The fight, as they say, is epic.
I fell. My place is taken... that's it.
What does personality mean here?

A volley, and after the volley – worms.
So simple and so logical
But in the conflict we'll be together again,
My people, because we loved you.

Nikola Vapcarov
(Written two hours before his execution by firing squad)

Life and Death on Grafa

"**Y**OU CAN starve a Bulgarian but you can't kill him," Tanya had once told me. The living embodiment of this fact was Stefan Grunchev, the violinist who sometimes played outside the window of my new flat on Graf Ignatiev Street.

"Love. That is the most important thing," Stefan told me, eyes swivelling to follow the retreating figures of a couple of young girls. He put his violin under his chin and played a brief exuberant scrap of a song from Carmen.

It was one of those unexpectedly warm spring days in Sofia when work in doors was particularly difficult to endure. The lime trees that lined the boulevards and shaded the narrow streets had just come into leaf. Soon the fresh, too sweet scent of their flowers would fill every boulevard and insinuate itself along every street, into every little courtyard.

I was sitting with Stefan on a low concrete and wooden bench next to the tramlines. This was his regular pitch. I walked past it every day to enter the dark tunnel-like archway which led to a dingy courtyard and the front door of my block.

Sometimes I was rushing to a press conference or an interview. But other times, returning home with time on my hands I would sit down at the other end of the concrete bench and talk with Stefan. The heavy grinding trams gathered speed as they trundled past us down the gentle incline, clanking their bells furiously at pedestrians who dared to stray off the narrow broken pavement into their path.

Young girls in revealing clothing went window-shopping arm in arm. A female American friend of mine once asked me protestingly, "Do their mothers know their daughters are walking the streets dressed as prostitutes?"

But Stefan loved them. They were always close to his thoughts. He put down his violin and mused about love.

"As you know Mr Jack, I am more than 80-years old, but I still hope to find a companion for my life. That is the reason I play. I don't play for money or for glory. I play for human relations."

Even so, people gave him money, and he needed it. I myself brought him small gifts; packets of cigarettes and food. I also smuggled bank notes into his little money bag when he wasn't looking. If I offered them to him directly he refused to take them.

Everything about the old violinist was battered and worn through. His scruffy yellowish shoes were torn on their uppers so the corns on his misshapen toes and the grey holey socks poked through. He wore the same pair of stained and ragged yellowish trousers every day and the same battered suit jacket in summer and winter. The grey nose of his broken violin case, held together with elastic, protruded from a striped canvas shopping bag with twisted wire handles.

But in spite of his dirty tramp like clothes, he managed to retain his dignity. He was not quite a broken old man. Although his body was hunched and crippled, his face was still lively. His dark eyes were sunk deeply in their sockets and his nose was bony and hooked, an exaggeration of its former youthful shape. His features were surrounded by a fine growth of fulsome, snowy white beard. It was much thicker than the fine white baby hair, almost as soft as down, which sprouted thinly from his pink scalp.

"My beard creates a good impression, eh?" he would boast, with a justifiable note of pride in his voice.

Stefan held himself aloof from the drunks with whom he sometimes had to share the bench. He reproved them sharply if they attempted to butt in on our sometimes lengthy conversations, which he insisted on conducting in beautifully enunciated English, acquired thanks to superlative schooling during the 1930s. His accent, although clearly foreign, was almost impossible to correct. As we talked, his ears strained for my words and he spoke them back slightly modified to my own pronunciation.

"Mr Jack! I like to find as many ways as possible of saying the same thing, " he told me, resting his bow on his knees. The heat of the day had dissipated with a light evening breeze. I had brought him down some home-made English fruit cake, from a recent trip home. As we talked I broke off small pieces and pushed them into his mouth to prevent his fingers from getting sticky.

"Tell me please. What is the opposite of humble. Unhumble?"

"Possibly. Or proud."

"Prrrroud, prrrroud," he tried the word making it sound in his mouth as if it had taste. It wasn't quite right for him. He shook his head in dissatisfaction.

"No, no. Another word please."

Several other alternatives were tried and rejected.

"What about bold?"

"Bold. Bold. Yes, I think you have given me the word. Yes. Yes!"

He laughed and then in his perfectly modulated accent redolent of Oxford, the books of Evelyn Waugh and the Home Service he cried: "Be bold! Be bold! Mr Jack, you must be bold!"

To emphasise his rallying cry he raised his fiddle and struck up the main theme from *Peter and the Wolf*, a tune I had I once told him was one of my favourites.

"I have been practising it for you," he confessed. "I play it when I go to bed and when I get up in the morning."

His face relaxed in pleasure. The scope of his life had narrowed to this last faithful relationship between man and instrument.

Anyone who is able to grasp a violin cannot be utterly a beggar. Even more importantly, anyone, like him, who is continually rebelling against his own terrible condition, attracts respect. Stefan was a well-known figure on the street, known to natives of Sofia simply as *Grafa*. He attracted neighbourly concern from a broad acquaintance. Sometimes a doctor would stop by for quarter of an hour to exchange a few words of Farsi – another of the languages Stefan had mastered. Another friend liked to speak to him in German. I had also found him conversing in French.

Bulgarians like to speak foreign languages. It makes them feel cosmopolitan and European. Stefan may not have looked like much but his erudition added a little bit of style to Grafa's mixture of glitz and tack. Further down the street there were neat chrome-plated cafés where sulky slender waitresses in uniform tight miniskirts and platform heels dishedout fruit melbas and little cups of coffee. Well-lit vitrines displayed sports gear by O'Niell and suits by Bitsiani and Hugo Boss. Mercedes with tinted windows sped past the orange trams. But between the shops, in doorways and narrow alleys, informal traders hawked pirate CDs and cheap Turkish-made clothing. A legless beggar, collected tiny coins from passers-by.

On the other side of the street was the vegetable market, half-shaded by the trees of the garden square. At this time in early summer, each market stall was topped with a great mound of the wine-dark cherries from Kiustendil close to the Macedonian border. From where I sat with Stefan they look like heaps of glistening purple caviare.

On one of the side streets by the market, grannies from the villages laid out little piles of home-produced vegetables, cheese and pickles on up turned soap boxes. They crowded under the lindens and called after passers-by in cracked, high voices:

"Hey, laddie, natural sheep's yoghurt only two levs. Cheese if you please, miss! A bit of salad for you hey?"

Beyond the trees in the garden was the domed church of Sveti Sedmochislenitsi – the seven Slavic apostles – one of the city's main orthodox Christian places of worship. It used to be a mosque and had been built by one of the greatest mosque builders of the Ottoman court. Beyond it was the unadorned grey facade of the Interior Ministry where dissidents had been imprisoned and tortured in both Tsarist and Communist times.

I liked to sit with Stefan on Grafa because it was here that the digital rapidity of the changes that had swept Bulgaria since the end of Communism were most obvious. The beneficiaries and the victims of those changes jostled side by side.

There were children playing football in the schoolyard opposite. On the back wall in the middle of a mess of graffiti I could read the foot-high message in English: "Fuck You Teachers!"

When they got older, would these youngsters' sole ambition be to emigrate, as it is for most Bulgarian youth today? Their yells mingled with the noise of the street, the trams and clack of people's shoes, and in the distance the wheeze of an accordion grinding out its unvaried familiar tune.

The ambling stocky shape of Bai Angel, the gypsy, in his old red baseball cap approached from the direction of the book kiosks in Slaveikov Square. The huge bulk of Gosho the brown bear, half his height again at full stretch was tethered to him by stout chains and a metal rod which had been fixed into the bear's nose. Bai Angel pummeled out the same wheezy tune on his red squash box over and over again. The bear moved with him in a shambling dance.

Both the bear and Bai Angel had better futures ahead of them. An Austrian charity had offered to buy Gosho for 10,000 Euro and to put him in a special reserve. You can't get into the European Union and still have gypsies leading bears through the streets on chains.

Stefan rested from his music and flexed his fingers. They were twisted with arthritis so he could hardly play. Both the effort, and the failure to play as he ought, hurt him. But it was still his greatest pleasure. As he twirled his wrist to bring his instrument up and under his chin again there was still an air of performance about him and the glint of a challenge as his eyes momentarily glanced up to heaven. For a split second his terrible stoop was forgotten.

He played me scenes from Mussorgski's *Pictures from an Exhibition*. The musical images seemed to comfort him. As he moved on from picture to picture he described them to me: the staccato notes of the prancing gnome, the heavy dark chords of the lumbering ox cart. But the strings on his violin weren't quite true. Also the hairs on his bow were frayed.

"The semi-tones are falsh" he lamented, slipping into anxious German in his distress. He pressed his wizened fingertips to the strings in a vain attempt to squeeze out a better sound.

"I curse the evil emperor who has brought me to this." He shook his bow at me in frustration.

"I used to be a maximalist, but now I am forced to be a minimalist."

With this he struck up another snatch of a song but after a few phrases trailed the melody off into an improvised ending to make up for his failing memory and fingers.

While Stefan was eking out the end of his life on his low bench, Bulgaria had actually completed the Social Affairs Chapter of the European Union's *acquis communautaire*. What did this mean I asked myself? There was virtually no social care in Bulgaria. Stefan received a supplementary pension from a German charity. Even so, if it were not for his neighbours, he would have perished. For the worst off in Bulgarian society, democracy had brought nothing but misery.

Stefan dealt with the problems of Bulgarian life by being a fantasist. He had many dreams. One was that we would make a fishing trip later in the summer.

"Mr Jack have you lately caught any troot?" he enquired one day when I had not seen him for a while. "I beg your pardon, I mean trowut." For some reason he always had trouble with this word. His idea was to take some wine and a picnic and a couple of girls and head up into the central Balkan Range, back to the mountain streams where he had fished for trout himself during the summer vacation. Inevitably he had to express this idea musically with flashes of Schubert's *Trout Quintet.*

"Can you hear the trowut swimming, Mr Jack?"

We kept this fiction going for weeks until the next idea came along

"How much is the cost of an aeroplane ticket to England? I would like to go with you next time you return home. I will play my violin to your father's cows."

"It will cost you at least $250," I told him regretfully.

"I can get the money."

The next suggestion was a simpler one. He invited me to dinner. I promised to come, smuggled a packet of cake into the old shopping bag and left him in the care of a pair of young girls. One had stopped to take pictures of him for a college photographic project. Later from my balcony as dusk fell I watched the two girls assisting his hobbling bent-double figure slowly down the street to the tram stop.

The invitation to dinner was the nearest we ever got to fulfilling one of his fantasies. I didn't realise how far-fetched it was until in early spring, arriving back the city after an absence of some months, I found a letter from him.

"Mr Jack," it read. "I am sick and cannot leave my apartment. Please visit me if you can."

I went to the address on the letter. It was a long way from the city centre. His door was five floors up in a block on the far edge of the Nadezhda (hope) quarter of Sofia. Never was a district more ineptly named. It is a forest of crowded, poorly built tenement blocks separated by patches of wasteland a good hour's journey by rattling tram into the city centre.

"Our only hope is to live somewhere else," was the feeble joke of desperate residents.

"KNOCK VERY LOUDLY."

The notice, whose thick letters had been laboriously scribbled in biro on a sheet of plain paper, was glued to the scuffed flimsy pale grey door.

I knocked loudly. There was no sound. I bashed at the door again as hard as I could, hurting my knuckles.

"Who is it? Who is knocking?" His voice was reedy, querulous, faint.

"Jack! It's Jack!" I yell.

A scraping sound.

"Who? Who are you?"

"Jack!"

This time I cupped my hands against the door and yell through them.

The scraping continued but louder. A key fumbled in the lock. Finally the door opened a crack. Stefan stared confusedly at me. We were almost at eye level as I had squatted down while I was shouting through the door and Stefan sat on a plastic upturned bucket. He didn't recognise me. I stood up and in my normal voice said:

"It's Jack."

"Ooohh! Mr Jack, Mr Jack! It is you. Why were you sitting down there. I thought you were a child. Come in. Come in Mr Jack Hamilton."

He reached out both hands to mine and pulled me in.

"If there is a God I thank him for answering my prayers!"

He held on to me hard as if to make sure that it is really me.

"But why are you wasting your time with me?"

He reached behind to an old wooden stool that looked like it had been nailed together from packing crates. With his other gnarled hand he grasped a knotted length of electric flex tied to the rim of his bucket where the handle used to be. Slowly, like a crab he dragged himself back across the bare concrete floor into the single room which was now his prison as much as his home.

You see how I have to live," he gestured and his high voice descended to a fretful mumble. The furniture was almost all broken. A tiny table was crammed with jars, bottled and the debris of elementary meals – crusts of stale bread, empty yoghurt pots. There were two broken beds piled with unwashed bedding, an old office chair with no back. Sheet music tumbled from a fallen-in book case. Worn out clothes were scattered everywhere, over the bed, chair and concrete floor. The only piece of cooking apparatus was a single ring electric hotplate on the floor by the door. The place smelt of sour dust, rotting food and unwashed linen.

It took five minutes for Stefan to inch back across the floor to the dirty bed, where he collapsed.

"Can you not bring back from England some painless way of letting me die," he begged. "They say here that that they cannot do this for me."

I couldn't. Instead I gave him some packs of extra strong Victory cigarettes. Unlike in George Orwell's 1984, the Victory brand in Bulgaria is a mark of good quality. Victory means luxury. From the empty packets scrunched on his table I could tell that Stefan had been making do with Arda, the cheapest brand of all, normally favoured by tramps and gypsies. The Victories were the best I could do.

He struck a match with a shaking hand and drew deeply. At once his face seemed to relax. Apart from the violin, this was one of the few things that brought an expression of physical pleasure to his face.

Stefan wore a loose woollen tank top and a very torn old tracksuit bottoms that did not do up. It was virtually impossible for him to appear decent. Whichever way he pulled his clothing he exposed another part of his anatomy. After a vain struggle to cover himself properly, he apologised.

"You must excuse my situation, but such are my possibilities."

Amongst the piles of sheet music which tumbled out of the broken bookshelf there were some photograph albums with pictures from the world-wide tours of the Sofia Philharmonic Orchestra. Stefan pointed himself out in London, Germany, Tehran. The man in the photographs was clean-shaven and plump, even sleek. His suits were well-filled, his brilliantined hair combed back in rippled waves. From these formal black and white prints I could just guess at the world and life that the stooped old man once lived in.

But he preferred to dream about the future rather than dwelling on the past. Trapped by his failing health, the fantasies had become more modest: to go down for one afternoon to play his violin on Grafa. But even this simple desire was beyond him. Even if he could get there, his fingers only just obeyed him enough to perform simple snatches of tunes. And then he could hardly hear what he was playing. His biggest fantasy was just to die.

"I have thought about taking my own life. But I cannot see how. My mental health will not allow me to commit suicide," he said.

His neighbour, Maria, who brought him food and medicine, had told me that he must care about his life very much because he held onto it so stubbornly.

"Tell her its isn't true," he begged. "I don't care about life. I want to die. Tell her that I want to die."

He seized my hand and squeezed it. It was impossible to tell him he was wrong. What could be better than death for him in his situation? There was no answer. But while I struggled to find some words of comfort, I was interrupted by an exclamation of surprise.

"You have such long fingers. Why did I never see them before? Oooh! Mr Jack. With fingers like yours I could have been the second Paganini! Measure here against mine. Och! Och! Now stretch your fingers like so. Yes, yes. First finger and third. Now second and fourth, bend and straighten."

In a trice his depression had vanished.

"Mr Jack, I have an idea. Are you prepared to try it? Pull my violin case from under the bed!"

I did as he said and slipped off the elastic which held it shut. We sat knee to knee, he on the edge of his frowsy bed and I on the office chair with his violin under my chin. Then one by one he took me through the finger positions on each string and their relations to each other. Obediently I followed his instructions as he patiently explained to me the essentials of playing the violin.

"You are getting tired? Eh? That's good. You must work hard."

It was a totally crazy plan, but also poetic. Somehow, indirectly through me, something of his talent and his memory could be preserved. He wanted to teach me the basics of playing the violin. Not in any hope that I might play – for me it was far too late – but that I might eventually be able to pass on his love and enthusiasm for the instrument to my niece, whose birth was expected in a fortnight.

"I am a good teacher. We don't have much time but I will show you what I know." He paused. This mention of time had thrown him back into melancholy.

"Ohh Jack. *Ars longa, vita brevis est,*" he wailed, eyes filling with tears. "This violin, this violin I bought it from the workshop on Hristo Botev street. I have played it for fifty years. It has a quotation inscribed on it. 'In the wood I was dumb, after they cut me I began to sing'. As he told me this he began to shake with grief.

"It is the opposite for humans," he sobbed. "After we die, we are silent."

Deep into the mountains

Vzemi ogun, zapali me

The whole world I have been round,
A girl like you I never found
Take a fire, Burn me up, turn me into ash
So I cannot look upon you any more.

Folk song

Who Can Stay?

THE GERMAN owner of the graphic design company where Yana worked had been using Bulgarian artists as cheap skilled labour for commissions back home. It seemed like a good idea. But the jobs hadn't come in or some bits of work had been rejected.

So for the past three months, Yana had been working like a bonded slave. Her boss had paid her for work which clients had then rejected. So he said that the payments were advances on her wages, which she was having to pay off.

There was nothing that anyone could do, she told me. None of the other design studios in Sofia were taking people on. One of her colleagues has gone to Hungary to work in an animation studio there. If things didn't get better, she would have to leave too.

My own career was also going through turmoil at this time. The proprietor of *The Sofia Independent* had turned all our lives upside down when he closed the newspaper down quite suddenly one Friday afternoon. He did so without warning and with immediate effect.

We had gathered for our regular editorial meeting, ready to plan the next week's issue. It took a few moments for thoughts of story proposals to evaporate. I mentally scrapped the piece I had been planning on the unknown Israeli company with no previous experience of aviation, that had bought the national airline, Balkan, for $150,000. The company had debts of $100 million.

Instead I found myself automatically composing a story in my mind. A headline: "EX-PAT WEEKLY FOLDS", then a strap-line below it "Staff laid off without warning". The lead continued the theme of personal drama:

The proprietor of the capital's largest English language newspaper admitted defeat last week in his struggle to..."

I got no further. What was the point?

"I will find jobs for you all in my other businesses," he promised. For some of the Bulgarian staff this was a welcome offer. Not for me, nor for Matei, who was going back to the US for a year. I didn't need the Independent any longer. Although, everyone still thought I was the correspondent for the *Financial Times*, and even told me that they read my my stories there, I had become a stringer for *The Wall Street Journal Europe*, the *FT*'s chief rival.

In its Brussels HQ I had found a group of journalists and editors were genuinely enthusiastic about this new frontier of Europe. Perhaps this was natural. The transformation of the east was the story that had brought many of them over from the US ten years earlier. They were not jaded by the chaos and problems which democracy had created. Instead they were excited about it.

"Bulgaria! What's going on there?" This was the enthusiastic response I got from Paul Hofheinz editor of the *Central Europe Economic Review*, a monthly supplement published by the newspaper. My excitement at getting stories published there was not just the pleasure of seeing my name in print in a serious publication. It was confirmation of what I had felt but until then had not been able to demonstrate even to myself. I was experiencing a great story. In my wildest dreams I had not imagined spending more than a couple years in Bulgaria, but now I could hardly imagine leaving.

Meanwhile, Yana's problems got worse. Her whole office was closed down. Worse still, she was in danger of losing half her artistic production. Her boss had taken a collection of her pictures hostage. It had been in the office because they were planning to arrange an exhibition. He had claimed about 20 pictures as final payment for the "advances" which Yana had not been able to repay.

She was already adjusting to the loss.

"I don't care about them. I'll paint some more. If he wants to take them let him have them. I'm glad he likes them."

I had moved into a big flat in the centre of the city. It was a spacious eerie in one of the stained, old-fashioned buildings that line Graf Ignatiev Street, which everyone called *Grafa*. It had no furniture, draughty windows and was indescribably dirty.

This meant I had rejected an idea that Yana had been trying to persuade me about.

"Why don't you move in with me? That will solve my rent problem for a start. If I do end up going to Prague for a bit, you can keep it for me," she had suggested.

"I don't think that's a great idea."

"Why do you want to live there, so dirty and noisy?"

"To feel engaged to things."

"You are just scared to live with me. You are so English!" she pouted, making it sound like an insult.

The subject hung between us like a grey cloud trapped in a valley, obscuring everything else. Yana couldn't find another job. I was working harder than ever. She was planning to find some work abroad. She wanted to leave and yet she didn't. We sat on her balcony, staring out through the security grill and argued with me.

. "I like foreigners less and less. Coming here and thinking that all they have to do is take from us."

"Not all foreigners are like that. I'm not."

"No, but it's all a bit of fun for you. The great adventure you are always going on about. Do you ever think that it isn't much fun to be living in an adventure?"

"I'm trying to make a living here too."

"Yes, writing about privatisations Mister Ten Percent."

Mr Ten Percent was the nick-name of the Minister of Industry. This was the cut he was rumoured to take on every state-owned property that was sold to a private investor.

It was like an unscratchable itch between us. My perspective on her country was moving further away from her's. The more I discovered, the more fascinated I became. She was growing more and more cynical.

The crisis arrived along with her mother who came down by train from the Danube town of Rousse. Yana went to collect her from the station, dragging me along unwillingly. Her mother was a solid flinty dame, short hair dyed yellow, nearing pensionable age with 30 years as an employee of the Bulgarian State Railway in her labour docket. She looked like she could lay a big man out cold with a blow from her very stout arm. Or a glance.

She looked me up and down with a look that weighed me to an ounce, like a parcel in the despatch depot where she worked.

She said nothing. We trundled back towards Yana's on the tram in strained silence. Her words of fury only broke when we were back through the door and a bare kitchen revealed that her daughter had forgotten to get in any food.

"Not even bread!" she stormed. Her dismay was real and deep. A house without bread is no house at all. It is no welcome. My bad influence was to blame. Yana went out to the shop miserably leaving her mother and me together in awkward silence.

I waited for her to try and drive me away from her daughter. But as soon as the door shuts she confronted me.

"My daughter needs you to move in with her," she growled through clenched teeth and without preliminary. I made an evasive answer.

"You are the man. The suggestion must come from you. I am relying on you for my daughter now."

The more she insisted the more reserved, evasive and "English" I became. I thought back to a conversation I had with a friend about Bulgarian attitudes to marriage. Bulgarians are still very traditional in regard to relationships she had told me. Particularly the way they look at women. If you get to a certain (quite young age) and you haven't got a man, then you are on the shelf. Then again divorce is pretty common too. It is as if once they are married they don't always take it very seriously. So the border between messing around and getting serious is a fluid one she had warned me.

Well it looked like I had just stepped over that border.

The evening ended frostily. Yana came out with me to the front door of her block. She was miserable.

"My mother thinks that you should be my ticket out of Bulgaria. To her, you just represent a European Union passport. I don't want that either. But I think I have to leave. I have found a company in Prague, which says it will give me a job. After this evening I have decided to take it."

So the future, like that for almost every ambitious young person in Bulgaria, had boiled down to a single question. Emigration?

It was a typical Bulgarian irony that it is she who went and I who stayed.

Over the following week I helped her pack up her flat. Everything was done with deliberation rather than excitement.

"It has been humiliating to feel that I needed you more than you needed me," she told me, as the last box is packed and ready to be collected. The observation was painful because it is not primarily an about rent, or money, or the possibility of working in a western European country. She was talking about a crucial inequality in the way that we loved each other. I didn't need her enough – an accident of love perhaps. But not entirely.

Yana was right about me in one other respect too. We were moving on different tracks. I was motivated by the quest for adventure, she by necessity. How small and frivolous that mades me feel. It was as if after trying to dig so deep into this country and to understand it, I had missed out on a vast aspect of life; something that ought to have been immediate and absolutely obvious to me. I only sensed it then because of its absence.

I helped Yana manhandle her large rucksack and bag down to the patch of bare ground behind the Novotel Evropa at the far end of Maria Louisa Boulevard, where hundreds of buses supplied the main link between Bulgaria and the rest of the world. Some individual operations sold tickets from the door, others had little booths plastered with the names of destinations: Paris, Frankfurt, Dusseldorf, Dresden, Madrid, Roma, London, Istanbul, Tirana, Belgrade and so on. There were buses to every corner of Europe. It was one of the great exit points from the country, probably more important even than Sofia airport. According to one estimate three-quarters of a million people or just under one-tenth of the population had emigrated in the past decade.

"It is not so bad," said Yana, meaning just the opposite.

"Out of my 20 classmates from the academy only three of us are still here. Now it will just be two." She smiled bitterly. "Of course, I'll come back."

Once again, I could not tell whether I should believe her. She reached up and kissed me tenderly on the cheek. Not like a lover.

"That's better. I don't think I love you any more. Perhaps I am even learning to hate you a bit for what you have done to me. Anyway, I don't think I shall ever see you again."

I pushed her bags into the hold under the coach and she climbed the steps. As she turned to say goodbye again the hydraulic door hissed shut behind her.

To marry young is early.
To marry old is late

Bulgarian proverb

Milk from the Matchmaker

SOUNDS of the Sofia night: the snap of stray dogs quarrelling in the square, the hacking cough of Angel, the widower who lives one floor down, the blare of car alarms, the cries and clangs of of the garbage disposal men clearing the debris of the market from the street below at two in the morning.

Even in sleep the city impressed itself on me. The dull roar rumble and metallic clank of the old heavy trams shook the bare floorboards under my thin mattress. The sound, transmitted and dulled by its passage through earth, foundations, walls, wood and cloth sound rumbled in my inner ear like a train rattling over points. The entire block shivered and a few more flakes of cement fell from the balcony's crumbling stucco.

Morning: The steel apartment door clanged: a faint thud and clink of glass, muttering, heavy breathing, shuffling feet.

Zlatka. It must be Zlatka, the landlady of my new apartment.

Her appearances were rare and unpredictable and normally related to requests for money or some minor intrigue she hoped to hide from Margarita, her crazy (certifiably crazy) daughter. By some sixth sense (perhaps the very one that she never tired of telling me about) she had divined my return to the city after a period of travel. Maybe she wanted to borrow money again.

I found her in the kitchen breathing heavily and tottering slightly. She was stout, sunburnt, grubby, moustachioed and never changing. Hardened by work, it was impossible to tell her age. Her younger daughter was barely 20 but she could have been anything from 50 to 70. Even her clothes were the same every time I saw her: the same flowery headscarf, broad skirt and seemingly endless layers of grubby sweaters and cardigans, in spite of the summer heat.

Somehow she had managed to tote a large cardboard box filled with jam jars up to the fourth floor. It sat in the middle of my kitchen with the ominous air of a new fixture. Wordlessly, and breathlessly she indicated a two-litre plastic Fanta bottle standing on the low kitchen table amongst the mess of rakia bottles and salads from the night before. It was filled with a creamy yellow liquid. A milk delivery.

"Give me a glass of water," she gasped.

We sat at the old table in the sitting room. She gulped the water.

"Boil the milk" she reminded me. "It is from my own goats, health-giving and fresh. Just like the milk you drank from your mother. Boil it before you drink it."

She smiled revealing copious glints of gold amid yellow teeth.

"That's very kind of you, Zlatka, but tell me, what are the jam jars for?"

"They won't get in your way." It was a statement of fact rather than a question.

"Just a little business I have to look after. You know my daughter..."

A furtive look crept into her expression and she glanced at me conspiratorially as if we shared some private joke too dubious even to laugh about openly.

"You're a good lad. We understand each other don't we?"

I was fairly sure we didn't. But I nodded anyway. I often speculated about the life of my peculiar landlady. She moaned perpetually about poverty.

"Life is very expensive, medecines, bills, taxes, repairs."

But she must surely have been extremely rich. Her entrepreurial philosophy was based on a twin track of hard work and *kelepir*, originally a Turkish word meaning approximately *"something for nothing"*. Nothing was too shameless for her. On rent days she would try to touch me for loans. I gave in once and found the money impossible to get back.

Enthusiastic as she was about money she was dismayed by capitalism and looked back on the old regime with nostalgia. It was not an ideological view point but simple regret for a comfortable system that she had milked better than most. She had, after all, acquired three city apartments at a time when there were long waiting lists for people even to get one. She also owned a good tract of farmland near Varna.

I paid my quite large rent in advance with a sheaf of $100 bills. These she stuffed inside the folds of her many cardigans, where somehow they stuck. Was this where she kept all her money, wrapped in her clothes? Or did it perhaps just flutter out again without her noticing as she stumped down the street to the tram stop, her stout arms full of the empty plastic bottles which I had put aside for her. I doubted it.

Plastic bottles and jars. She was obsessed with them, collected them from wherever she could find them and filled them with milk or yogurt. Matei had seen her rummaging for bottles in the garbage dumpsters by the market alongside the tramps, beggars, gypsies and street children. Now for some inscrutable reason she was hiding her empty jars from her daughter. There could be no explanation.

But Zlatka's life was full of secrets. As far as rent and bills were concerned she tried to ensure there was no verifiable history. She was anxious to have as few official documents as possible which might force her to pay taxes, so things like receipts were anathema. All our money transactions became hopelessly embroiled in the blizzard of water, heating and electricity bills which she insisted that I paid through her, instead of directly.

The biggest conspiracy in Zlatka's life was her daughter.

"She hasn't been round again has she?"

No name was necessary, when Zlatka asked this question during one of her unannounced visits. She was asking about her elder daughter. The crazy one. Margarita. I had only ever told her about one visit, the first. After that I kept quiet about them. So I had my own secrets from Zlatka too.

One morning, I had found a little note squeezed into the crack of the door. The slip of paper, torn from a diary note book enclosed a passport photograph of a woman with glassy heavily kholed eyes, sucked-in cheeks, and no smile.

In thick pencil the message read: "For Jack". And on the back of the photograph: "With Love. Margarita".

I didn't mention it to Zlatka because she was always threatening to send her daughter back to the "Fourth Kilometre", the asylum on the edge of the city on the main road towards Turkey. Tiresome as Margarita was, I did not wish that on her.

I had met Margarita the first time I went to pay the rent. She had offered me in quick succession cigarettes and *boza,* a repellent drink the consistency and colour of thick chocolate milk, manufactured from sour fermented malt. (It tastes of armpits. The only people who can stomach it are those whose mothers have fed it to them since their earliest years).

She poured me a full glass of it from one of her mother's plastic bottles. It slopped over the table. I pushed away the glass and proffered cigarette as politely as I could.

"Why do you not smoke," she drawled. "It is sooo good. It is good for you. It is better than sex even."

This brief encounter was the start of trouble. Margarita began trying to evict me. She would appear in the early morning outside my door like a witch in a cloud of smoke, fag tightly clasped between wild, gesturing fingers. There was something spazmodic and exaggerated about her, augmented by the aura of stale tobacco and cheap scent.

"I am not crrrazy," she would tell me in heavily accented English.

"She has a yellow card. Do you know what that means?" Zlatka asked me.

It is the special identity card issued to the mentally ill. "Her exhusband hit her on the head."

I had threatened to leave, but on that subject Zlatka was implacable. I had paid several months rent in advance. So I had to stay.

Occasionally, guiltily, I would pretend that I was not at home. Sometimes, I would leave my flat to find the entire stairwell thick with cigarette smoke. I wondered if she had been there, staking me out, loitering silently in the early dawn? Or did the nervous fingers that had flung the unextinguished fag butts over the sooty ash streaked floor belong to the anxious clients who sometimes waited on the landing for the lawyer's office to open next door.

But why wait so early? And who was stealing my post? I was getting as paranoid as Zlatka herself.

Or maybe not quite that paranoid. After all, she had gone into hiding from her daughter in the flat of her friend whose daughter was the lawyer who was attempting to get Margarita committed to the lunatic asylum.

At rent paying time I had to hunt her out there. It was less seedy than Zlatka's own home but even so there was a solid frowst. It smelt like windows had not been opened for many months.

"We have all be sick for the past ten days. Flu," said Zlatka.

She had been looking after an invalid, also resident there, who tottered briefly out into the corridor in her nightie, looked around and retired again.

Zlatka offered me a slice of cake and a glass of thick yellowish goat's milk at the table cluttered with jars and dishes. She sat on her unmade bed amidst disordered piles of clothing and questioned my about my love life. Now that Yana was no longer around she hoped to get me fixed up again. At the top of the list was her younger daughter. Every time I saw her she wanted to check that I hadn't got into a new relationship.

"*Ah taka!* That's the stuff! Don't rush into anything, you've plenty of time. Zlatka will see you right!" The calculating match-making glint illumined in her eye.

"My other daughter isn't mad you know," she reminded me. She gave me flattering reports of her university career in agronomy and the responsible position she had achieved in a firm which manufactured aluminium cooking pots.

"They are very good value. Just 100 levs for this roasting dish."

Like a conjuror she pulled one out from under the table.

"Just 100 levs. May be your mother would like one?"

I declined as gracefully as I could.

She also had a niece, she told me, a lovely trainee police psychologist from a village on the slopes of Mount Vitosha. Apparently she would do very well for me. I wondered if she would collect a commission on a successful deal.

As I left, the hall was filling with acrid smoke from the kitchen. I guessed the milk had over boiled. The smoke was thick and black. It must have been burning for a while, but Zlatka barely noticed.

"A bulb must have gone," she muttered in the gloom. More greasy black clouds billowed out.

"Now don't worry. You just have to be patient. You won't lose out I promise," she reassured me. I turned to walk down the stairs and she watched me from the door way enveloped in a bitter haze of charred milk.

"We've understood each other haven't we. After all we could be relatives one day."

Hubava si moe goro

My forest, you are beautiful
You smell of youth.
But always in our hearts
Sorrow and ruth.

Whoever once has seen you,
He ever grieves
That he cannot lie for always
Beneath your leaves.

Lyuben Karavelov

Gypsy Love

I ESCAPED I escaped into the vast forests of the Rhodope mountains. I hitch-hiked my way southwards slowly through their rain-drenched heart, on my way to the almost mythical village of Kovachevitsa where Johnny and Tanya (whose apartment in Sofia I had just left for one of my own) had a house. Tanya had given me the key to it, or rather the keys, a whole bunch of them inside a plastic bag and a long list of instructions about the dozen locks that I would have to unlock before I could get inside.

The key bag was in my rucksack and I was waiting for a lift in the one-horse village of Shiroka Poljana. It was a genuine one-horse village. I was watching the horse in question, its front legs roughly hobbled together, as it grazed on the other side of the road where a fresh meadow of grass and flowers leads to a mountain lake.

Because of the rain, the mushrooms had come up and the hills round about were filled with mushroom hunters. They had been coming into the hamlet all day. Judging from their dark looks and shabby clothes most of them were gypsies. Several traders had set up stalls along the side of the road. The place had begun to look a little like a wild west gold rush town, only it wasn't gold dust but fungus being weighed in the scales. In the little shack behind me a young girl was serving kebabs and little bottles of *mastika* to the entirely male clientele.

Living in the mountains is not easy. A man in the bar had told me about the *"gorski"* mountain people. They have a reputation for independence and toughness. One year *mutri* from Sofia had arrived in a fleet of four jeeps and announced that they were taking over the mushroom trade. In future no one would be allowed to sell mush-

rooms except to them, they said. The locals had responded by blocking the road with trees. They had smashed up the jeeps and set fire
to them.

Hitchhiking on those mountain roads means a lot of time hang-
ing around on deserted hillsides, sometimes getting rained on, sometimes not. Most traffic through the mountains is just from one village to the next, or from the high forest and pastures back down to
the village. As they drove by, drivers of the ubiquitous Russian-made
cars made downward jabbing motions with their index fingers and
shrugged their shoulders. It was a way of saying they were local, that
they couldn't take me anywhere that I'd want to go.

There was no back seat to the Moskvitch belonging to a trio of
Romany mushroom gatherers that juddered to a halt on the rain-
slicked road.

Three moustachioed men jumped out. They had seen the camera
slung round my neck and wanted to have their photos taken. Their
clothes were thin and sun-bleached. One of them opened the boot
and showed me plastic bags full of the spongy greeny-orange fungi.
Cepes to the French, *porcini* to the Italians, these boletus mushrooms
would fetch good prices in the delicatessens of Milan and Paris. The
trio had spent all morning collecting them and planned to sell them
to traders who would pack them into refrigerated lorries. They would
be across the border by this evening.

I took their pictures and got into the car. There was no back seat,
so I crouched in extreme discomfort on the dirty metal floor and held
on to what I could with my rucksack on my lap. My leg was totally
dead after five minutes.

The car looked personally acquainted with every pot-hole and
rock on the road. At the crest of every hill the driver switched off
the ignition to save on petrol. We free-wheeled down the other side,
barely in control. In some places we passed muddy roads twisting up
through steep valleys, whose sides had been stripped of trees. The
mess of uprooted stumps, logs and branched lay every way across the
bare hillsides. Felled trunks had scored dark earth channels down
from the high ridges to lie in immobile wooden cascades on the edge
of the road. But mostly the forest was uncut. As we crossed each
pass into the next valley, we gazed out across the evergreen sea with
huge waves of dark pine stretching into the distance in every direction.

The driver was a born-again Christian. He turned frequently to ask me about God, and each time he did this I mentally put my trust in Him, as the car hurtled round another corner on the wrong side of the road.

"Are you Christian?"

I told him I was. It seemed to please him.

"What is the first commandment? And the second?"

I struggled for a while with the translation of "graven image". Watching me flounder he began to embark on a sermon, gesticulating with his free hand.

"There is nothing more important than the Ten Commandments..."

But his two companions shouted him down.

"No, no! Shut up you! We aren't interested in that stuff! Tell us about American girls. Are they are as beautiful and as liberal as they seem on TV?"

There was no point in explaining that I wasn't American.

"*Frenski Lubov*? Do they give French love?" asked the man squashed in the back of the car next to me. He sniggered and made an obscene gesture.

I blushed.

"You are American. Do you have a Bulgarian girl? Why would you want Bulgarian when you could have American?"

"Do me a favour," interrupted the man in the front seat. "Next time you come from America bring me over a nice 16 or 17-year-old with green eyes and long hair. S he must be a virgin, mind. But from a poor family. A rich American girl would never want to get married to a gypsy and live in these mountains would she?"

"Probably not."

"You don't have to tell her it's for marriage. Tell her that you're bringing her on holiday."

In spite of its absurdity, it was an enlightening conversation. The way the Roma in Bulgaria live couldn't be further from the western world. Even life in Sofia seems a million miles away from their existence. Yet somehow, probably through TV, they had acquired two extreme contradictions from the west: a comically erroneous impression of American girls and belief in evangelical Christianity.

I saw how far away my new friends' lives were from the luxurious West that they so happily imagined, when we arrived at their village, if it could be described that way. It was a gypsy ghetto, half logging camp, half slum on the edge of nowhere, nothing more than a bunch of shacks made from scrap. There was not a single dwelling which one could call a proper house. Half a dozen roughly hobbled horses grazed along the verge. Mangy dogs stalked through the trees where several old cars and some carts with rubber wheels and tarpaulin covers wee ranged about.

Multicoloured lines of clothes, like flags of all nations, fluttered gaily from strings that decorated the front of every dwelling. In Bulgaria, Roma are considered to be filthy people, but I had never passed by one of their communities without seeing long lines of clothing, flapping in the breeze. Keeping clean in those conditions however, must have been an endless losing battle.

The smoke from cooking fires tended by squat babas mingled with the rain. Inquisitive young faces sprouted from the opening of shelters improvised polythene, tin, bits of wood and brick. Grubby children ran everywhere. They stared at me, smiled and shouted. A group of them freewheeled down the hill, three to each brakeless rusty bicycle. They clustered round me begging for money and to have their pictures taken. Shaking myself free I waved a good bye to the Christian and his sex-obsessed friends and strode out of the hamlet.

"Remember! A nice American girl!" one of them shouted.

"I won't forget," I promised.

The next place on the road was Gorno Drianovo, a bustling village ten kilometres up the mountain. A local man returning from the nearest town dropped me in the centre of the village. Houses crowded on the winding central road from above and below. All the village life was concentrated on this narrow strip. Cows and goats returning from the pastures meandered back to their stables, men unloaded thick logs from a heavy Russian truck in to a wood store. The road was littered with sawdust and cow pats. Beautiful, unusually pale and blond little children ran everywhere.

There was an old whitewashed mosque on the edge of the tiny village square. Its stubby minaret was crowned with a cone of dull grey galvanised metal. This was a village of Pomaks – the name given to ethnically Bulgarian Muslims. A long line of old and middle-aged men in thick coats and woollen caps sat on a low bench by the mosque wall. They watched me curiously and returned my greetings politely.

"You have a nice village. There are so many children," I told them. It was true. Compared to the deadness of most Christian villages, this one was full of life.

"Nothing to do here but..." said a man wearing a pompom hat, with an obscene gesture and a wink. His fellows chuckled.

"How far to Kovachevitsa?"

"Six kilometres," said pompom hat, gesturing open handedly up the slope.

"Who will you stay with there?"

"The Pojarlievis."

"Who?" They conferred amongst themselves.

"Ah, you mean Bai Ivan, the professor?"

Everyone knows everyone else in these mountains and the Pojarlievis had been coming here for decades.

"You will have to walk from here," they said, pointing which way I had to go.

As I walked away from the village night was falling. But it was a clear night and my way was illuminated on either side by the winking of thousands and thousands of fireflies. By chance I had stumbled across their summer mating spectacular.

The Pojarlievis owned the second house in the village. They had come to this village in the early seventies to escape from socialism. A playwright friend of theirs had stumbled across this forgotten place high in the mountains during the early seventies while looking for a location to shoot one of his films. It had been abandoned by all but a handful of its inhabitants because of its inaccessibility. There was no work there and no way of getting to it apart from a mud road which sometimes slid down the hill after big floods. No one wanted to live in such a godforsaken backwater. No one, that is, except Sofia intellectuals in search of a place so remote that it had been passed over by the dead hand of the regime.

"It is one of the most beautiful places in the country," Tanya had told me.

The next morning revealed why Kovachevica was so special.

Tanya's house was small and simple, a stone cottage with a yard. Many of the other places in the village were much grander. Some were huge, bigger by far than many town houses in wealthier areas of the country. But they were crammed together, fitted like jigsaw pieces along winding stone streets. They were heavily built, full of architectural gems and quirks, rising three, four or even five storeys, the upper floors overhanging the lower ones. Huge balconies – *chardaks* - both jutted out beyond the walls and also stretched back into the depths, sometimes taking up virtually an entire storey. Staircases branched out of the centre of these great chardaks or zigzaged up the front of them. Hearth stones, insulated by half-domes of clay and buttressed by curved beams stuck out from the upper walls like clay goiters - this way fires could burn safely outside the main wooden structure of the houses. They was even an elementary form of indoor plumbing. Upstairs privies were connected to an elementary sewer under the central cobbles of the street via stone flues, built inside the high exterior walls.

I walked to the top of the village. From here I could see the slant- ing grey-green roofs, made from stone slabs that overlapped like fish scales. From a distance it looked like the stones and slates had been worn down by time to blend with the rocks and earth. Half the houses were deserted. Brambles had pulled down the heavy roofs and overrun the walled courtyards. Others, many of them carefully restored, were locked with heavy padlocks. The owners lived in Sofia or Blagoevgrad, the regional capital.

The valley fell sharply away below the houses. From the rotting balcony of one of the last and tallest unrestored houses at the top of the village, I could see the line of the stream some way below and a pattern of tiny meadows and potato fields.

I headed down again. A riot of wild flowers in the long grass nearly obscured the path leading out of the village into the valley. The gentle slope was criss-crossed with bushes, fruit trees, stone walls demarcating tiny grazing plots, orchards, potato fields and tiny meadows where lines of cut hay dried in the sun breathed out an intoxicating odour.

A scythe-man and a boy with a motorbike lolled by a water trough. Old women led donkeys piled with crazy mounds of hay so that they looked like walking haystacks. Plump grannies in flowery baggy pants and scarves stretched up to pull down the pink-orange cherries from the trees in the ridged potato fields and pushed the fruit into their mouths while they picked.

"*Dobur Din*! Good Day!" they giggled, like naughty children. Their colourful trousers showed that they were Pomaks from the Muslim village down the hill..

I went down to the river. It was dark in the shadow of the rocks and overhanging trees. A wild dog (or was it a wolf?) skulked in the shadows and crept up the slope into the trees as I approached. The humped roadway of an old Turkish bridge had long since collapsed into the water. The pale limestone blocks were covered with lichens and are fitted together so closely that it appeared to be made from one unbroken piece of stone.

I had brought a fishing rod and so I picked my way from boulder to boulder along the stream that cascaded through a narrow wooded gorge, dabbling vainly in the pools. A couple of men were already fishing a large and deep pool under a cliff, fed by a waterfall that spouted through a gap between two great boulders. It was the best place, they told me, offering me freshly grilled trout and rakia. They were also Pomaks from the village further down. The Pomaks were the only people who still lived and worked in this part of the mountain. Except these men didn't have any work so they spent their time fishing and gathering what they could from the land.

As we talked a thunderstorm broke, drenching us in minutes. We headed back down the river together towards the villages. The wetness, combined with tiredness and slight drunkenness made the route back into an obstacle course. My new companions expertly pulled themselves up an especially hard wall of rock. I started after them and one offered his hand. I reached up and he pulled. In surprise at his strength I lost my footing and he simply hoisted me up as though I were a sack of potatoes.

At the broken bridge we parted company. The fishermen headed down to their village. When they were gone, I threw off my clothes and leapt into the water. The water was so icy cold that I felt it thicken my blood and my heart boomed in my chest. Then I hunted for fresh water crayfish, but they burrowed themselves into the sand at my approach and I couldn't get any. The rain had passed and I dried myself on a sunny rock.

Back at Tanya's house, I draped my clothes on the stove. It was a low rectangular box made of thin black metal. They are known as "Gypsy Love" by Bulgarians, because they flare up quickly to a great heat, but also die fast if not tended.

Nostalgia for Barbarians

*For what are they waiting, still gathered in the squares –
They moved out yesterday the barbarians, they are no more.
They even left us their flags, flags fringed with gold
And some sort of message – covered in signs.*

*What old things did he whisper in the ear of his wife –
Did he not send her to arrange the couch of the guest.
She now displays gifts – a beautiful vase
And the habit of undressing when she's alone with a man.*

*What is happening at the back of the court – with the king –
God make his years fruitful, barbarians – or children.
But they have broken the jester, the queen sets the dogs to bark
And what is this bounty, to throw gold at beggars.*

*So much they did, those barbarians,
what barbarians they were...
We dream of their hands – beautified with rings.
If only they return some day – our sons sang to us
and they went after them to become barbarians.*

Hristo Stoyanov

An Awkward Dissident
in Democracy

MOST of my friends in Sofia didn't understand why I was such close friends with Hristo Stoyanov, the poet, novelist and cigarette addict who had introduced me to Vladimir the tramp.

He was a vast bear of a man in his mid-forties with the powerful chest and forearms of the foundryman he had been in his youth. He had a shock of thick black hair and a thick black beard flecked lightly with white. Physically he betrayed just two signs of weakness. The first was a lack of teeth, the second – trembling fingers. At times of high stress his hands would shake like leaves so he had to hold his lighter with both hands to ignite a cigarette.

"He is a *razboinik*, a ruffian! I'm sorry that I ever introduced him to you," grumbled Aglaya my friend at the private BTV television station.

Aglaya normally loved introducing me to people and took pride in the friendships that I had made thanks to her. But maybe she had a right to be pissed off with Hristo at that moment. Since she had become Assignment Editor for BTV news he had been pestering her to get himself featured on the programme. He was hoping to get free publicity for his latest "aggressive novel" about contemporary Pomak life and wouldn't take no for an answer.

"We don't do news stories about book releases," Aglaya had insisted. But he paid no attention.

Even so, her description of Hristo was perfect. He had recently resigned from the Bulgarian Writers' Union in typically scatologi-

cal fashion, presenting its members with his own award: "The Galvanised Zinc *Ibrik*".

In the age of running water, these little watering cans are not
much found, but Hristo had liberated one from the outdoor privy of
the grandfather of the mayor of a Muslim village.

"It's for washing away posterior thoughts," he told the annual
meeting of the union, and plonked the zinc can with its little spout
onto the podium in front of the chairman. It was a bit like someone
chucking loo rolls around at a meeting of the Royal Society of Arts.

Having created his sensation, he left. The union was probably
glad to see the back of him, even at the expense of receiving this flam-
boyant insult. I got the impression that many people in Bulgaria's
literary world disliked Hristo as much as he disliked them.

"The fact is I am fighting for the right for those bastards, my
colleagues in the newspapers and in the Writers' Union, to express
themselves. But they can't see that. They never lifted a finger to defend me," he had told me afterwards.

The reason I liked him was precisely the same reason why Aglaya
was angry with him. Hristo was truly a ruffian – one of nature's born
fighters and a master of excessive unreasonable behaviour. He was a
six-times divorced self-taught author, journalist and poet who introduced himself to people with a business card which read

"Hristo Stoyanov – *Bulgarin*".

He told bad jokes, chatted up anything in a skirt and was prepared to start an argument with anyone who challenged him – one
reason why he seemed to be perpetually in conflict with the government and the courts, not to mention half my friends. But he was also
loyal and would drop everything to travel half way across the country
to see a friend.

That was why I had dropped everything to travel down to Smolyan to see him. Hristo was suing the local prosecutor for abusing his
right to free speech. He had asked me to be there and invited me to
stay with him in his tiny bedsit.

This was located in a bare concrete block of flats hard up against
the mountainside. The single room was kippered with the smoke of
thousands of cigarettes. I wondered how long I could stand it.

Apart from the smell, the room was like the outward expression
of its owner's mind. A bookcase lined one wall from floor to ceiling.
Open any volume and a cloud of stale tobacco would puff out at you.

Hristo had read every tome: the classics of Russian and Bulgarian literature, and also translations of writers from every major European country including poets, philosophers and historians.

There was a table with an old typewriter on it by the window. A bed was pushed against the bookshelves. During the day it doubled as a sofa. In the corner of room behind the bed head was a collection of stout pine staves, each more than six-foot long and stripped of its bark to reveal the yellow wood beneath.

"I collect a new staff every time I go mushroom hunting," he told me. They looked like items for self-defence. Something in his tone of voice made me think perhaps they were.

The wall opposite the bookcase was covered in paintings – works begged from many of the leading contemporary artists alongside Hristo's own works: mostly of large breasted women metamorphosing into snakes. Sometimes they had coiling scaly green tails where legs should be. Otherwise snake heads emerged from human necks. When I first met Hristo, he was working on his seventh divorce. His girlfriend at the time was less than half his age.

"I can still keep her satisfied. I have great energy," he had told me with a proud chuckle. Like I said, the room was a physical manifestation of his mind.

He had roasted a chicken and baked a *pitka*, a round flat traditional loaf, in honour of my arrival, so for a while the fresh smells of cooking predominated over the fug of tobacco. He pulled out several dusty bottles of fake Savoy Club whisky and gin from a dusty cupboard at the side of his desk. They had been there, untouched, since Hristo had given up alcohol several years before. He was delighted to find someone to try them on.

I thought that former boozers didn't normally keep the stuff knocking around in case they were tempted, but Hristo was too bloody-minded to be knocked off any course he had decided to take. In any case, the drink was filthy – probably concocted by Tsar Kiro, the gypsy king, out of industrial spirit and flavourings. I selected the gin.

We talked late into the night about the Pomaks, about Christians and Muslims in the Rhodope Mountains, about Islam and about communism and its continued influence on the intelligentsia. He grumbled about poets, writers and artists who sucked happily on the communist teat until it ran dry and who then transferred themselves with scarcely a break to the Open Society teat, where they drank the money of George Soros.   I drank the cheapo gin while he talked and smoked and told me about his past in the steel mills and copper foundries.

He had married a girl, simply because she had got pregnant by another man and he felt sorry for a child that would be born without a father. He started to read books and to write poetry. He also built a reputation as a hell-raiser.

"I would drink twenty vodkas in one sitting. I could do that every night," he boasted. The confession had little of the self-pitying *mea culpa* of the wistfully sober.

"I only drank *na X*" he said. That means, down in one.

Several marriages and children, later the authorities sent him back to Smolyan. He was arrested for writing a jeering poem about Todor Zhivkov. Then democracy came and he became a novelist and a journalist and eventually a one man publishing phenonmenon: author, publisher and distributor all in one.

He had decided his publishing house was ripping him off, so he withdrew from his contracts and went into *samizdat*. Each winter he wrote another book. Normally it took him a few months. By spring it was printed. Then all summer and into the autumn he distributed it.

When he started on this idea, he didn't know how to drive. Aged 45 he passed his test and took to the road. His first car was a 15-year old Skoda, which he had acquired for the equivalent of a hundred pounds or so.

The day after he passed his driving test, he loaded the boot and the back seat with hundreds of copies of his latest book (dedicated to me and my friend and sometime research and travel companion the political scientist, Robin Brooks). And careered onto the highway for his first grand book tour of Bulgaria.

Eventually, the story of these tours became a book itself. It was a catalogue of prangs and near misses and near death experiences, intertwined with scandalous and embarrassing recollections from his alcoholic past. For Hristo, every mishap was a treasure.

"Och! I was nearly done for. I tried to turn round and the car jumped up on the central barrier," he lamented, as if his vehicle were a horse that had taken off on its own accord. "Luckily a lorry with a rope came by and they pulled me to the side of the road."

These sorts of accidents inevitably led to expensive visits to garages. A new axle, a new drive shaft and so on, quickly ate up profits from the first tour. Hristo dealt with less serious prangs himself with a spray can of yellow paint. After any ding he would jump out and sprays over the mark as if he were treating a wound with spray-on antiseptic. The front and side panels gradually acquired a dubious blotchy and scabrous patina.

It seemed crazy from a commercial point of view. He certainly sold books. And he made himself a well-known face to almost every bookshop in the country. But did he make any money? One of his new girlfriends drank away the profits of one book. He spent half the profits of another on buying a new car – well, a new old car, a 20-year old Lada which broke down a week later, and thereby consumed the other half of the profits.

After a good deal of fake gin, even Hristo's stories couldn't keep my eyes open. So Hristo gave up his narrow single bed to me and roll himself in a plaid rug on the floor. Even with clean sheets I was wrapped in a cloud of tobacco. Tobacco was everywhere; the smell of smoke always in my nose. The last thing I saw before falling asleep was a little column of smoke twisting up from beyond my feet.

I woke early, at six am, and the smoke was still there in my nose, coiling up in the shaft of early morning sun bright through the uncurtained window. And Hristo lay stretched on the floor in his blanket, staring at the ceiling, cigarette in mouth, a crumpled packet next to the brimming ashtray. He had been smoking for hours waiting for me to wake up, waiting to have someone to talk to.

We went to the court house in the massive concrete civil complex at the bottom of the town. It was like the little brother of London's National Theatre, but no one had been looking after it. Concrete was moulting from the walls. None of the lights worked and there were no windows. It would have made a good prison.

I sat in the second row of benches in the gloomy court room. Hristo's neighbour had come to listen and a journalist from the local newspaper. There was a female judge, two men from the prosecutor's office, Hristo and Zdravka Kazaldjieva, his lawyer.

Hristo appeared as his own witness. His fingers shook as he described to the court what had happened. The conflict with the local prosecutor had begun after the publication of his most notorious book. *The Secret Life of a Pomak Girl* was a harrowing, sexually explicit drama of abuse, alcoholism, domestic violence, ignorance, poverty and exploitation. It was set in a Pomak village and completely overturned the standard idea of how the Rhodope Pomaks lived.

It was the story of a poor abused girl who murders her baby and is driven to suicide, told against a background of mutual antagonism between Pomaks and Christians. The chief abuser of the story was a Pomak policeman who became a Christian priest and travelled the villages converting the Pomaks back to Christianity. His corruptly funded campaign was a cover for money laundering and sexual predation.

Hristo claimed it was all based on fact. He had written many of the articles himself and had the yellowing press clippings in a box to prove it. But the Pomaks hated the dirty unflattering portrait he painted of them. So did the priest he had modelled his character on. The government authorities also hated the book. Its depiction of unbridgeable divisions between Muslim and Christian undermined the official version of ethnic and religious harmony, which was being energetically promoted as a model for other Balkan countries. The fact that he had filled the book full of sex and violence made the whole thing worse.

So the city prosecutor had denounced him as a criminal and pornographer and warned the people of Smolyan not to buy or read the book. Then he launched an investigation into Hristo. The police had come round to his flat and arrested him. They told him that while he was being investigated, he could not leave the town.

This was not the communist period. These events took place in 1998. Yet, for nearly a year, Hristo had sat at home, grinding his teeth and chain smoking cigarettes with shaking fingers, thanks to this illegal and unenforceable edict. Rebel that he was, he had never dreamt of defying the order. Why not? He couldn't explain.

"Then one night a group of men even beat me up as I was walking home. I was threatened on the telephone. Women called me in the middle of the night and said they will kill me."

He had brought a cassette player into the court and played the recording that he had taken of one of these threats on his answering machine. A woman's harsh voice, shrill with anger, cursed him, promising him trouble and beatings and that he might be killed.

"They even threatened my mother, my poor mother!" he burst out. This last outrage had hurt him most. The recollection of it almost drove him to tears as he stood in the witness stand.

"My teeth all fell out too," he complained baring stumpy gums.

The hearing was quickly over. Afterwards, we went to Hristo's local café which contained most of what passes for intellectual life in the town. There were a couple of poets and a man who made pornographic films in Germany.

"He's a genuine pornographer but no one cares about him," Hristo pointed out.

Zdravka, the lawyer, one of Bulgaria's most successful human rights advocates, told him he was a child. She predicted that the judge would reject his claim and then they would have to appeal. again and again and again.

"We can't have prosecutors and other court officials publicly denouncing people as criminals before they have gone through the court process. People like Hristo must have the opportunity to defend themselves. Unfortunately Bulgarian judges can't see that yet," she said.

I wondered why Hristo had embarked on this long and difficult path.

"There is a Bulgarian saying that you should know about. It isn't very pleasant but it explains why I have to fight. The more you struggle, the deeper they shaft you. And so most people don't fight. They just let the state fuck them over. But I am struggling" he growled, thumping the table, eyes flashing with passion.

He paused and looked at me mischievously.

"And you know what? I'm even beginning to enjoy it!" He burst out laughing, at his own crudity, then his shoulders slumped.

"I know that I'm getting fucked a lot of the time."

Declaration of the acceptance
of Islam in the name of a priest

Your Majesty, honour and mercy, to you my Sultan! Good health to you! I, your humble servant, come from enlightened and educated people. I was dignified with the honour of accepting Islam under your guidance and I beg you, my lord for the following. Because until now I have not been given clothes, and I am not circumcised, please deign to indicate to me the most suitable place to carry out my circumcision, after which please number me amongst your glorious court attendants. The command belongs only to my honoured and merciful Sultan.
Your humble servant: the new Muslim and former priest.

1 January 1721
From the Ottoman archives

A Struggle for Souls

I DIDN'T take the straightest road eastwards from Smolyan to Kurdjali. Instead I turned my little car onto a potholed track that wiggled along the side of narrow valleys and through thick woods, tracing a great southwards loop towards the Greek border.

I was going to meet Father Bojan Saraev, charismatic priest and leader of the Movement for Christianity and Progress. Since 1990, Saraev had been campaigning to convert the Pomaks of the Rhodopes "back" to Christianity. Pomaks are ethnically Bulgarian Muslims. They are one of the most intriguing of Bulgaria's minorities.

My journey would take me into the heart of a knotty and little understood religious conflict, the battle for the soul of a dying region.

It was hay-making time. In the bottom of the valleys nearby villages, I passed families hard at work in the herb and flower-strewn meadows. Men wearing faded blue overalls, or sometimes stripped to the waist and bathed in sweat, swung scythes like metronomes. Short, work-toughened women in bright red and green, with gaudy patterned head scarves, tossed the cut hay with long wooden pitch forks, or piled it into wobbling souffléd mounds on carts pulled by tiny patient donkeys.

Late in the day I walked into Father Saraev's compound on the edge of the scruffy town of Kurdjali. The man driving the Christian revival of the Rhodopes greeted me with a broad confident smile. He was a broad and physically imposing man with a round face, full lips, a flat nose that could have been broken, thinning, long, fine sandy hair and striking pale blue eyes. His voice was low and melodious. He had a big laugh which he broke into easily. He looked like he might be quite good at converting people to his beliefs.

The priest led me to the veranda of his little cottage next to the bright new stone and plaster church. All around us building work was in progress, creating what would become a modern monastery with a soup kitchen, a school, a dormitory and comfortable guest quarters. This was no empty church in the making, Saraev was building a complete religiously-based social services centre.

"I wanted to meet you," I started, "Because you are..."

"...someone who has changed his religion?" he interrupted.

"Ye-es." I was taken aback by this direct approach. Saraev had been born a Muslim. He had served as an officer in the State Security in various villages in the eastern and central Rhodopes during the latter years of the Communist era.

I asked him why he was converting the Pomaks.

"Pomaks have a spiritual discomfort. They feel they are not Bulgarian because of their religion. To feel properly like Bulgarians they need to return to their original faith. The Orthodox Church has entered the genes of Bulgarians. A Bulgarian cannot be anything but an Orthodox Christian."

In other words, the Pomaks carried a psychological wound handed down from their many times great grandparents and only conversion to Christianity would make it go away. It sounded like a load of nonsense to me and I had other reasons for being suspicious of the idea.

The ideas this priest was putting forwards now were not new, nor were they particularly spiritual or religious. They belonged to a long tradition of nationalism, whose roots lay 300 years in the past.

The ancestors of the Pomaks of today probably abandoned Christianity for Islam between the 16th to 19th century. According to popular legend, the Janissaries, the Sultan's most loyal troops, converted the Pomaks to Islam forcibly and with great cruelty as punishment for rebellion and disloyalty.

Signs of this legend are everywhere. As you travel round the country, and especially in the Rhodopes, it can sometimes seems that every jagged outcrop of cliff near a village is called the "Maiden Rock", from which a damsel flung herself rather than join the harem of the local Turkish Bey.

Then there is the legend of the "Dividing Field". According to this, in some villages every male inhabitant was invited to choose between Islam and Christianity. On one side was a cauldron of stew for those who chose the turban, on the other a swordsman and his block waited to behead the stubborn wearers of the Bulgarian *kalpak*.

One of the most famous folksongs from the region celebrates the idea of sacrifice in blood curdling detail.

Do you give, do you give, Balkansko Yovo,
The beautiful Yana to the Turkish faith?
Alas, Voivodo! My head I will give
But beautiful Yana I will not give
to the Turkish faith!

They cut off his hand and then they asked him.
Do you give, do you give...

And so on. The song repeats itself verse after verse until poor old Balkansko Yovo has been utterly dismembered, arms legs, ears and nose while still refusing to hand over his girl to Islam. Finally they chop off his head. The song doesn't say what happens to beautiful Yana. Perhaps she chucked herself off the nearest cliff.

This idea, the myth of the forcible conversion of the Pomaks, the idea that they had not embraced Islam willingly, was the chief idea that lay behind Saraev's campaign. The major problem with it was that it is wrong. The Christian peasants who accepted Islam did so for economic and social benefits, which at that time included serving in the army, owning land, not paying tax and so on. In those days it was better to be Muslim.

Similar economic motivations probably lie behind the modern day voluntary conversions of many Pomaks back to Christianity. The pendulum has swung back the other way.

But nationalists like Saraev are giving it a hefty push and have been doing so for the past 100 years. During the 20th century there have been more than half a dozen attempts to "bulgarize" the Pomaks, changing either their names, their religion or both. The sinisterly-named "Regeneration Process" of the Communists was only the last and most violent of them.

In 1972, the Politburo ordered all Pomaks to change their Islamic names. This meant that Ibrahim, Hasan, Ahmed and so on had to become Ivailo, Ivan and Alexander for example. Islam, Islamic practices, traditional rituals and clothing were all banned. Circumcisions, the celebration of festivals such as *Kurban Bairam* (Eid) and Ramadan were criminalised. It was an awful period in modern Bulgarian history. And Saraev stood at the end of it. He was carrying on the Regeneration Process in the democratic era.

This at any rate is what my friend Hristo Stoyanov had accused Saraev of doing. Hristo and Saraev loathed each other deeply. Hristo had based the character of the abusive priest in his scandalous Pomak novel on Saraev. I had to admit that the priest seemed a better man than the cynical and probably libellous portrait that Hristo had painted of him.

But Hristo's view was important because he was a witness. He was the only "outsider" I knew who had seen the "Regeneration Process" first hand. He and his mother had arrived in Smolyan, in the middle of the Rhodope mountains, in the early 70s. They had come there from Gabrovo, an industrial town in the heart of the Balkan Range.

Most of Hristo's classmates at school were Pomaks.

"If a student came to class with his Muslim name, he would be sent home. And the next day, and the next day. Then he would be punished for not having done his classes. This was meant to put pressure on the parents, of course."

Adults were also turned away from work if they did not have a Bulgarian name. Finally, if they continued to resist, the police would visit in the middle of the night to summarily issue the whole family with new names.

Some villages in the west rebelled and the army was sent in. Soldiers and tanks surrounded the rebel villages and armed police were sent in to enforce the name changes. Dozens of people were wounded, a few were killed, many were sent into internal exile. 550 men and women were incarcerated in the notorious Stalinist concentration camps on the Danube island of Belene and at Stara Zagora, which had been specially reopened to receive them. From the communist point of view, the campaign was a great success. The programme was carried out in such great secrecy so that few people in Sofia, let alone outside the country, knew about it at all.

How much had Saraev's conversion campaign inherited from this nationalistic episode? The priest denied there was any link at all. He had resigned from the State Security, converted to Christianity and took holy orders in 1990. Since then he had almost single hand-edly, created and led the campaign to convert his fellow Pomaks. He wouldn't commit to how many people he had converted.

"No one can count the number," he said.

He claimed to have made 50,000 converts during 1993, nearly three-quarters of them in the Central and Eastern Rhodopes. His plan had been to convert three-quarters of the Pomaks by the end of the century. This was not going to happen. The evidence suggested that the numbers of converts was tailing off.

Saraev thought he knew the reason for this. There was some-thing much more sinister going on in these mountains he said. His work was not just about reclaiming the Pomaks for Bulgaria. He saw himself also as a bulwark against the Islamification of the Rhodopes.

"Arabic countries are paying for the restoration of mosques and the training of Imams, who are being sent into the villages. The Po-maks are falling under foreign influence. They are becoming the vic-tims of Islamists," he told me.

"Go to the villages and see."

I left Kurdjali and Father Saraev and continued my journey through the mountains. At one place a crowd had gathered to watch a wrestling match on a bare field just outside a village. The specta-tors had gathered in a large ring about 30 feet across. They were squashed three or four deep. Those in front squatted on the ground so the people at the back could see. Wrestling – *ketch* – is the na-tional sport in this part of the country. Everyone came to watch from old women to young boys many of whom were struggling with each other in their own play contests outside the ring.

The wrestlers themselves were bare-foot, bare-chested youths. The bouts were quick and violent. It seemed primitive. Perhaps this was because it was happening out of doors on the dusty earth, with no gymnasium accoutrements.

I gave two of the contestants a lift to the next village. One of them had a red bandanna round his forearm. He had won the com-petition for his age category. He would celebrate his 18th birthday on the next day and was going to his parents' house to say goodbye because on Monday he would enrol on national military service.

I dropped him and his friend in front of the huge new white church that overlooked the red tiled roofs of the village of Nedelino.

It was the biggest church to be built in Bulgaria since before Communism and had cost about $1 million, provided by a charitable foundation run by the wife of the Prime Minister. It had been built on the site of the Muslim cemetery.

The church symbolised Nedelino's position as the centre of Saraev's conversion movement. In 1993 about one-fifth of the population of had converted in a mass baptism, presided over by the priest.

The verger was in a little café on the main street. He told me that he had converted at the mass baptism. His name was Nikolai. It was notable that he has chosen a true saint's name rather than, as many former Muslims do, a name derived perhaps from a flower, stone or some other inanimate object or idea, which would still be within the Islamic canon.

He unlocked the main door the church and led me inside. It was more like a modern protestant church than an orthodox one – partly because it had not been decorated, but also because of the light which flooded in from large windows. Most 18th and 19th century orthodox churches are places of dim mystery, dark as caves, illuminated by the yellow light of candles and narrow shafts of light that glimmer through tiny slit windows – if it shines in at all. The Nedelino church had smooth, high white walls. In a few places work had begun on simple brightly-coloured murals. But they seem perfunctory and inexpressive, offering no connection to life outside the church walls. The iconostasis was plain and virtually unornamented.

The church could easily fit five hundred worshippers. Nikolai told me that on average 70 worshippers attended each Sunday. The church shared its priest with the neighbouring village where they were also building a new church. Nikolai was delighted that large amounts of money were being spent on churches in his region, even if there weren't enough priests to go around.

This was a point which had made my friend the hell-raising author Hristo Stoyanov furious when we had discussed it in Smolyan. He had told me there were only six priests in the region – and sixty-eight churches. Dozens of churches had been locked up and no one entered them for months at a time, let alone a priest who might only appear for the occasional funeral. Many of them were collapsing and thieves had stolen the icons from the iconostasis and the crosses from the altars.

"So what are they doing about it? They are building new churches that's what!"

Nikolai didn't see it that way.

"The arrival of Father Saraev in the village was a great piece of luck to us. He met individually with every person who wanted to talk to him."

About 1,600 people in the region had decided that they must really have been Christians all along.

"I had felt for a long time that I was not really a Muslim."

What had made him feel that? I wondered. He shrugged.

"It was always with me." He paused, trying to find his words. "There are some things. We have in my family some things, passed down from my great, great grandparents, which make me think they did not accept Islam willingly."

"What sort of things?"

I had heard of this before. Islamic gravestones marked with secret crosses, icons built into cupboards or hidden within secret recesses; Christian symbols incorporated, encoded, into the decoration of buildings. It was even said that that the sunburst designs carved by the old woodworkers as ceiling ornaments, were sly expressions of Christian faith. But much as these things had been described to me, I had never actually seen them.

Nikolai's old relic was a box with a cross-carved into it. It had been in his family for generations, a reminder, to his mind, of the family's origins. Nikolai genuinely believed that he suffered from an unjust conversion to Islam forced upon his forbears by the Ottomans 300 years ago. He had finally put this psychological wound behind him.

OK. Maybe one genuine convert for Saraev, I granted him. Now wanted to test the other side of this religious divide. Was Islam really making a come-back in these mountains, as Saraev had said?

I passed through mostly Pomak and Turkish villages. Many of them had bright new mosques, whose domes and sharp minarets were roofed in brand new tin that dazzled in the sun like the foil from a just unwrapped chocolate bar.

At least some of these mosques had been built with money from Turkish or Saudi charities. One of the biggest new mosques was in the town of Rudozem, north of Nedelino, formerly a major centre for lead and zinc mining. The mines had been closed and so the town was dying. Its mosque was brand new – a huge square temple of light set aside from the rest of the town.

Its front veranda had space for hundreds of pairs of shoes. I left mine there and went inside. The young Imam was in the main hall. He was wearing a clean pressed tracksuit and white skullcap. His beard was and hair were neatly clipped. He told me he was 26-years old and had been Imam in the town for six years already. His name was Nejadin Hasan Uzun. He was ethnically Turkish and had qualified as an Imam in Turkey before coming back to Bulgaria.

As we talked an old man came from behind a pillar where he had been praying. He was the old Imam, Nejadin told me. He had a long grey beard, crooked teeth and a black skull cap. He wore typical peasant clothes and said nothing, although he shuffled after me and his younger colleague and listened to everything which we said.

Nejadin's fervent, well-spoken religiosity seemed strange and almost out of place beside the rough laconic silence of the older man. They represented two faces of Islam in Bulgaria. The old one was rustic, unobservant and tied up with local superstitions and traditions. The new one, now replacing it, was energetic and orthodox, less at home but also more determined to hold its place.

This new face of Islam had grown stronger in reaction to the decades of oppression during the communist era but also in reaction to the strange blend of evangelism and orthodoxy proselytised by Father Saraev. They both seemed to me to be equally mistaken, equally based on fraudulent myths, and equally irrelevant to the true needs of the local population.

I asked Nejadin whether any Muslims in Rudozem had been converted to Christianity. There was no question of this happening, he said. Such conversions only happened where religion was weak generally – as it was in some nearby towns and villages.

As for the story that the Ottoman authorities had forcibly converted Christians to Islam in the 16th and 17th centuries, it was a complete myth. He led me the centre of the sparkling white mosque where light streamed onto the soft pattered carpet from the windows under the dome. Raising his voice into a chant he quoted in Arabic from the Koran and the words echoed round the walls.

"There is no violence in religion," he translated. Forcible conversion cannot have happened. And in any case, Islam had come to Bulgaria perhaps even before the Proto-Bulgars had crossed the Danube and founded the first Bulgarian state in 681.

"The mountain people of the Rhodopes have never been Christian."

I stopped for the night in the town of Ardino. Its single hotel was an unheated draughty concrete block. There was no reception, and no light just a echoing staircase ascending into shadow. The concierge was in the restaurant chatting to a young man behind the grubby aluminium servery that was simultaneously kitchen and bar. She looked like she had long since given up hope of attracting any guests.

I couldn't tell whether the lights had been switched off for atmosphere or economy. The only source of illumination, the neon striplights in the servery cast their sickly glare into the blue smoky chiaroscuro and revealed a particular sort of etiolated revellry which is typical of towns where absolutely nothing happens. In the far corner a middle-aged crooner cranked out pop folk standards to a metallic beat from his synthesizer. His formulaic ululations blanked out any need for the ennui of conversation. Half a dozen customers stared sullenly at one another as they fiddled with cups of coffee and tumblers of rakia. They looked like they had been nursing the same drinks all evening.

I lugged my rucksack across the bar and sat down at a table. In a while, the concierge came by and dropped a key onto the table and the young man produced a large salad of raw cabbage and carrots and glass of cheap rakia – the sort which tastes of instant hangover. I smothered the salad in salt, vinegar and sunflower oil and bolted it down.

Sleep was not easy in the too short lumpy bed. The wailing of the *chalga* man penetrated the thin floorboards and broke my shallow dreams. I woke and slept and woke again. When it finally stopped I lay and listened to the utter and dramatic quiet: no traffic, no distant hum of factories, no wind – the babble of a solitary passing drunk, and perhaps the faint whisper of the river.

The next day I went exploring in the hills. I followed a narrow valley out of the town. Just before the path curled round the first shoulder I glanced behind me. To the south were snow capped mountains wreathed in cloud. Every detail stood out clearly, illumined by the morning sun. I trudged on higher and higher up the valley until I rounded a shoulder of the hill.

I crossed the ridge. Far below through the trees I caught my first glimpse the river Arda, a pale ribbon snaking through a steep gorge. The track criss-crossed down the steep valley side and eventually I came out of the trees. And then I saw the Devil's Bridge.

According to local myth it claims a life every year. I had been warned.

"Don't be tempted to swim in the pool below the bridge."

My clothes were sticking to my skin and the water did look cool and inviting. But I did not succumb to temptation. I sat on a rock and dabbled my feet in the icy water.

It was one of the most impressive Ottoman bridges in Bulgaria, built at the beginning of the 15th century. Its huge central arch vaulted the stream, supported by two smaller arches on either side. The inside of the arch was a perfect semi-circle whose reflection in the still water of the pool made a complete O. The road above made a gentler curve from one bank to the other, tracing the shape of a yoke. The point at the centre of the bridge where these two curves meet was impossibly thin, just two stones thick only, the heavy keystone covered with a single paving slab. And yet its perfection meant the bridge was strong and had stood for centuries.

I had come across many similar bridges all through these mountains. Every encounter was a delight. Sometimes I caught just a brief glimpse of a little redundant arch to one side of a busy concrete road bridge. Or I found a perfectly intact narrow loop of stone bridging a stream on an ancient track through the mountains, forgotten or ignored by road builders for centuries. These bridges were a testament to the engineers who built them. Time had whittled them down to their purest elements. Take away a single stone and the entire structure would fall into the water. Some bridges, I had heard, had no cement in their construction. Sometimes a thin layer of moss covered the worn stones, fitted so closely together that the perfect semi-circle seemed to be carved out of one piece of rock.

For me these bridges had come to symbolise the old life of the Rhodope mountains. They showed how people used to pass through these mountains in a different way, along routes which no longer matter. They pointed the ways that every autumn the herdsmen drove their flocks from the upland summer pastures down towards the Aegean Sea and its warm lowland grazing.

Under one of the smaller arches of the Devil's Bridge a pair of boys threw a small square net stretched between two poles into the pool. Then they hurled rocks to scare the fish into it. It is tempting at such times to speculate that one has found a pre-modern paradise and to eulogise it. How can such ways of life – donkeys and square fishing nets still survive?

The answer is with difficulty. Economic pressures and the brutality of communism had already destroyed the nearby villages. Such life that remained would not last long in the era of capitalism. What I was witnessing was the last thin vestiges of what had been before.

But everything was changing in this cut-off part of the country. The Ministry of Energy was threatening to build a complex of three massive hydro-electric dams one of which would rise up almost exactly where I was sitting. The great gorge would become a lake.

As I wondered about the future of this place a man on a donkey ambled across the bridge and disappeared into the woods on the other side. There was no point in just going to a bridge, I told myself. One has to cross it.

So I followed him, tracking the dainty imprints of the donkey hooves on the muddy path up through a pine forest. As I breasted the ridge of the valley, it opened out into a network of pastures. My path had led me to a simple farmyard and primitive peasant house, made entirely of wood and wattle and daub. It was a two storey building. Downstairs was the barn, where the animals lived. It opened straight into a muddy yard, shored up by rocks and wooden palings. Chickens, some goats and a cow roamed through the dung.

At my approach an old woman had scurried inside and appeared on the broad balcony, strung with rows of wrinkled reddish-brown peppers, yellow bunches of maize and bushels of herbs hung on hooks to dry. She looked at me curiously and croaked a *Dobur Den*, before settling down cross-legged to some work.

A man appeared from behind the house. He was the same person who had been riding the donkey. He welcomed me with a smile. It was a surprise for him to see a stranger in such an out of the way place, he shouted at me hoarsely in heavily accented Bulgarian. He was very deaf and evidently unused to not speaking in Turkish.

This *mahala* was called Latinka. Four or five families still lived on this side of the bridge. They were all Turks, he said. The only way to get here was by foot or by donkey. It was two and a half hours to the nearest town.

"Only some old grandfathers and grandmothers have stayed. We were too old to move away. Our children are now over there."

He gestured eastwards with a kind of chopping motion. Some had gone no further than Ardino or the main regional city of Kurdjali, others all the way to Instanbul.

Turning northwards to towards the pine-covered hills he spread out his hand.

"There is no one there. That land is entirely empty."

The nature was very beautiful, he agreed.

"But here there is no life. Thank God, one of my sons still lives in Ardino. He works in the tobacco factory. Every weekend he comes out here to help us. We cannot manage on our own any more."

He shrugged his shoulders sadly and looked around at the little patches of vegetable garden he had carved out of improbable slopes. The earth of these tiny plots was richly black, enriched by the dung of generations of animals and painstakingly watered, hoed and sown by hand. The rows of potatoes, peppers and onions stood out like little oases against the bleak rocks and scrub of the mountainside.

On my way back from the bridge, I walked through the village of Diadovtsi. Twenty or thirty white-washed houses were ranged around the crest of a hill looking southwards towards the mountains of Turkey. They looked like cottages from a fairytale. The setting sun reflected pink and orange from their white walls and grey slate roofs making them bright against the lush green meadows that surrounded them.

A second look produced a more ominous impression. Straggling fruit trees spread unpruned between the buildings. Brambles had overcome the fences and scrambled up onto the roofs. It was a garden run wild. The windows, black squares in white walls, stared blankly. Doorways gaped. The only sounds came from a gurgling spring, the jangling music of goat bells from some far-off herd of goats and birdsong, which was everywhere. The only thing that moved aside from myself was a single brown cow that ruminated lazily under a mossy plum tree.

Maybe someone still lived here, I wondered, or perhaps they just came here from somewhere else for the grazing. Whatever the truth, I saw no one. I wandered the silent paths between the old stone houses. They had been plastered on the inside with mud and straw and fitted snugly and aptly into their places. Some of them were perfectly intact, although windowless. Others had dangerously leaning walls. Sometimes nature had asserted herself from above; rotten beams had collapsed depositing the heavy weight of stone slates through the building. Or else she had pushed up from below. Here creepers, brambles and bushes had undermined and pulled down a wall. There a tree had taken root indoors and thrust out through the windows and gaping roof.

The houses were completely empty. Not a stick of furniture, a tool or item remained as a clue to what sort of life had gone on here. On the dirt floor of one house I found a single child's shoe and a small blue plastic ring. Traditionally these rings are supposed to ward off the evil eye.

It was amazing to me that anyone could bear to abandon such a beautiful place. There was good pasture all around and no shortage of water. Several good springs had been enclosed in neat stone arches built into the hillside – a technique I only came across in the eastern Rhodopes. But for the ethnic Turks who lived here, it must have become a prison.

On Christmas Day 1984 special police and army units had descended on Turkish villages throughout eastern Bulgaria. The Communist Party had decided that Turks were also Bulgarians "forcibly converted" to Islam and ordered them to take Bulgarian names. The speaking of the Turkish language, traditional dress, and customs were also banned. These strictures were strictly enforced.

It took one month to complete the initial name-changing process, but the repression continued for the next four years in response to continued low level resistance. Estimates of the numbers killed vary wildly from the twenties to the thousands.

The government failed to keep its repression secret unlike when it had done the same to the Pomaks. News of the atrocities being committed against the Turks was publicised internationally thanks to information gathered by the Turkish secret service, which had informers amongst the Bulgarian Turkish community.

In May 1989, First Secretary Todor Zhivkov admitted defeat in his attempt to control the rising tide of civic unrest in Turkish districts and opened the border. More than 300,000 Turks fled the country in the so-called "Great Exodus". Villages, like this one, throughout the region were completely deserted. Its former inhabitants had fled the country to find new lives in the outskirts of Istanbul and the other industrial towns of Northwest Turkey.

No one has ever been brought to justice for these Regeneration Processes. Neither for the one that crushed the Pomaks in the 70s nor the one that a decade later was inflicted on the Turks.

. . .

Only once did I ever discover a man prepared to admit his part in the Regeneration Process. He lived in the village of Beden, west of Smolyan. I had turned off to visit the place on a whim because of its name, which in Bulgarian means "Poor". I found it is tucked in a cleft of the mountains between pastures of thin grey grass and potato fields.

There were not many people about. In the centre of the village four old men sat on a bench in front of the old mosque. The building was locked although it was Friday. It had boards nailed over the windows and looked like it was never used.

At the bottom of the village an old couple sat companionably, enjoying in the warmth of the autumn sunlight, in a small paddock by the school house. A cow grazed near them. They looked like a sweet old pair. The old man was happy to talk to me. He had been the village teacher. Would I like to see around the school? We left his wife with the cow.

"She is a descendent of Bulgarian Mohammedans. Her Muslim name was Fatme but she doesn't like to use it. I call her Sevda. I am a Christian, originally from Lovech," he said. He had come to Beden in 1949 as an assistant teacher, married a local girl and stayed.

"The regeneration process was not repressive at all. It was patriotic and progressive. Here in this village it was very successful. We had a big educational campaign. We sent the children to high school in the town, even if this was against the wishes of their parents. Often they were opposed to education, particularly for the girls. Sometimes we would collect them in a jeep and take them to the town without their parents' knowledge. These girls have now become doctors and professors and live normal lives. Do you think, they would want to go back to being Mohammedans?"

We looked at a dusty black and white photo exhibition dating from the communist era. It stood in the school passage way and shows pictures not only of Thracian finds from the 4th century AD from the near the village but also gravestones with crude crosses carved on them and other old Christian artefacts. A map showed the village and surrounding land. The fields were all marked with Christian names such as Goliama Churkva and Mala Chorkva (big and little church).

"This shows, the village was once Christian before the Turks converted it. But now things are turning back. Many of the children have no knowledge of their Muslim origins. If you ask them about their Islamic family names they could not answer. We are not Christians or Muslims here. We believe in common humanity. We are Europeans, modern Europeans. Humanity is the most important thing."

It seemed ironic, even funny. But the grinding poverty of the place didn't encourage laughter. This old man in his old clothes clung onto that distant hope that somehow he was moving into a grand European utopia where the ancient conflicts between Christianity, Islam and Judaism would be a thing of the past.

We emerged from the school to find that the square had begun to fill with people.

"There will be a funeral," the old teacher told me. The men and women clustered separately. I stood by a group of old women and listened to their gossip and complaints about their own and their neighbours' health as we waited for the procession to pass.

"Not many people will turn out," a woman told me. "Not for an old baba. 80-years-old, *leka i prust*. Light be her dust. It's her family and friends who have come mostly. Only when young people die does everyone attend the funerals. We have lots of funerals here. But there hasn't been a wedding for 15 years."

The corpse of the deceased woman was wrapped in an orange blanket and carried on a wooden trestle by a crowd of old men. Every few steps a new man would step in to shoulder the load, relieving one of his companions. When the men had gone by the women followed. I waited until the procession had left the village on the narrow path that led to the graveyard and then I quietly walk back through the empty streets and left the village behind me.

A Bride, a Golden Apple

How sweet it is to see
Folks become kin!
A mother raised, she raised –
She didn't know what she was raising:
She raised a golden apple
To sweep another's house
To carry water for another.
Her father-in-law has an empty purse
But his house is merry
And his water is fresh.
Her father has a full purse
But his house is forlorn

Traditional folk song
Translated by Thomas Butler

What is a Dowry Worth?

GLORIOUS period of Indian summer at the end of October –
what the Bulgarians call gypsy summer – was just beginning
when I arrived in the village of Breznitsa. During my dozen or
so visits over the past couple of years I had never seen so much going on. A long summer of work was coming to an end, the final crops
were being brought in and stored, forage gathered for the winter,
wood stores replenished. Trays of penny bun mushrooms, speckled
beans, bright yellow maize and racks of tobacco leaves on long strings
drying in the sun, blocked the narrow pavements and half the streets.
Everyone was out in front of their houses working, preparing, sorting
fruit, shelling beans, packing tobacco.

Pale eyed, fair-haired children, heading home from school, abandoned their rucksacks to turn great skeins of dark hay with wooden
pitchforks before going inside to eat. In a few weeks nearly all agricultural work would cease. This was the last opportunity to get it
done before the winter set in with snows and ice.

Breznitsa was inhabited by the same minority that Hristo Stoyanov wrote about. The same people whom I had met in the central Rhodopes, whom Saraev was trying to convert. But no religious
foundation had ever attempted to convert or reconvert its populace.
No one had offered to build a great new church or mosque or tried
to divide the community against itself. The church and the mosque
stood on the main square on either side of the main street, where
they had always stood.

I had come to Breznitsa in search of the *Pomakluk*. This is a word
that describes the entire Pomak culture, history, identity and a way of
living. Some folklorists reckon that the Pomakluk is the oldest and

purest form of Bulgarian culture still existing. If this is true, it is a paradox. It would mean that the Pomaks are more Bulgarian than the Christian Bulgarians themselves. But it is possible that these folkorists are right and that the Pomaks have kept alive a way of life long forgotten by the rest of their country. This is because of the remarkable isolation in which these few traditional Pomak villages have existed, not just in recent times but for almost all of their history.

Breznitsa is one of about a dozen Pomak villages in the mountainous south western part of Bulgaria. They are grouped in three clusters spread across the upper reaches of the Mesta valley: one on the eastern slopes of Pirin, a second in the south western part of the Rhodopes and a third in the northern Rhodopes. They are all located high up in the hills, hidden away from travellers passing along the main route by the river.   Each village cluster has its own network of forest tracks and dirt roads. So travellers going between them on horse or by foot can travel directly, while those visiting by car have to take the long, winding and round about tarmac routes that join them to the main highway and to the main stream of Bulgarian life.

The region feels like the last area of the Balkans where the pre-19th century, multi-ethnic, multi-religious society still exists in all its muddled uneasy glory. It is poor, but also vibrant and growing. Here, finally, I had found what had been so depressingly lacking in the etiolated formerly Pomak societies further east. I had found Pomaks who were proud of their name, who had no time for mealy-mouthed evasions like "Bulgarian Muslim" or worse the old-fashioned "Bulgarian Mohammedan". They might as well have been a million miles away from the retreating, withering communities that I had witnessed being buried along with the old woman in the drear village of Beden.

Privately, I classed these villages into a mythical "Pomakistan". Pomakistan is not a political or geographical entity. Nor could it ever be one. No Pomak village is exclusively Pomak. They all have a few Christians, some Roma and possibly a few Turks living with them side-by-side. And the villages themselves have Christian villages as their neighbours. Pomakistan has no borders, no political parties, no desire for autonomy or seccession. It is both part of Bulgaria and separate from it, and as intangible as the roots of Pomak identity.

The first person I saw as I entered the village square was my friend Salih, a large man with black curly hair and a broad open face like a child's that revealed every emotion that he felt. He was younger than me by about a year, but looks older. People living in villages and working on the land always age more quickly, I have noticed. Still, it was hard to get used to Salih's respect for me, even calling me "*Batko*", as if I were his elder brother. He was born exactly in the year that the regeneration process began. Until he was eighteen, he had only been able to use his real name, Salih, in private.

He rushed across and embraced me in a great hug. I would stay in his house, he insisted. He and his wife Umi would move out of their bedroom to give me the best bed to sleep in. They always did this. I could never persuade them that it wasn't necessary.

From the outside, their house was a basic concrete rectangular frame filled with rough bricks. The principle of its construction and of every other house in the village had probably not changed for hundreds of years. The only difference now was that concrete had replaced wood and breeze blocks mud. It was built against the side of the mountain. A vegetable garden climbed up behind it and round the back of the ground floor was also low foetid barn, almost dug in to the steep sloping hillside where they kept a cow and a donkey. Out front and to one side, jutting out from the first floor, was a broad concrete terrace almost half as large as the house itself. This was where the maize and the tobacco could be dried.

It also provided a large covered area that was filled with a great mess of motorbike parts and Salih's father's huge and ancient Russian motorcycle of the type which all the villagers use to take them up the steep dirt tracks into the mountain forests. There was also a large apple barrel, food for the chickens and rabbits, a hay store, bunches of pale yellow corn cobs, strings of purply-brown wrinkled peppers a huge pile of firewood, an old cart, some mattocks, hoes, shovels, pitchforks and brooms. Around the door was a great clutter of rubber galoshes, clogs boots and broken trainers for outdoor wear and flip-flops and slippers for indoors.

As in all Muslim households it was forbidden to enter with shoes on. On my first visit, Umi had provided me with a pair of woollen bootees to keep my feet warm indoors. The concrete floor and corridor were covered with a few hand-woven chergi – multi-coloured striped wool rugs – but they were old and faded. Salih's parents lived on the ground floor, but they were still in Greece working as migrant labour on the EU subsided tobacco farms. Upstairs, Umi's part of the house was mostly furnished with new and unblemished modern machine-made fabrics and materials.

This was more than a generational gap. It was a direct result of the way that the village had opened up in recent times. Umi and Salih Bukuvian were some of the first people in the village to consciously reject the Pomakluk in favour of everything modern that was rushing into the village for the first time.

Umi's taste for the modern extended to her personal dress. I don't think I once saw her wear *shalvari*, the voluminous, lurid bloomers worn by most women in the village. For the older, more traditional part of the village, these garments were like a uniform, even down to the limited choice of design, so you could easily see the same clashing purple flowers on orange a dozen times during an afternoon. She didn't like them

"I prefer to be modern. We can all choose now."

Up to a point anyway. At home Umi sometimes wore jeans, something almost unheard of for a married woman. But in the street she wore modest skirts, appropriate for going to work at the hospital in the town of Gotse Delchev. Once, in the early nineties, caught up in the feeling of liberation, which had come to Breznitsa the same as everywhere else in the country, Umi had taken the bold, foolhardy decision to step out in the street wearing a mini-skirt. She had brought it back from the university in Blagoevgrad.

"I remember the first time I wore it into the street. No one had ever seen one here before. Scandal! The men just stared at me, but the other women shouted at me and chased me home. I had to run back and change straight away. That was ten years ago but I haven't dared try it again and nor has anyone else. The whole village talked about it for months afterwards."

She giggled and reddened at the memory, laughing with the laughter of hindsight. But it had not been funny at the time.

Salih and Umi were one of the most progressive couples in the village, thanks to the fact that they had both gone away to study in the most important regional town. Salih became an engineer, Umi a nurse. Education had been kinder to Umi than to her husband. She had found work in the hospital in the local town of Gotse Delchev. This made her one of the few women in the village with a proper salaried job. She would never have to work in the exploitative cut and stitch workshops that now clustered at the top of the village. Owned by Greek and Italian firms they used underpaid Pomak labour to turn out clothes and shoes for the European market.

But education had given Salih ambition, with hardly the means to achieve it. Work for an electrical engineer in such a small village was sparse. His best hope would have been emigration. He had tried it at the beginning of the 90s, masquerading as an ethnic Turk he had tried to get across the eastern border. He was apprehended and returned. When I first met him, he was running a small kiosk near the square, which sold sweets and cigarettes and cheap packets of biscuits.

Sharply sensitive of its bad side, he liked to ask me what I thought of the village, but it seemed to me that he rarely expected a positive answer. It was as if he couldn't believe that someone in my place could find anything to admire in a simple village. As we walked through the streets he gestured with dismay at the rubbish that lay in neglected piles, tumbling down the banks of the stream.

Once Salih had been elected village treasurer. He had tried to institute fines for littering. It had done no good, except to make him unpopular. So he was not re-elected.

"We must modernise ourselves. It isn't good to be so backwards."

There were many many projects that if only he had money he would like to do. He would like to set up a bar on the square, an internet café, he said, or a little tourist hotel. But there were already a couple of places where the youngsters went to play games and surf the net. Who would visit his hotel?

I could neither encourage nor dissuade him from his fantasies, including a mad plan to emigrate to England.

"My friend, do you know what I have decided?" he asked me once, grasping me by the shoulder as if he needed reassurance.

"No Salih, tell me what."

"I want to go to England, to London. When I am there I will learn English."

"Are you sure that's a good idea?"

"Of course. Nowadays a man must know English to be successful. Don't you think it's a good idea?"

"What would you do? How would you live? How will you get there?"

"I can do anything. There is no work I will not do. The hardest and dirtiest. When you go back to England will you find out for me how I can do this? Can you get me to England?"

He begged me with an expression of naive hope and longing on his face. He looked like a child telling his father that he could climb a tree. Could he? Could he?

"I can't stay here," he said, the begging look changing to one of petulant frustration. "I don't know what it is but this village life is not for me. It constricts me."

Ironically he was dreaming of what most people loath about the modern world. To him, the idea of a mechanised 9-5 existence was the epitome of luxury, much as his own pure existence in the mountains might seem like utopia to most wage slaves.

"I want someone to tell me when I should work and when I should rest," he said.

. . .

About a year before I had helped Umi sell her dowry. These were the possessions that came with her when she left her parent's house and moved into Salih's. It was on my second or third visit to the village, by which time I was becoming an established guest at the Bukuvians, that Umi threw open the twin doors of the dresser to show me her traditional wealth. It was filled with rugs and blankets and aprons and cloths, woven in the startling bright colours that distinguish all Pomaks designs. She heaved large plastic bags of thick woollen socks, all decorated with flower patterns and geometric designs onto the floor. Bundles of headscarves followed, and sheaves of bootees, patterned pillow cases, baby carriers, embroidered linen cloths for bundling food, long quilted wedding robes like Joseph's many-coloured coat. Her mother had started making this stuff for her as soon as she was born, and she herself had joined in with its manufacture as soon as she was old enough to count the passes of the shuttle through the loom. Then she started unfolding the rugs, which seemed to contain every imaginable colour from night-deep blue and blood crimson, through the brown of crushed dark olives and a startling, luminous, iridescent pink which is the trademark colour of the Pomaks.

These heavy tightly woven rugs were called *chergi*. The classic *cherga* is a simple design of bright stripes, a bit like a multi-coloured barcode. The colours and width of the stripes vary according to a not always obvious underlying pattern. The big chergi are made of several thinner strips sewn together. Even when they follow the same pattern, the frequency of the stripes of each section never exactly match. So after a few drinks the waves of colours on a good cherga can seem to actually shift in front of the eyes.

Umi flicked them open over the floor and onto the bed so I could see them in full. It was like being in an Istanbul carpet shop when the salesman tries to dazzle you with choice, knowing inevitably that something will take your fancy. But she was not a saleswoman. She didn't know what her rugs were worth, if anything at all. She just wanted to find out whether people in Sofia, or the foreigners who sometimes travelled past the turn-off to the village might buy them. She had noticed how foreigners always fell in love with the bright colours, the fine embroidery, geometric patterns and flowers. But as she laid out each rug with nervous pride, and told me of the many hours that had gone into making it by hand on wooden looms, she could not equate this lifelong labour with any price.

She scoffed at my suggestion that she and the other women in the village should make more of them to sell. No one would do it. Having spent long hours of her youth creating these things, she knew they were rare and special. But they were also useless.

"Heavy and difficult to clean. You have to protect them from moths. And they take so long to make. No one can be bothered with all that any more."

Selling them for whatever money they could raise would was the limit of her ambition. She was in love with modernity, modern furnishings mass-produced in Turkey, cheap to buy and easy to look after.

And would they sell? I was certain about it. I arranged for Umi to bring some of her rugs up to take part in the British Embassy's Christmas bazaar. She and Salih arrived in the city as nervous provinicials, in an ancient village car, weighed down with rugs. It was a grand success. They raised nearly 500 pounds without selling nearly everything. Although not a large amount in absolute terms, it would go a long way in the mountain economy.

The result was, however, not exactly what I expected. One day I arrived at Salih's house to find he wasn't at home. In spite of all her modernity, there was a slight uneasiness about Umi as she received me without her husband. In a more traditional household this would have been harder still. But Umi's expression was not all embarrassment. There was disappointment and reproach in it as well.

"He has gone out with his friends. Hunting."

"Hunting?" I didn't know that Salih was a hunter.

He wasn't Umi explained. Not until recently…

The story came out. Salih had taken the money raised by his wife's dowry and spent some of it on learning how to be a driving instructor. So far, so good. But the remainder, more than half of it, nearly 300 pounds, he had blown on a sporting rifle and the very expensive course of instruction and licence that is necessary before you join the Bulgarian Hunting Union and can be accepted into the village hunting club. Salih was now spending every Saturday and Sunday during the autumn and winter chasing for rabbits, deer and boar.

I suddenly felt very guilty. I had told him many times of my en-thusiasm for hunting. When Umi, in her modern way, protested that she didn't like her husband going out to kill wild animals, I could only shrug in embarrassment. When the man himself arrived back in his khaki clothes, and full of excitement as any schoolboy my embarrass-ment only grew. He told me how wonderful it was going to be now that he could go out hunting and I could come with him. I shrugged in embarrassment again. Was this the reason why I had helped them sell their past?

• • •

Further north, beyond the headwaters of the Mesta in the very north of the Rhodopes I had seen what the dowry could mean to a traditional Pomak family. I had visited the village of Draginovo in the summer and made friends with the mayor's secretary, a cheerful plump woman called Diunya, who held court in the village hall, be-hind a high counter piled with registration papers.*

Diunya had introduced me to some friends. Osman, a young man from the local furniture making factory, was marrying Adije,

---

* If you know the village secretary, you know everyone. It is her job to register all births, marriages and deaths. In Pomakistan this job is made more difficult by the confusion over names. Since 1989 most villagers had reverted to their old Islamic names but not all of them. Some kept their new Bulgarian names, a few went by both names. As she told me:

"It can make the simple business of writing a birth certificate for a new child quite difficult. Everything has to match."

daughter of Mahmoud, the local car mechanic. She took me along to the wedding.

Mahmoud's small front room was like Ali Baba's cave. His daughter's dowry was stacked along the walls on every side, a riot of colour. The wall facing the window was piled with striped chergi, like rainbow barcodes. The hairy goat-hair rugs and woollen patterned blankets were stacked so high that they nearly touched the ceiling. The other walls were hung with hundreds upon hundreds of scarves of every possible pattern and hue, on top of them were hung a regiment of socks, knitted from thick wool with bright geometric patterns. Not an inch of space was uncovered.

In the centre of all this attention was Adije. Mahmoud's daughter was getting married and she was surrounded by her dowry. In fact, officially she was already married. The bride price had been paid and the divorce price had been set and agreed to by all parties. All that remained was for the groom to take the bride and her dowry from her family house into his own.

The bride price had been fixed the night before in this very room. At one time this might have been a serious commercial discussion. But time had mellowed it into a pleasing humorous tradition. The groom had pretended not to have any money and, Adije's family had pretended to throw him out. Slowly and surely from sewn up pockets, from his socks and shoes, from the waistband of his trousers the groom had assembled a great pile of banknotes. The assembled guests had then made their own contributions.

The divorce price was more serious. I had sat in the back of the mosque and watched the ceremony earlier in the day. The mosqe was a simple square building, the interior painted egg-shell blue and the walls lined with medallions containing Koranic script picked out in orange on a dark blue background embellished with swirling acanthus leaves.

The young couple sat cross-legged in front of the Hodzha, a plain grizzled man, neither a young zealot nor a doddering pensioner. In simple language he had lectured them on their obligations under Islam, describing the law set down in the Koran but also the demands of life.

"Are you ready to mature? To grow old?" he asked them.

They nodded happily and then they took their marriage oath.

"Now you are married, you must not show a hair of your head," the hodzha told Adije. He concluded with the rules for divorce. Osman could divorce Adije whenever he liked but that would not absolve him from supporting her. Divorce would come at a price that had to be fixed. A friendly haggle finally settleed on the price of a cow. The hodzha knocked down the price from 650 levs to 630 levs, just over 200 pounds sterling.

Now the dowry room was full of fuss and gossip. It was crowded with women, curious youngsters, and attentive grannies full of memories of their own weddings, all of which had followed this exact same ritual since a time that no one could remember. The bride sat on a straight backed wooden chair in the middle of the room.

I sneaked in at the back, and an old woman kindly showed me a place to sit. Nothing could hide the fact that this was predominantly a female affair. Most of the men were outside working, drinking, loitering, or cooking the wedding feast.

Aged just 18, Adije was like a child who had dressed up. She was dressed in the richest finery she would ever wear. Her short deep royal blue jacket with tippets of rabbit fur covered a couple of elaborately hemmed waistcoats and an embroidered shirt with a golden bodice clinking with coins. She must have been wearing several layers of shirts underneath it because a confusion of overlapping sleeves protruded from beneath her underrobe. The broad, flared cuff of each sleeve was richly patterned with minute and colourful embroidery. Each pattern built on the rest until all together they melded into a whirl of forms. The underrobe itself was patterned with thin vertical stripes of red and gold. It was held in tightly at her waist by a woollen belt and spread out like a skirt below her knees. On her legs she wore crazily patterned wool socks, a riot of multi-coloured geometry.

Her hair was covered with a red embroidered skull cap from which hung a fringe of gold pieces, including a huge golden medallion in the centre of her forehead.

"It is Turkish. Pure gold," her mother had told me definitively. "With a picture of the Sultan."

I took a closer look. It was not the Sultan. The head belonged to the bearded and imperious Tsar Alexander II of Russia who defeated the Sultan's forces and kicked the Turks out of Bulgaria.

Just below the medallion at the point between her eyebrows, she wore a single red sequin. So did her mother, sister and all her cousins. They looked more Hindu than Bulgarian or Muslim.

Remarkable as Adije now looked, the wonders had only just begun. All attention was now on her face and on a thin, middle-aged
woman who has set to work on transforming it into the image of a
goddess. Adije had the same round open face as her mother but not
yet its firmness. This, however, was about to change.

First the thin woman covered Adije's face in thick white foundation. Next she coloured her forehead, cheeks and chin each with a
large red spot. Then, starting in a star shape around these red spots,
she built outward a shining mask, leaf by tiny rectangular piece of gold
leaf. It was a long and painstaking process. It took more than an hour
for the thin carapace of gold to covers the bride's entire face, including
her eyelids. Then the woman carefully placed over the top a smattering
of shiny multi-coloured sequins, like a glittering case of the measles.

While this performance was going on Adije was forced to sit perfectly still on the hard wooden chair and forced herself into complete
immobility, in spite of the excitement which she must have been
feeling. For her, there could be no more running around the room
hugging and kissing her sister, her mother, aunts and grandmother.
Although everyone was fussing around her, she could do nothing.
She had been forbidden to speak, smile or make any expression lest
it spoilt the effect of the gold and possibly dislodge some of the sequins.

A few beads of sweat dotted her forehead but she pressed her
lips together and stared straight ahead, woodenly, only glimpsing
from time to time with sly, scarcely perceptible swivels of her eyes at
the reflection of her face in the little plastic mirror she gripped in her
left hand. The face that shimmers back at her in the dim glass was
not her own.

Adije had been turned into a sparkling doll of gold and porcelain, or a church icon come to life. The transformation hardened the
shape of her face, which before had been sweet and unremarkable.
The effort of holding still her face, and perhaps the pride of the moment too, had accentuated the shimmering line of her cheek bones
and given her lip an imperious curl. She was indeed no longer a
rosy-cheeked peasant girl, but an empress for the day, enthroned in
state with the rich hangings of her dowry ranged about her and all
the women of her family twittering in attendance.

"I was painted on my wedding day too. Of course, I was. We all
were. It is difficult," said the old woman, who had showed me to my

seat. "The clothes are heavy. When she leaves the house her eyes will be shut. But it will be all over by this evening. It has always been done like this. It was the same for my parents, my grandparents. No one can remember a time when we did not do this. It has always been the same."

Someone once described this ritual to me as a sight to make the eyes fill the soul. It is one of the great mysteries of Bulgarian culture. How could people who are so poor produce a vision which is so rich? Where did the tradition come from?

I don't know the answer to this. Nor does anyone else. The anthropologist who first told me about this ritual, showing me grainy photographs of golden-faced brides taken in the early 90s at one of the first weddings to be held openly after the fall of the regime, was entirely unable to explain where the tradition had come from. It is definitely not Islamic or Turkish. Nor is it Bulgarian or Slavic. Its origins must lie somewhere deep in the roots of the Pomak's self-reliant folkloric culture. It has passed down by word of mouth and tradition within their villages for centuries. It is one of the central mysteries of the Pomakluk.

The idea of an alternative source of Pomak culture is particularly important in the village of Draginovo, as the village sits in the centre of the controversy about who the Pomaks really are. The village used to be called Korova. In the 19th or early 20th century, it was renamed after a priest who came from the village and who had written an eye-witness description of how the Turkish Janissaries forcibly converted the population to Islam in the 17th century.

"The turkification lasted until the feast of the Virgin Mary [mid-August]," wrote Pop Metodii Draginov. "Of those who were not turki-fied, some were slaughtered, others fled into the forests and their houses were burnt down. Then, as a provocation, Hasan Hodzha made the new converts destroy all the churches from Kostenets to Stanimaka, in total 33 monasteries and 218 churches."

This is the golden document of Bulgarian nationalist theory. It is the only potentially verifiable historical evidence that the Pomaks were forced on pain of death to abandon Christianity. But, unfortunately for supporters of this theory it is most probably a forgery. The ancestors of today's Pomaks may well have been Christian, but the idea that they were converted by the sword is almost certainly a myth. Draginovo, with its painted brides, is where the tragedy of the Pomaks can been seen in all its bitter irony. They have been subjected to a century of forced, often violent assimilation campaigns, thanks to a lie.

But I didn't have time to think about this historical puzzle. The loading of the dowry had begun. This was done slowly and deliberately, one piece at a time. Everything had to be shown off and treated with respect. While the men did the moving, the women gathered in the front room and sang. The songs were sad. The bride may only have been going to the other side of the village but she was departing from her family house forever. I retreated from this act of farewell into the garden.

As I watched the bridal goods being loaded onto the back of the two huge Russian trucks I though about how much of this wedding had been about money. The whole extended ceremony had revolved around questions of property. There was the bargaining for the bride price, the giving of presents, the dowry, the attaching of money to the bride's costume, the cost of any divorce and finally the transfer of the bride and her trousseau to the groom's house. Even the bride's golden face could be seen as a symbol of wealth. And yet the Pomaks are so poor.

Adije and her mother stared out, half veiled by the curtains, as the material for her future home was transferred out of the house. Only when it was all loaded did the bride herself emerge. Her mother and sister led her, one on each arm. Her eyes were shut. Three scarves covered her bowed head: one red, one white and one yellow. Over all of these was thrown a red and gold gauzy veil. She walked with tiny faltering steps and humbly bent head, like a Japanese doll and was gently placed in a car, so heavily bedecked with coverings that the occupants, including the driver, could hardly see out.

The procession honked and blared through the muddy streets to the groom's house. The rest of the wedding party followed on foot. The bride alighted at her new home, and with humble step crossed the threshold with bowed head, where finally her husband met her, although only briefly.

She was escorted to an upstairs room where, flanked by two attendants, she stood to receive her dowry. It was unloaded with the same slow formality that it was loaded. And when every last pair of socks had been taken upstairs, the guests filed in to give their own presents. Meanwhile, the groom had an easier time. He wandered outside, smoking cigarettes, chatting with his friends and and appeared on the balcony from time to time to let fly from the hip with a stubby, stockless shotgun.

In the street outside the music and dancing had begun. Adije could only watch. I lost myself in horo after horo until in the darkness of night it was time to drag myself away. In a way I had not found answers to my questions. Who were the Pomaks? I still didn't know. But what I did know was that even the most elementary facts about their past, the historical bedrock, had been falsified and forged and mingled with myth too often to be relied on at all. Yet some things cannot be destroyed, even if they also cannot be explained. This inexplicable marriage ritual hinted at the possibility of some other mysterious origin lost in the confusions of history.

But there are no answers these questions. Bulgaria is very good at hiding the solutions to its mysteries.

The silhouettes of houses clambering up the slopes on either side of of the dark street loomed black in the night blue sky. A truck, laden with tree trunks, growled through the darkness, obliterating for a moment every other smell but that of dark cloying diesel. Then magically a breeze from the mountain freshened the cool air which was again crowded with a complex mix of cooking smells, pine wood smoke and the sweet stench of animals in their byres. A cow, breathing heavily, nudged past me on its way home.

The End

Glossary

Baba	Grandmother
BCP	Bulgarian Communist Party
Bei	A friendly form of address. The equivalent of "mate".
Borets, Bortsi	Literally, wrestler. Stocky intimidating men in dark suits and dark glasses
BSP	Bulgarian Socialist Party, formerly the BCP
Chalga	Pop-folk music. Normally a brash mixture of eastern and western styles. It is popular with taxi and bus drivers
Chardak	A deep veranda on the upper floor of a traditional house
Chenge, chengeta	Cop, secret policeman
Cherga	Traditional striped woven rug
Cheta	Partisan or revolutionary band
Chicho, chichovci	Uncle, uncles
Diado, diadovci	Grandfather, grandfathers
Dobur Den	Good Day
Durzhavna Signornost (DS)	The Communist era State Security Service
Groupirovka	Business conglomerate with mafia-type connections and political influence
Hodja	Imam of a mosque
Horo	Ring dance
Komunistichisko Delo	Official organ of the Bulgarian Communist Party
Krutchma	Bar, tavern, eating house
Kuker	Masked reveller who plays the part of a good spirit in spring and winter rituals
Lelya	Aunt
Mahala	Hamlet or district of a village or town
Mastika	An ouzo-like spirit
Meze	Food to go with alcohol
Mutra	Gangster, heavy, bandit

Narodno Subranie	The National Assembly
Neblagodarnik	Ingrate
MRF	Movement for Rights and Freedoms, the party of the ethnic Turkish minority
Nazdrave	Cheers
Pomak, Pomaci	Member of an ethnically Slavic, Bulgarian-speaking Muslim minority
Pich	Dude
Pop, popove	Priest, priests
Popadia	Priest's wife
Rakia	Distilled spirit made from fermented grapes, plums and almost any other fruit you can think of.
Rabotnichesko Delo	Official organ of the Central Committee of the BCP
Shalvari	Baggy trousers worn by Muslim peasant women
Stotinka	Small coin. One hundredth of a lev
Tsiganin	Gypsy. Epithet for a Rom
UDF	United Democratic Forces. The original anti-Communist coalition, created just after the fall of the regime.
Vrachka	Fortune teller

Notes